PARALLEL HIGH PERFORMANCE PROGRAMMING WITH PYTHON

Unlock Parallel and Concurrent Programming in Python using Multithreading, CUDA, Pytorch, and Dask

by

FABIO NELLI

First published: April 2023
Published by: Orange Education Pvt Ltd, AVA™
Address: 9, Daryaganj, Delhi, 110002

ISBN: 978-93-88590-73-0
www.orangeava.com

Dedicated to

My wife Pamela and my son Valerio
who have been by my side throughout the development of this book

"I'm personally convinced that computer science has a lot in common with physics. Both are about how the world works at a rather fundamental level. The difference, of course, is that while in physics you're supposed to figure out how the world is made up, in computer science you create the world"

LINUS TORVALS

About the Author

Fabio Nelli holds a Master's degree in Chemistry and a Bachelor's degree in IT and Automation Engineering. He is currently working at several research institutes and private companies, where he presents educational courses on data analysis and data visualization technologies. In addition to his professional work, he contributes to the field by writing articles on the web, specifically on his website meccanismocomplesso.org, and by authoring in-depth books on the subject.

Technical Reviewer

Prashanth Raghu is a technology enthusiast who is focused on understanding the impact of open-source technologies in large-scale applications. He graduated from the PES Institute of Technology and later from the National University of Singapore, and is currently working as a software architect at Zeta Technologies. In addition to his passion for technology, he has interests in art, playing the Carnatic flute, and sports.

Acknowledgements

There are a few people I want to thank for the continued and ongoing support they have given me during the writing of this book. First and foremost, I would like to thank my wife for continuously encouraging me to write the book; I could not have completed this book without her support.

My gratitude goes to the Orange Education team who have been with me throughout all the stages of the development of this book. Special thanks goes to Shali Deeraj and Shubha Murthy for their support.

Preface

This book will introduce you to the various techniques currently available for parallel and concurrent programming with the Python language. There are many libraries and techniques that allow you to take advantage of different architectures available to make the calculations more efficient and performing (GPU, cores, resources distributed on the network, etc.). This book will try to gradually introduce the readers to the concepts behind these techniques with example codes.

Chapter 1 will start with an introduction to parallelism in Python and then will explain how the operating system handles multiple processes and threads. Its purpose will be to introduce you to the concept of **parallel programming** by talking about all the fundamental concepts that are involved, and which are necessary to fully understand the features and uses. Once these general concepts have been introduced, you will see the peculiarities of Python in this area, especially with threads, talking about the **GIL (Global Interpreter Lock)** and the problems it introduces. We will also learn about standard Python library modules such as *threading* and *multiprocessing*.

Chapter 2 will cover parallel programming in Python that uses Threads as concurrent elements. Specifically, the chapter will deal with the threading module that allows us to easily implement threads and provide a whole series of useful tools for their synchronization.

Chapter 3 will cover parallel programming in Python that uses Processes. There are two main approaches by which processes can be implemented in parallel programming: the multiprocessing module of the standard library and the mpi4py library which extends the MPI protocol also for the Python language. Both libraries will be treated in detail, with a series of examples that will show how they work and their main characteristics.

Chapter 4 will cover aspects of asynchronous programming in Python including the AsyncIO library as an example library.

Chapter 5 will cover the distributed systems as they fall within the scope of parallel and concurrent programming and can prove to be a valid solution. The Celery library is the reference point in Python for the realization of distributed systems. With a series of examples, we will see how to use this library to perform multiple concurrent operations, called tasks, and how these are distributed and executed in parallel on a Celery-based system. In addition, we will subsequently move on to other alternative solutions, starting from a very similar one, such as Dramatiq to a simpler one, but which conceptually differs from these, such as SCOOP.

Chapter 6 will cover GPU programming since these processors are designed to process vector data extremely quickly and efficiently for image rendering, 3D engines and manipulation of polygonal primitives. Python offers good solutions with various libraries such as Numba (CUDA) and PyOpenCL.

Chapter 7 will introduce you to the world of parallel computing applications, showing how this approach is now present in many scientific and professional disciplines.

Chapter 8 will cover parallel computing specifically with regard to Data Science. Many of the libraries commonly used in Data Science such as Numpy, Pandas and Scikit-learn can be extended to parallel computing thanks to the Dask library. This library provides objects such as nparrays, dataframes and machine learning api designed to work in parallel. There are many other scientific libraries that can be integrated with Dask.

Chapter 9 will cover another very interesting field of application, which in part extends to what was said in Data Science: Artificial Intelligence. Machine Learning and Deep Learning are subsets of Artificial Intelligence and they provide us with a good tool to explore data. Lately, these techniques are expanding enormously by exploiting parallel and distributed computing.

Chapter 10 will show you how developments and trends of this way of programming are fitting perfectly with the most innovative new technologies.

Downloading the code bundles and colored images

Please follow the link to download the
Code Bundles of the book:

https://github.com/OrangeAVA/Parallel-Programming-with-Python

The code bundles and images of the book are also hosted on
https://rebrand.ly/3127a9

In case there's an update to the code, it will be updated on the existing GitHub repository.

Errata

We take immense pride in our work at Orange Education Pvt Ltd and follow best practices to ensure the accuracy of our content to provide an indulging reading experience to our subscribers. Our readers are our mirrors, and we use their inputs to reflect and improve upon human errors, if any, that may have occurred during the publishing processes involved. To let us maintain the quality and help us reach out to any readers who might be having difficulties due to any unforeseen errors, please write to us at :

errata@orangeava.com

Your support, suggestions, and feedback are highly appreciated.

DID YOU KNOW

Did you know that Orange Education Pvt Ltd offers eBook versions of every book published, with PDF and ePub files available? You can upgrade to the eBook version at www.orangeava.com and as a print book customer, you are entitled to a discount on the eBook copy. Get in touch with us at: **info@orangeava.com** for more details.

At **www.orangeava.com**, you can also read a collection of free technical articles, sign up for a range of free newsletters, and receive exclusive discounts and offers on AVA™ Books and eBooks.

Piracy

If you come across any illegal copies of our works in any form on the internet, we would be grateful if you would provide us with the location address or website name. Please contact us at **info@orangeava.com** with a link to the material.

Are you interested in authoring with us?

If there is a topic that you have expertise in, and you are interested in either writing or contributing to a book, please write to us at **business@orangeava.com**. We are on a journey to help developers and tech professionals to gain insights on the present technological advancements and innovations happening across the globe and build a community that believes Knowledge is best acquired by sharing and learning with others. Please reach out to us to learn what our audience demands and how you can be part of this educational reform. We also welcome ideas from tech experts and help them build learning and development content for their domains.

Reviews

Please leave a review. Once you have read and used this book, why not leave a review on the site that you purchased it from? Potential readers can then see and use your unbiased opinion to make purchase decisions. We at Orange Education would love to know what you think about our products, and our authors can learn from your feedback. Thank you!

For more information about Orange Education, please visit **www.orangeava.com**.

Table of Contents

## CHAPTER 1

Introduction to Parallel Programming

In this first chapter of the book, we will introduce the concept of *parallel programming* by talking about all the fundamental concepts that are involved, and which are necessary to fully understand the features and uses. We will first talk about the hardware components that have allowed execution in parallel on new computers, such as CPUs and cores, and then about the entities of the operating system that are the real actuators of parallelism: processes and threads. Subsequently, the programming models of parallelism will be illustrated in detail, introducing fundamental concepts such as *concurrency*, *synchronicity*, and *asynchronicity*.

Once these general concepts have been introduced, we will see the peculiarities of Python in this area, especially with threads, talking about the **Global Interpreter Lock (GIL)** and the problems it introduces. We will mention standard Python library modules such as **threading** and **multiprocessing** which we will cover in more depth in the next chapters. Finally, we will close the chapter by talking about the evaluation methods of a parallel program, such as speedup and scaling, and discussing the problems that can be introduced by programming in parallel (*race condition*, *deadlock*, and so on).

By the end of this chapter, you will have understood all the fundamental concepts and terminology behind parallel programming. You will have built a general scheme in your mind in which all the protagonists of the parallel execution will be present and how they act to achieve it. Then, you will be ready to tackle the practical part of programming covered in the following chapters.

Structure

In this chapter, we will discuss the following topics:

- CPU and cores
- Processes and threads
- Parallel and concurrent programming
- GIL and threads with Python
- Speedup and Scaling

Parallel programming

If you are reading this book, it is certainly because you have already understood the need to increase the potential of your code, discovering the limits of traditional models that follow, for historical reasons (limit of old computers), a serial approach.

The advent of new hardware technologies has given us the opportunity to be able to run multiple programs simultaneously on our computers. In fact, our computers, even the simplest ones, have a *multi-core system* that allows programs to run in parallel. *Why not take advantage of this architecture then?*

Too often you have found yourself developing a Python program to perform a series of operations. Often in the scientific field, it is necessary to implement a series of algorithms to carry out very laborious calculations. But at the end of your work, by running the program on your computer, you will find with disappointment that it is not as fast as you hoped, and the execution times become too long as the size of the problem you are processing grows. But it's not just a speed issue. More and more frequently, today, we have to deal with ever larger amounts of data, and with the calculations related to it, programs need ever greater memory resources, which, despite their power, our computers do not manage to deal with.

Parallel programming allows you to execute parts of the code of one of our programs simultaneously, significantly increasing performance. Programming in parallel, therefore, means reducing the execution time of a program, using resources more efficiently, and being able to perform more complex operations that previously would have been prohibitive.

Technological evolution of computers and parallelism

Today, for many programmers, parallel programming is still an unfamiliar thing, since it is still a fairly recent technique. In fact, only a few years ago, all computers available to developers were equipped with a single **Arithmetic Logic Unit (ALU)** and serial programming was the only conceivable. The program instructions were executed one at a time in a sequential manner (see *Figure 1.1*):

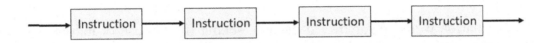

Figure 1.1: *Serial execution*

Many of you will in fact remember the characteristics of the computer generally indicated with the frequency of the processor in **Hz**, which indicates the instructions that can be *executed per second*. The power of a computer was primarily measured by its computing frequency. The higher this value was, the faster the programs ran.

The concept of *parallelism* is a concept that was gradually created with the evolution of the hardware present inside computers. Until 1980s, computers were very limited: they ran *one program at a time*, instruction after instruction, in a strictly *sequential manner*. It is clear that in such a technological environment, the concept of parallelism could not even be imagined in the slightest.

With the advent of the *Intel 80386 processor*, the possibility was introduced for the computer to interrupt the execution of one program in order to work on another. Consequently, concepts such as *pre-emptive programming* and *time-slicing* were born. This technological advance introduced a pseudo-parallelism effect since the user saw multiple programs working at the same time. With the subsequent *Intel 80486 processor*, the situation was further improved by introducing a pipeline system based on the subdivision of programs into subtasks. These were performed independently, alternating between the various programs. Furthermore, the internal architecture made it possible, for the first time, to assemble several different instructions (even from different programs) and execute them altogether at the same time (but not simultaneously). And this is where the real development of concurrent programming took place. The instruction portions of the different subtasks are completed in order to be executed as soon as possible (see *Figure 1.2*):

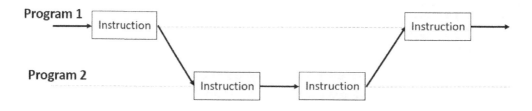

Figure 1.2: *Concurrent execution*

The situation went on for over a decade, seeing the release of increasingly powerful processor models, able to work at higher frequencies than the previous ones. But this situation soon went into crisis due to a series of problems and physical limitations. Increasing the frequency of execution means at the same time increasing the generation of heat and the consequent energy consumption. It was clear that the frequency boost would soon reach its limits.

And that's how processors took a leap of innovation, with the introduction of cores in their system. These, also known as **logical processors**, are allowed to simulate the presence of multiple processors within a single CPU, resulting in multi-core CPUs. In practice, one could have a multiprocessor computer capable of executing instructions from different programs simultaneously, in parallel. And it is therefore in the *early 2000s* that parallel programming was developed, giving the possibility for developers to be able to simultaneously execute different parts of the same program.

CPU, cores, threads, and processes

To understand the concepts that we will cover in this book, it is essential to first know what **threads** and **processes** are, and how they are closely related to the execution modes by the CPU and cores.

These are not *abstract* concepts, but real entities existing in our operating system. So to get familiar with them we can go and take a look directly at our operating system. For example, if you are working on *Windows*, open the **Task Manager** and click on the **Performance** tab.

You will get a window very similar to the one shown in *Figure 1.3* where it is possible to monitor in *real-time* the consumption of the various resources, such as the CPU, *memory*, and *Wi-Fi network*:

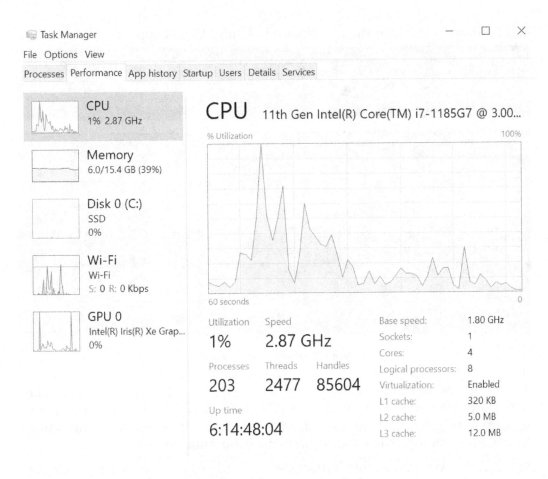

Figure 1.3: *Task manager in Windows*

In addition, a variety of information such as the number of processes and currently running threads are also shown. On the right, are listed some characteristics of the system we are working on such as the number of cores.

If, on the other hand, you work on *Linux* systems such as *Ubuntu*, you can have a corresponding application by writing from the terminal:

```
$ top
```

A screen very similar to the one shown in *Figure 1.4* will appear:

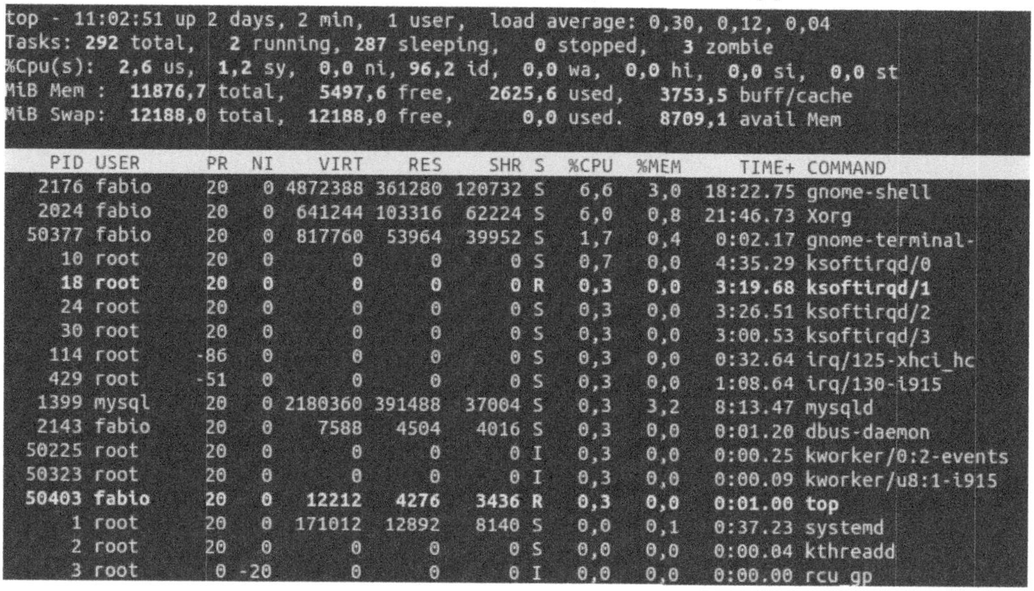

```
top - 11:02:51 up 2 days, 2 min,  1 user,  load average: 0,30, 0,12, 0,04
Tasks: 292 total,   2 running, 287 sleeping,   0 stopped,   3 zombie
%Cpu(s):  2,6 us,  1,2 sy,  0,0 ni, 96,2 id,  0,0 wa,  0,0 hi,  0,0 si,  0,0 st
MiB Mem :  11876,7 total,    5497,6 free,    2625,6 used,    3753,5 buff/cache
MiB Swap:  12188,0 total,   12188,0 free,       0,0 used.    8709,1 avail Mem

  PID USER       PR  NI    VIRT    RES    SHR S  %CPU  %MEM     TIME+ COMMAND
 2176 fabio      20   0 4872388 361280 120732 S   6,6   3,0  18:22.75 gnome-shell
 2024 fabio      20   0  641244 103316  62224 S   6,0   0,8  21:46.73 Xorg
50377 fabio      20   0  817760  53964  39952 S   1,7   0,4   0:02.17 gnome-terminal-
   10 root       20   0       0      0      0 S   0,7   0,0   4:35.29 ksoftirqd/0
   18 root       20   0       0      0      0 R   0,3   0,0   3:19.68 ksoftirqd/1
   24 root       20   0       0      0      0 S   0,3   0,0   3:26.51 ksoftirqd/2
   30 root       20   0       0      0      0 S   0,3   0,0   3:00.53 ksoftirqd/3
  114 root      -86   0       0      0      0 S   0,3   0,0   0:32.64 irq/125-xhci_hc
  429 root      -51   0       0      0      0 S   0,3   0,0   1:08.64 irq/130-i915
 1399 mysql      20   0 2180360 391488  37004 S   0,3   3,2   8:13.47 mysqld
 2143 fabio      20   0    7588   4504   4016 S   0,3   0,0   0:01.20 dbus-daemon
50225 root       20   0       0      0      0 I   0,3   0,0   0:00.25 kworker/0:2-events
50323 root       20   0       0      0      0 I   0,3   0,0   0:00.09 kworker/u8:1-i915
50403 fabio      20   0   12212   4276   3436 R   0,3   0,0   0:01.00 top
    1 root       20   0  171012  12892   8140 S   0,0   0,1   0:37.23 systemd
    2 root       20   0       0      0      0 S   0,0   0,0   0:00.04 kthreadd
    3 root        0 -20       0      0      0 I   0,0   0,0   0:00.00 rcu_gp
```

Figure 1.4: *top on Ubuntu terminal*

As we can see, at the top all the resources in use are shown with their values which are updated in a current way. In the lower part, there is a list of all active processes in the operating system. As you can see, each process is identified by a unique number, the **process identification number (PID)**.

Since Linux systems are much more *flexible* and *powerful*, especially thanks to the numerous shell commands, we can also monitor all the threads related to every single command. For this purpose, we will use a more specific command to monitor processes: `pid`.

`$ pid -T <PID>`

The `-T` option is used to indicate that the threads that are realistic to the process will be shown. The `pid` of the process that you want to monitor in detail is then passed to the `pid` command. In my case, choosing for example the process with **pid 2176**, I will get the result as shown in *Figure 1.5*, in which all the threads of the preceding one are shown with their identification number, **SPID**:

```
(base) fabio@fabio-Lenovo-ideapad-310-15IKB:~$ ps -T 2176
   PID    SPID TTY         STAT    TIME COMMAND
  2176    2176 ?           Ssl    17:36 /usr/bin/gnome-shell
  2176    2185 ?           Ssl     0:04 /usr/bin/gnome-shell
  2176    2187 ?           Ssl     0:20 /usr/bin/gnome-shell
  2176    2188 ?           Ssl     0:00 /usr/bin/gnome-shell
  2176    2190 ?           SNsl    0:00 /usr/bin/gnome-shell
  2176    2192 ?           Ssl     0:00 /usr/bin/gnome-shell
  2176    2195 ?           Ssl     0:04 /usr/bin/gnome-shell
  2176    2196 ?           Ssl     0:04 /usr/bin/gnome-shell
  2176    2197 ?           Ssl     0:04 /usr/bin/gnome-shell
  2176    2198 ?           Ssl     0:04 /usr/bin/gnome-shell
  2176    2653 ?           Ssl     0:00 /usr/bin/gnome-shell
  2176    2654 ?           Ssl     0:00 /usr/bin/gnome-shell
  2176    2655 ?           Ssl     0:00 /usr/bin/gnome-shell
  2176    2656 ?           Ssl     0:00 /usr/bin/gnome-shell
  2176    7152 ?           Ssl     0:00 /usr/bin/gnome-shell
  2176   50433 ?           Ssl     0:00 /usr/bin/gnome-shell
```

Figure 1.5: *pid command results on Ubuntu terminal*

The **Central Processing Unit (CPU)** is the real brain of our computer and basically, it is the place where our code is processed. The CPU is characterized by cycles, that is, the time units used by the CPU to perform an operation on the processor. Often we indicate the power of a CPU considering the *frequency of cycles per second* (see the **2.87GHz** speed value in *Figure* 1.3).

The CPU can have one (*single-core* CPU) or multiple cores (*multi-core* CPU) inside. Cores are data execution units within the CPU. Each core is capable of running multiple processes. A **process** is essentially a program that runs on the machine and to which a section of memory is reserved. Furthermore, each process can in turn start other processes (*sub-process*), or run one (**MainThread**), or *more* threads within it. A diagram of all this is shown in *Figure* 1.6:

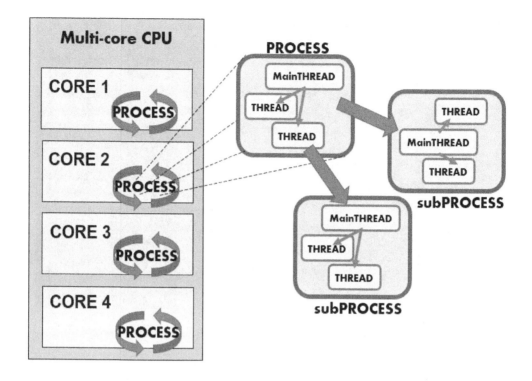

Figure 1.6: *CPU, core, process, and threads*

Threads, in turn, can be considered sub processes that run concurrently within a single processor. Like processes, threads also have a series of similar mechanisms that manage their *synchronization*, *data exchange*, and *state transitions* during their execution (**ready**, **running**, and **blocked**).

This is the general framework that we must have in mind to better understand how the processes and threads within our machines operate and consequently model the programming in parallel in the best possible way.

Concurrent and parallel programming

There is often confusion between *concurrency* and *parallelism* and it is not uncommon for the two terms to be used interchangeably, but this is incorrect. The two concepts, although closely related, are different in the context of parallel programming, and it is very important to understand the differences.

Let's start with the things the *two* concepts have in common. Both concurrency and parallelism occur when we have a program that must perform multiple tasks at the same time. But this is precisely the meaning of concurrency.

Concurrency means managing (and not executing) *multiple tasks* at the same time, but they won't necessarily run simultaneously.

So a program that will have to perform several tasks at the same time, can do it even by processing only one task at a time. As soon as it has finished executing the instructions relating to a task or a portion of it (*subtask*), the program will move on to the next task, and so on. One task after another, alternating between them, will be concluded and the program will complete its task. If it helps, you can think of tasks as *competing* with each other for execution.

So in this case, even if our computer has a single core CPU, a competing program can easily run (see *Figure* 1.7):

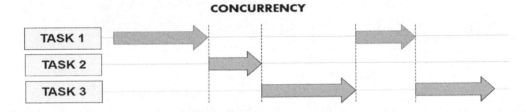

Figure 1.7: Concurrency in a single core CPU

From the outside, the user will see several tasks being performed simultaneously, but internally, only *one task at a time* will be executed in the CPU.

But concurrent programming also extends to *multi-core* CPUs or *multi-processor* computers. In this case, you could have a competition case as follows:

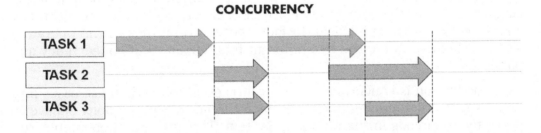

Figure 1.8: Concurrency in a multi-core CPU

As we can see in *Figure* 1.8, things get more complicated. Since there are multiple processing units (multiple cores), subtasks can be assigned to each and executed simultaneously. We, therefore, have the phenomenon of parallelism.

Parallelism means performing *multiple tasks* at the same time simultaneously.

Hence parallelism is a *special case* of concurrent programming.

Parallelism occurs when a program assigns each task to a core CPU so that each of them can be processed simultaneously, that is, in *parallel*, as shown in *Figure 1.9*:

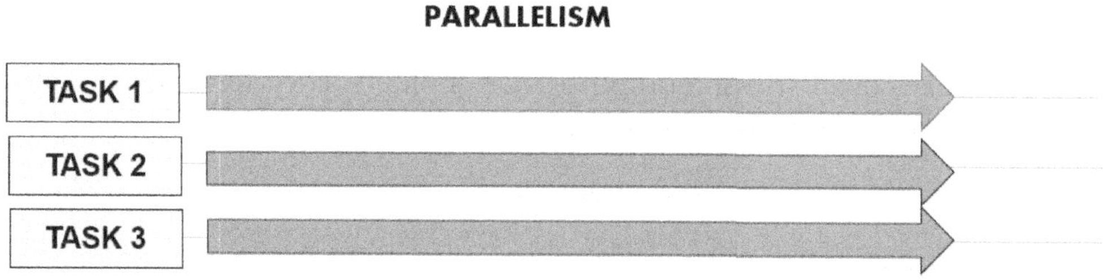

PARALLELISM

Figure 1.9: *Parallelism in a multi-core CPU*

Hence, parallelism requires hardware with multiple process units, essentially a multicore CPU. In a *single-core* CPU, concurrency can be mimicked but not parallelism.

Threads and processes in Python for concurrent and parallel models

Having now understood the difference between concurrent programming and parallel programming, let's take it a step further. In many programming languages, it is common practice to associate threads with concurrency and processes with parallelism. In fact, these two entities of the operating system will incorporate the two different functionalities of concurrency and parallelism.

As far as Python is concerned, however, it is good to divide these cases into two distinct programming models. In fact, threads in Python don't behave as perfectly as threads in the operating system. Threads in Python cannot run concurrently, and therefore cannot operate in *parallel*. Working with threads in Python is like working with a single-core CPU, although this is not the case.

Python thread problem: the GIL

The fact that threads in Python, unlike other programming languages, cannot be executable simultaneously on two different cores, is closely linked to the Python interpreter itself. In fact, the interpreter on which Python code has always been running was implemented in **CPython**, and during its implementation, it was realized that it was *not* fully thread-safe. That is, the more threads tried to access a certain object in common (the memory is shared between the threads), it often ran into a state of inconsistency, due to the phenomenon of the *race condition*. To avoid this huge problem, the **Global Interpreter Lock (GIL)** has been included within the interpreter. The Python designers therefore made the choice that within a process, only *one thread can be executed at a time*, eliminating the parallelism of this type of entity (no *multithreading*).

GIL is only acquired by one thread at a time while all other threads are waiting. As soon as the thread has finished its task, the GIL is released which is thus acquired by the next thread. There is, therefore, a real concurrent execution. **Concurrent programs** are generally less costly in terms of resources than parallel programs, as creating new processes is much more expensive than creating threads. It should be borne in mind, however, that the operations of acquisition and release of the lock affect slowing down the execution of the entire program.

But things are not that bad. In fact, later we will see how to adapt this peculiarity of the Python language threads in parallel programming models. Furthermore, many external libraries do not rely on the GIL, since they have been implemented with other languages such as **C** and **Fortran**, and therefore will take advantage of internal mechanisms that use multithreading. One of these libraries is precisely `NumPy`, a fundamental library for numerical computation in Python.

Elimination of GIL to achieve multithreading

As for the possibility of removing the GIL from the Python interpreter, it has always been a *hot topic*. However, this possibility has become increasingly difficult with time since it would be too difficult to remove the GIL without excluding many official, and third-party packages, and modules used in Python.

Another possibility could be to use other Python implementations other than CPython. The most widespread of these, **PyPy**, famous for its greater performance, has unfortunately also implemented a GIL very similar to that of CPython. Instead, **Jython**, a version of Python implemented in Java and **IronPython**, implemented with .NET, do not have GILs in them, and can make use of multithreading, and therefore take advantage of the presence of multiple cores or processors.

Threads versus processes in Python

Summarizing then, *threads* and *processes* are the tools that Python provides us for the implementation of programs in concurrent and parallel form, respectively.

In *Table 1.1*, you can see some characteristics of the *two* entities compared with each other and which must be taken into account during programming.

Threads	Processes
Memory sharing (of the process)	No memory sharing
Light consumption of resources	They require a lot of resources
Quick creation with little load	Slower and heavier creation
Synchronization mechanisms required	No synchronization needed

Table 1.1: Threads versus processes in Python

Concurrency and parallelism in Python

Therefore, for concurrent programming in Python, taking into account the behavior of the threads in this language, we can correct the definition of concurrency previously given, eliminating the possibility of *parallelism*.

Concurrency means managing multiple tasks at the same time, but they won't necessarily run simultaneously.

So we can imagine concurrent programming in Python with threads that each perform their tasks independently and in competition with each other for execution. They will alternate with each other in the general flow of execution until they are completed, as shown in *Figure 1.10*:

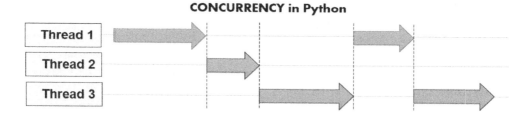

Figure 1.10: Concurrency in Python

While for parallel programming in Python, *processes* are perfect for executing tasks simultaneously, that is, in *parallel*. Each of them will be assigned a task and all together at the same time will be able to execute the instructions inside them, until the completion of the program, as shown in *Figure 1.11*:

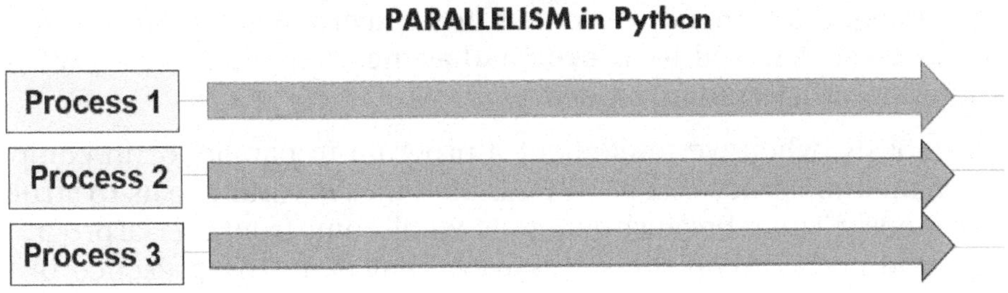

PARALLELISM in Python

Figure 1.11: *Parallelism in Python*

It is therefore clear that while for other programming languages the terms *concurrent* and *parallel* could lead to confusion, in Python, concurrency and parallelism not sharing the same common aspects of simultaneity, are two completely different concepts.

The light concurrency with greenlets

As we have just seen, the competition finds in threads a valid tool to implement its programming models.

But in addition to *threads*, Python offers another possible alternative: **greenlets**. From the point of view of competition, using greenlets or threads is equivalent, because in Python the threads are never executed in parallel and therefore with this programming language both work perfectly in concurrent programming. But the creation and management of greenlets are much *less expensive* in resources than threads. This is why their use in programming is defined as light concurrency. For this reason, greenlets are often used when you need to manage a large number of simple I / O functions, such as what happens in web servers. We will see how to create and manage greenlets with a few simple examples later in the book.

Parallel programming with Python

Understanding the role that threads and processes can play in Python. We can delve into *parallel programming* closely related to the Python language.

In this language, therefore, parallel programming is expressed exclusively on processes. A **program** is then divided into *several* parallelizable subtasks which are each assigned to a different process. Within each of them, we can therefore choose whether to perform the various steps *synchronously* or *asynchronously*.

Synchronous and asynchronous programming

In this book, and in much of the online documentation regarding parallel programming, the terms *synchronous* or *asynchronous* are often referred to, sometimes also referred to as **sync** and **async**. In all these cases we refer to two different programming models.

Unconsciously, when we implement a program in parallel or in competition between multiple processes or threads, it comes naturally to us to structure it synchronously. This is because generally, we all come from a serial programming background and tend to think this way. That is, in the presence of two or more processes (but they could be threads as well as simple functions within a program), a process (**PROCESS 1** in *Figure 1.12*) goes on with its execution, up to a point where it will perform an external call, passing the execution to another process to obtain a service, a calculation or any other operation. The other process (**PROCESS 2** in *Fig.1.12*) will be performed to complete its task and then will return the outcome of the service to the initial process that has been pending in the meantime. Once the necessary result has been obtained, the initial process will resume its execution:

Synchronous programming

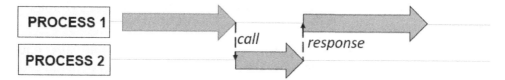

Figure 1.12: *Synchronous programming*

But in reality, *asynchronous programming* models are actually much more efficient than synchronous ones, both for more efficient use of computing resources and for the amount of time spent running the program. Let's look at the previous case together but this time seen asynchronously, as shown in *Figure 1.13*:

Asynchronous programming

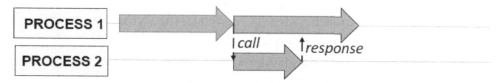

Figure 1.13: *Asynchronous programming*

As in the *synchronous* case, the *initial* process (**PROCESS 1** in *Figure* 1.13) will continue its execution until the call that will start a *second* process (**PROCESS 2** in *Figure.1.13*). But this time, the initial trial will not interrupt its execution to wait for the completion of the second trial. It will continue going forward with its execution, regardless of when and how it will obtain the outcome of the second trial.

As we can guess, *asynchronous programming* allows us to take advantage in many cases in which we would waste a lot of time waiting for operations that require an external response or a long execution time. It is therefore important to know both models well if you want to make the most of all the potential of parallel programming.

As for its practical implementation, although not yet completely intuitive for us, it is perfectly possible. All programming languages have internal mechanisms that allow them to be implemented. We will cover asynchronous programming in depth in *Chapter 6, Maximizing Performance with GPU Programming using* CUDA.

Map and reduce

A scheme widely used in parallel programming is that of the *Map-Reduce* which is mainly based on two phases:

- Mapping
- Reducing

The first phase, that of **mapping**, is based on the subdivision of the *tasks* to be carried out by a program into several parts (tasks) and then assigning them to different processes that will execute them simultaneously, that is, in *parallel*. Often the execution of each process leads to obtaining a result. So there will be a subsequent phase to the one strictly linked to parallel execution, in which all the results must be recombined together, that is, the **reducing** phase. *Figure* 1.14 shows a diagram that can help you better understand what was just said:

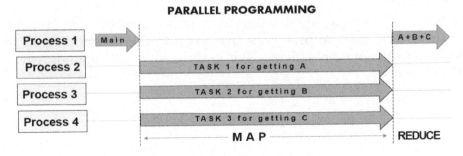

PARALLEL PROGRAMMING

Figure 1.14: *Map and reduce pattern in parallel programming*

CPU-bound and I/O-bound operations

During the *design* phase of a parallel program, however, attention must be paid to the individual tasks, evaluating whether among them there may be some that require too long an execution time. If this were the case, there would be a *high-performance degradation*, as all other processes would be waiting to complete the mapping phase. In fact, to pass to the *reducing* phase, all the results obtained from each process will be required. Let us consider a case like the one represented in *Figure 1.15* where one of the parallel processes requires too much execution time compared to the others. In this case, we will have all the other processes waiting to continue the execution and to pass the results to the *reducing* phase. In this case, *parallel programming* is no longer performing:

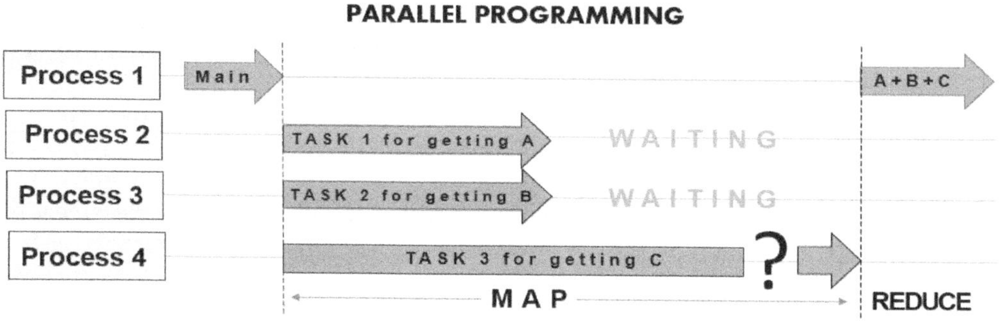

Figure 1.15: *Parallel programming with low performance*

So in these cases, we have to consider the various operations that are performed in every single process (*task*). These tasks could include internal operations such as reading a file or calling an external web service. In this case, the process will have to wait for a response from an external device and therefore the execution times can be unpredictable. This type of operation is called **I/O bound**. While operations that only involve internal CPU calculations are called **CPU bound**.

In parallel programming, when dealing with subtasks or CPU-bound operations, then the use of multiple processes that execute the instructions in parallel makes the program more *efficient*. But in the case of I/O bounds, we have to work differently.

In this case, the most suitable programming is *concurrent programming*, and this is where threads come into play. Within the process, we can create multiple threads. One will continue to take care of the CPU-bound operation while the others will take care of the various I/O bound operations. When one of these threads containing bound I/O operations waits for data or a response from an external source, the other threads will continue to perform their operations.

In this case, by running the threads concurrently we save execution time:

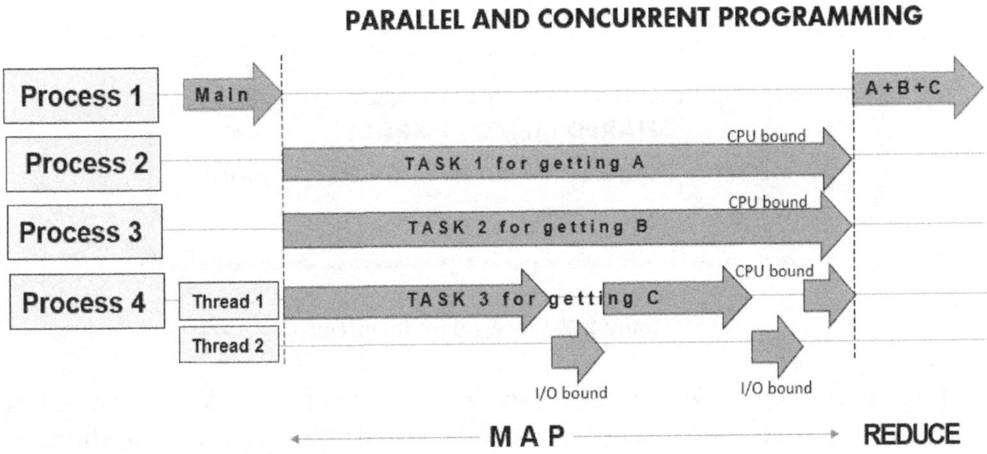

PARALLEL AND CONCURRENT PROGRAMMING

Figure 1.16: *Concurrency by threads for I/O bound operations*

As you can see in *Figure 1.16*, the creation of an additional thread, in addition to the **MainThread** (this is always present in a process), allows you to manage (asynchronously or synchronously) the I/O bound operation separately, allowing the **MainThread** to continue in the meantime with data processing.

Additional precautions in parallel programming

When dealing with concurrent programming, particular attention must still be paid when using threads, in particular with regard to the management of shared data. As shown in *Figure 1.17*, in fact, the threads within a process have both their own individual memory (not accessible to other threads) and a shared memory space, where there are objects accessible to all threads:

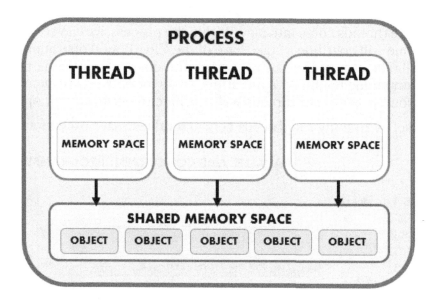

Figure 1.17: *Process with its threads*

Despite the presence of GIL in the Python interpreter working with multiple threads, it will still be necessary to lock the global objects present in the shared memory space if you do not want to fall into data inconsistency problems. But *how is this possible if the GIL guarantees that only one thread is executed at a time within a process?*

The fact is that the interpreter will only take care of the internal objects of Python, but as regards the objects we define and create during the execution of our program, there will be *no control* or *lock*, managed independently. It will be up to us to manage the locking of the global objects we create, to ensure that we do not get unexpected results.

In this regard, as we will see shortly, there are modules of the standard Python library that, in addition to implementing processes and in particular threads, provide a whole series of tools that allow us to manage also the locking of *global objects* to which we refer here we report.

Threading and multiprocessing modules

Moving on to the actual implementation, we can take advantage of both concurrent and parallel models with *threads* and *processes*, using two modules that the standard library makes available to us: **threading** and **multiprocessing**. These modules provide a set of functions in Python that interface with the operating system to *create*, *execute*, and *manage processes*, and *threads* with Python.

Note: If you notice, there is no specific module for threads it is not called multithreading, like that of processes, since Python is not actually multithreaded, but can only execute one thread at a time.

The **threading** module offers an abstraction layer to the `_thread` module which is a low-level module that provides primitives for working with multiple threads. In addition, it also provides a whole host of tools that help the programmer during the difficult task of managing concurrent systems such as threads: **lock**, **condition**, and **semaphores**. The functionality of this module along with these tools will be covered in depth in the next *Chapter 2, Building Multithreaded Programs* with a whole series of example codes that will help you understand how and when to use them.

The **multiprocessing** module, on the other hand, offers a valid API for the implementation of *process-based parallelism*. In addition to the creation and management of processes, this module also offers a large number of features that help manage the coexistence of multiple processes within a program. For example, **Queue** and **Pipe** are objects that allow the exchange of information (objects) between the various processes, or the pools that simplify the management of multiple processes at the same time. Also, this module and its functionalities will be extensively discussed in the *Chapter 3, Working with Multiprocessing and mpi4py Library*.

Memory organization and communication

So far we have discussed parallel programming, exclusively with regard to execution when approaching hardware systems that allow parallel execution is analyzing how the memory is organized.

In fact, even if we have a very powerful and fast CPU, with the presence of numerous processing units such as *cores*, the performance of a program will also greatly depend on how the memory organization is.

All operations involving data transfer into memory are generally not as fast as those in the CPU, and during these operations, the memory remains occupied until the end of the *memory cycle*, and no other component can use it.

A concept closely related to memory organization is the communication between the various components involved within the program. The forms of communication will be strictly related to the particular memory organization, and therefore the perfect functioning of a parallel program will have to better manage the passage of information between the entities in execution such as *processes* and *threads*, which takes place thanks to the memory. Depending on the memory organization, different mechanisms must be used to synchronize the passage of information between the various program objects in order to avoid the risk of data inconsistency or other problems such as *deadlocks* and *erroneous behavior*.

So it is clear that memory plays a very important role in the performance of parallel programming and it is, therefore, important to evaluate its behavior during our projects.

Memory organization within a process

For Python, there are essentially *three* different memory organization models possible within a program:

- Embarrassingly parallel
- Shared memory
- Message passing

These models are explained as follows:

- The first model, **embarrassingly parallel**, refers to the particular case in which the program entities, whether *threads* or *processes*, do not require any exchange of information and are able to carry their execution to the end, where the single results will be combined together. In fact, there are particular algorithms that respond to this behavior and are called precisely embarrassingly parallel.

- **Shared memory** is the model of memory organization typical of threads in Python. The threads within a process can communicate with each other through a shared memory made available to the process itself. There are several possible communication mechanisms that respond to this model, some valid and others not, and we will see some of them throughout the book.

- **Message passing**, on the other hand, is the memory organization model of processes. These in fact have no shared memory and therefore their only way of communicating is through messages. There are several solutions to this, often offered in the form of *ready-made packages* called **Message Passing Interface (MPI)**. The standard Python library itself offers an MPI module totally dedicated to this task.

Memory organization between multiple processors

So far we've been thinking about a single *multi-core CPU machine*. But the reality of parallel programming naturally extends to the use of multiple CPUs. These may be present on a single machine or on different machines connected in some way to each other.

It is clear that here too the organization of memory comes into play in the perfect functioning of parallel computing.

The *two previous models*, shared memory and message passing, are also extended in this area in the form of these *two* models:

- Shared memory

- Distributed memory

In the systems that follow the *shared memory model* that exists, all the processors present can access a particular memory area to share data and pass information. Systems of this kind are normally based on a physical bus that allows the connection of a certain number of physically separate processors (but they can be on the same machine or on different machines) as shown in *Figure 1.18*:

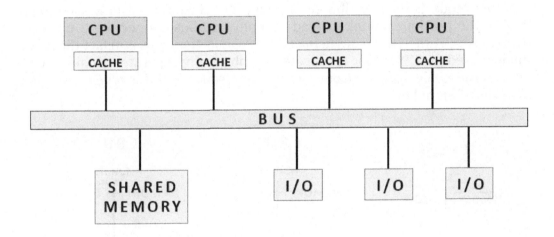

Figure 1.18: *Shared memory systems*

Each processor has its own local memory represented by a cache, generally with *high performance*, since the exchange of data between the CPU and this memory area is very frequent. But this area is limited and also often the various processors will have to share data to work on and this can only be done using the shared memory connected to the bus.

This is where the situation becomes delicate. The programmer will have to carefully manage the synchronization of the data used simultaneously between the various processors.

One of the CPUs will take the value of data from shared memory and copy it to its cache to process it in some way. In the meantime, another CPU will need the same value, and it will also make a copy of it from the shared memory to its cache. After some time, the first CPU will finish its processing and write the result to the shared memory, updating the value inside. In the meantime, however, the second CPU is processing a value that is no longer valid, and therefore here that the data coherency is lost. It is therefore clear that *concurrency management mechanisms* and *synchronization* similar to that of threads within a single process must be implemented (via hardware or programmatically).

So *why use this model?* Well, the main reason is that shared memory systems are very fast, as they rely heavily on hardware rather than software. In fact, many control and synchronization mechanisms on access to shared memory resources by the CPUs can be resolved through hardware.

Another model is the **Distributed Memory** model which is widely used today. Unlike the previous model, instead of a physical bus connecting the various CPUs to each other, there is a *network interconnection*. This is in fact the model mainly used for CPUs that are located on physically separate machines, even at a considerable distance from each other. A scheme of this type of system is shown in *Figure 1.19*:

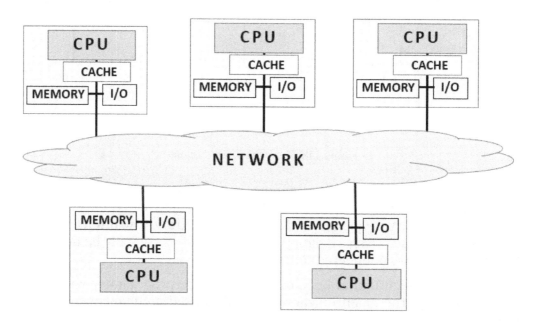

Figure 1.19: *Distributed memory system*

In this type of model, each CPU in addition to having its own dedicated cache also has a *local memory*, which it can normally use at full load. When there is a need to share data with another CPU, the data will be sent over the network. In this way, there will be no more data coherency problems, as each processor is responsible for its own data. Another *advantage* is that since there is *no* longer a physical bus, but only a *network connection*, the number of CPUs that can be added to this system is theoretically infinite.

The *disadvantage* of this model, however, is the fact that the network connection is not as fast as a physical bus, but above all, a **message passing** mechanism is required for communication and data exchange between the various CPUs. The management of messages, with their creation, sending and reading by the individual CPUs, on the one hand eliminates coherency problems, but significantly slows down the execution of programs.

Distributed programming

The existence of complex models such as distributed memory has led to further evolution on the part of parallel programming, so much so that it is defined as distributed programming. In fact, a program can be executed in parallel by different processes that run on different machines connected to the network. Today this system is very widespread and used, so much so that there are many Python packages that offer solutions in this regard. In this book we will also deal with this further extension of parallel programming, using some packages freely available on the net, dedicating an entire chapter to them, *Chapter 5, Realizing Parallelism with Distributed Systems*.

Evaluation of parallel programming

An aspect strictly related to parallel programming is the need to develop a whole series of methods to evaluate its performance. This evaluation is essential during the development of a program to decide if the choices made are convenient or if it is necessary to consider some other solution.

When you decide to use parallelism it is because you have been driven by the need to solve big problems in the shortest possible time. To achieve this goal, however, many factors come into play, such as the degree of parallelism used, the hardware and above all the programming model. It is therefore necessary to carry out a *performance analysis* to evaluate the validity of our choices during the development of the program.

There are a whole series of performance indices that can be used by evaluating their numerical value to measure the performance of our program. These are nothing more than numerical values obtained through appropriate calculations, which allow us in a systematic and precise way to compare programs or algorithms with each other. Among these indices, the best known and most used is **speedup**.

Speedup

Speedup is a number that expresses the difference between the *performance of two systems* that are running the same problem. In our case, the speedup S can be considered as the ratio between the time taken in the execution of a serial program *ts* with the time *tp* taken by our parallel program created to perform the same operations. The time *t* taken is a function of the number of processing units N, which can be CPUs, cores or GPUs, but N is generally referred to as the number of processors. And therefore, the time taken in a parallel system can be expressed as *t(N)*, while that in a serial system as *t(1)* since it is equivalent to a system with a single processor:

$$S = \frac{t_s}{t_p} S = \frac{t_s}{t_p} = \frac{t(1)}{t(N)}\frac{t(1)}{t(N)}$$

In other words, the *speedup* gives us information on what the performance benefits have been for having adopted the solution in parallel, compared to the serial one. Furthermore, if we compare the number of N *processors* with the speedup index, we can further classify our algorithm or program:

- If S = N then the speedup is **linear** or **ideal**
- If S <N then the speedup is **real**
- If S> N then the speedup is **super real**

The speedup index is also linked to **Amdahl's law**, widely used in parallel computing. This law is used to predict the maximum speedup achievable by a program while using *infinite processors*. It describes how in a program the percentage of serial code present determines the maximum achievable speedup value:

$$S \leq \frac{1}{1 - \alpha}$$

Where S is the speedup index and α is the portion of the time taken by the part of the program implemented in parallel.

So, if we have a program that takes 90 *minutes* to run the code in parallel, and 10 *minutes* to run the code in serial, so 100 *minutes* in total, then α = 0.9. So in this case the maximum obtainable speedup will be:

$$S \leq \frac{1}{1-0.9} S \leq \frac{1}{1-0.9} = \frac{1}{0.1} \frac{1}{0.1} = 10$$

The maximum *speedup* obtainable by our program will be 10. By gradually adding *cores* or *processors* to the execution we will have a gradual improvement of the performance of our program until we reach a speedup close to 10. Once we reach that value, even if we add more processors or cores to run in parallel, we will not have any further improvement. See the graph shown in *Figure 1.20*:

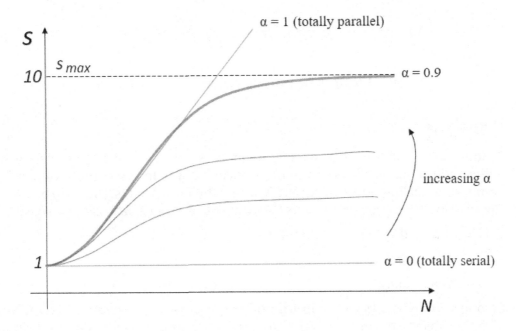

Figure 1.20: Amdahl's law

Therefore, if we want to improve the speedup of a program or an algorithm more and more, it will therefore be necessary to reduce the serial code parts as much as possible. Only in this way, by increasing the number of processors (or cores), we will have an ever more linear performance improvement.

Furthermore, once the parallelizable part of the code has been *maximized*, the next task would be to find the right compromise in which the speedup is as high as possible but using the correct *number of processors* (see *Figure 1.21*).

This avoids unnecessary workloads with too much unnecessary *parallelism* due to the addition of too many processors:

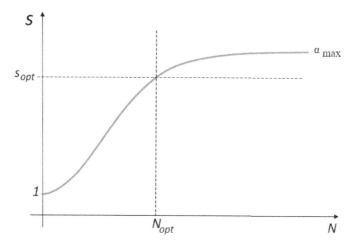

Figure 1.21: *Optimization of the number of processors needed*

Scaling

Scaling is the ability of a system to increase its computing efficiency by adding additional hardware (number of processors). In the context of parallel computing, scaling refers to parallelization efficiency, that is, the ratio between the *real* and the *ideal* speedup, as the number of processors used increases.

Scaling can be divided into *two* types:

- Strong scaling
- Weak scaling

Strong scaling occurs when the number of processors increases while the size of the problem remains constant. In ideal situations, this should result in an increasingly reduced workload for each processor.

Weak scaling occurs when the number of processors increases with the size of the processors. In this case, the workload for each processor should remain constant.

We have seen a strong scaling measure with the application of *Amdahl's law*, where the speedup is calculated by keeping the size of the problem constant and increasing the number of processors. Already, in this case, the law has shown us how speedup still has a maximum limit due to the impossibility of parallelizing 100% *of the code*. In addition, there are many other factors that come into play, which make it increasingly difficult to maintain a good strong scaling as the number of processors increases. For example, the latter, increasing in number, will require an ever-increasing load of work necessary to communicate with each other.

As for weak scaling, the speedup in this case has no upper maximum limits and therefore can grow indefinitely (in theory). This is confirmed by *Gustafson's law*, which defines the speedup calculation differently from *Amdahl's law*:

$$S = (1 - \alpha) + \alpha * N$$

In fact, *Gustafson* sensed that by increasing the size of the problem, only the speedup of the parallel part of the code α increased with the increase in the number of processors, while the serial one (1- α) did not. In fact, the graph shown in *Figure 1.22* shows the trends of the various speedups growing linearly with the addition of processors gradually, and therefore without ever reaching a *limit*:

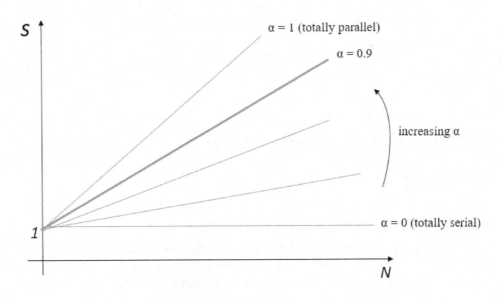

Figure 1.22: *Gustafson's law*

Thanks to the concept of strong and weak scaling, and the two laws of *Amdahl* and *Gustafson*, useful considerations can be drawn: for small problems, it is better to use small systems, for big problems it is better to use large systems.

Benchmarking in Python

The action of systematically testing performance under different conditions is called **benchmarking**. So far we have seen the evaluation of the performance of a program from a theoretical point of view. *But from the practical one?* Well, in Python there are a whole series of tools that allow us to measure the performance of a program or a piece of code.

In the following chapters, we will see some practical examples of how we will make these measurements. For example, to calculate the time taken (also useful for calculating the speedup) for the execution of a portion of code we will use the time module of the standard Python library. This module provides access to several types of clocks and using the call to the **time()** method we will get real stopwatch readings. Then, by making differences between the *times read*, we will obtain the time taken by the code included between the *two calls*:

```
started = time.time()

# Code here

elapsed = time.time()
print("Elapsed time=", elapsed - started)
```

Profiling

The analysis of which parts of the program contribute to performance, and identifying any bottlenecks is called **profiling**.

In Python, there are currently several tools in this regard, each useful for its peculiarities. Regarding the consumption of memory resources, it is possible to use a powerful tool: the **package memory profiler**. This module allows you to monitor the memory consumption of different processes/jobs in Python. In addition, it is able to perform a *line-by-line analysis* of the code for the consumption of resources and therefore can also be useful as a line profiler.

Conclusion

In this chapter, most of the concepts underlying parallel programming have been discussed in detail. Parallel programming has evolved over time in line with the available technologies, sharing the concepts and entities that have gradually developed. The processes and threads that run within the operating system are matched in parallel programming using process and thread objects that can be implemented with the *threading* and *multiprocessing* modules of the standard Python library. In the next two chapters, we will see how to use these two modules for parallel programming and to make the most of all the features they offer.

Points to remember

- **Concurrency**: This means managing multiple tasks at the same time, but they won't necessarily run simultaneously.

- **Parallelism**: This means running multiple tasks at the same time simultaneously.

- **Threads**: Threads in Python cannot run concurrently, and therefore cannot operate in parallel.

Questions

1. What is the difference between parallelism and concurrency?

2. What are the advantages and disadvantages of a distributed memory system?

3. When and how are weak scaling and strong scaling maintained?

References

- https://wiki.python.org/moin/GlobalIntepreterLock

- https://www.udacity.com/blog/2020/04/what-is-python-parallelization. html

- https://www.infoworld.com/article/3542595/6-python-libraries-for-parallel-processing.html

- https://en.wikipedia.org/wiki/Monkey_patch

- https://greenlet.readthedocs.io

- https://www.koyeb.com/blog/introduction-to-synchronous-and-asynchronous-processing
- https://medium.com/fintechexplained/advanced-python-concurrency-and-parallelism-82e378f26ced
- https://sebastianraschka.com/Articles/2014_multiprocessing.html
- https://medium.com/fullstackai/concurrency-in-python-cooperative-vs-preemptive-scheduling-5feaed7f6e53
- https://carpentries-incubator.github.io/lesson-parallel-python/
- http://code.tutsplus.com/articles/introduction-to-parallel-and-concurrent-programming-in-python--cms-28612
- https://en.wikipedia.org/wiki/Speedup
- https://hpc-wiki.info/hpc/Scaling
- https://www.meccanismocomplesso.org/python/

## CHAPTER 2

Parallel Programming with Threads

In this chapter, we will cover threads and their concurrent programming. In the standard Python library, there is a **threading** module that allows us to easily implement threads and provides a whole series of useful tools for their synchronization. The entire chapter will be dedicated to the illustration of this module, introducing one after the other all the classes provided and their functionality.

Structure

In this chapter we will discuss the following topics:

- Threads
- Lock and RLock
- Semaphore
- Condition
- Event
- ThreadPoolExecutor

Threads

The main protagonists of concurrent programming are precisely the threads, and in this regard, the **threading** module provides the `Thread` class:

```
class threading.Thread(group=None,
```

```
                    target=None,

                    name=None,

                    args=(),

                    kwargs={},

                    *,

                    daemon=None)
```

The `Thread()` constructor takes a number of arguments, among these of greatest importance and use are **target** and **args**. The function to be invoked within the thread is passed to the **target**, while the arguments to pass to it are passed to **args**. We can immediately see the functionality of this type of object with a practical example. In the program, we define five threads that will act in competition with each other. All of them will target the same function, which we will call **function()** for convenience. This function will not perform tasks, but will only occupy a short period of time, just to simulate the time spent in executing a set of instructions:

```python
import threading

import time


def function(i):

  print ("start Thread %i\n" %i)

  time.sleep(2)

  print ("end Thread %i\n" %i)

  return


t1 = threading.Thread(target=function , args=(1,))

t2 = threading.Thread(target=function , args=(2,))

t3 = threading.Thread(target=function , args=(3,))

t4 = threading.Thread(target=function , args=(4,))

t5 = threading.Thread(target=function , args=(5,))

t1.start()

t2.start()

t3.start()
```

```
t4.start()
```

```
t5.start()
```

```
print("END Program")
```

As we can see in the code, first of all, five instances of the **Thread** class are defined, corresponding to as many threads using the variables **t1**, **t2**, and so on. The execution of the threads will then be started later by invoking the start() method. By running the program, we will get:

```
start Thread 1
```

```
start Thread 2
```

```
start Thread 3
```

```
start Thread 4
```

```
start Thread 5
```

```
END Program
```

```
$ end Thread 1
```

```
end Thread 2
```

```
end Thread 4
```

```
end Thread 3
```

```
end Thread 5
```

If we look at the result of the execution, we can see some things. First, we see that the program starts all five threads at the same time and then closes without waiting for them to finish their execution, causing the prompt to enter a new command to appear. Actually, the five threads continue their execution in the background, continuing to give their output on the command line.

Another interesting thing that can be seen in the output is that the closing order of their execution differs from the starting one and can vary from execution to execution. This is normal behavior with threads since they are running concurrently. Their duration of execution and their order is seldom predictable. Therefore, it will be important to use synchronization methods that we will see later in the chapter.

join() method

In the previous case, we have seen that by starting threads within a program, one observes the behavior of seeing the program finish before the threads. This can be solved very easily since the threading module provides the **join()** method for this purpose. This method, launched on a thread, causes the program to wait for its execution to finish before closing. So, having multiple threads, we will call the **join()** method on each of them.

Then apply it to the previous case:

```
import threading
import time


def function(i):
    print ("start Thread %i" %i)
    time.sleep(2)
    print ("end Thread %i" %i)
    return


t1 = threading.Thread(target=function , args=(1,))
t2 = threading.Thread(target=function , args=(2,))
t3 = threading.Thread(target=function , args=(3,))
t4 = threading.Thread(target=function , args=(4,))
t5 = threading.Thread(target=function , args=(5,))
t1.start()
t2.start()
t3.start()
t4.start()
t5.start()
t1.join()
t2.join()
t3.join()
t4.join()
t5.join()
print("END Program")
```

In this case, by running the program we will get the following result:

```
start Thread 1

start Thread 2

start Thread 3

start Thread 4

start Thread 5

end Thread 3

end Thread 1

end Thread 2

end Thread 4

end Thread 5

END Program
```

As we can see, the program will now wait for all threads to finish their execution before closing.

But let's think about it further. Calls to the **join()** method can be used at some point in the program, as a simple synchronization example. For example, we want only a part of the code of the main program to be executed and then wait for the execution of the threads to start. To then restart, perform other operations, or start other threads.

Let's see a simple example by modifying the previous example code:

```
...

t1.start()

t2.start()

t1.join()

t2.join()

print("First set of threads done")

print("The program can execute other code here")

t3.start()

t4.start()

t5.start()

t3.join()

t4.join()
```

```
t5.join()
print("Second set of threads done")
print("END Program")
```

By running the newly modified code we will get the following result:

```
start Thread 1

start Thread 2

end Thread 2

end Thread 1

First set of threads done

The program can execute other code here

start Thread 3

start Thread 4

start Thread 5

end Thread 3

end Thread 5

end Thread 4

Second set of threads done

END Program
```

As we can see, you can add, using the **join()** methods, a point in the program where you wait for the execution of the threads to start, and then start again with the following lines of code.

Common thread synchronization pattern

In the previous examples, using multiple threads you can see identical lines of code being used multiple times. Each time we have defined for each thread a call for the **start()** and **join()** methods, writing numerous similar lines. The situation gets worse as the number of threads increases. However, there are other more convenient ways to write code.

In our example involving the 5 threads,, we can write the code as follows:

```
import threading
import time
```

```
def function(i):
  print ("start Thread %i" %i)
  time.sleep(2)
  print ("end Thread %i" %i)
  return


n_threads = 5
threads = [ ]
for i in range(n_threads):
  t = threading.Thread(target=function , args=(i,))
  threads.append(t)
  t.start()


for i in range(n_threads):
  threads[i].join()
```

In this form, the code is much more *readable* and *simpler*. By using a for loop that iterates for as many threads as desired, we avoided defining each thread individually (**t1**, **t2**, **t3**, ...), and calling the **start()** and **join()** methods for each of them.

By executing we will obtain a result identical to the previous examples:

start Thread 0

start Thread 1

start Thread 2

start Thread 3

start Thread 4

end Thread 0

end Thread 1

end Thread 2

end Thread 3

end Thread 4

Note: Be careful not to write this unless it is intentional:

```
for i in range(n_threads):
  t = threading.Thread(target=function , args=(i,))
  threads.append(t)
  t.start()
  t.join()
```

By placing the call to the join() method within the same for loop. We will not have the previous case where all threads are started at the same time. But it will be a serial situation. In this case, the first thread is launched and only when it finishes its execution will the second thread be started, and so on.

The concurrent.futures module and the ThreadPoolExecutor

In addition to the **threading** module, there is another module in the standard library that can provide us with a useful tool in the case of threads, and we will see it in the next chapter, also for processes. This module is called **concurrent. futures** and represents a *high-level interface* for asynchronously executing *callables*.

Inside, there is the **ThreadPoolExecutor** class which is very useful for managing several threads simultaneously. In fact, when there are many threads to manage within our program, the most efficient way to do this is by creating a **ThreadPoolExecutor**.

Let's take an example in which we want to launch four threads simultaneously, all linked to one or more functions. Instead of writing the definition of four instances of the **Thread** class, then four invocations to the **start()** method and four invocations to the **join()** method, it is much easier to use a **ThreadPoolExecutor**.

An example of what has been said is the following code:

```
import concurrent.futures

import time


def thread(num,t):
  print("Thread %s started" %num)
```

```
    time.sleep(t)
    print("Thread %s ended" %num)


with concurrent.futures.ThreadPoolExecutor(max_workers=4) as t:
    t.submit(thread(1,10))
    t.submit(thread(2,1))
    t.submit(thread(3,10))
    t.submit(thread(4,4))


print("Program ended")
```

Running the code we will get a result similar to the following.

.

Thread 1 started

Thread 1 ended

Thread 2 started

Thread 2 ended

Thread 3 started

Thread 3 ended

Thread 4 started

Thread 4 ended

Program ended

Threads are executed consecutively and executed apparently separately. From the extremely neat result, the **ThreadPoolExecutor** provides some sort of synchronization system inside it. Even if there shouldn't be any inside it. If instead, we write the previous code, without using a **ThreadPoolExecutor**, like the following one:

```
import threading

import time


def thread(num,t):
```

```
  print("Thread %s started" %num)
  time.sleep(t)
  print("Thread %s ended" %num)


t1 = threading.Thread(target=thread, args=(1,10,))
t2 = threading.Thread(target=thread, args=(2,1,))
t3 = threading.Thread(target=thread, args=(3,10,))
t4 = threading.Thread(target=thread, args=(4,4,))
t1.start()
t2.start()
t3.start()
t4.start()
t1.join()
t2.join()
t3.join()
t4.join()
print("Program ended")
```

By running it, we will find a totally different behavior:

Thread 1 started

Thread 2 started

Thread 3 started

Thread 4 started

Thread 2 ended

Thread 4 ended

Thread 1 ended

Thread 3 ended

Program ended

Here, the threads are started *simultaneously* and *concurrently*. The execution time of each running thread, therefore, depends on its duration.

In this example, we have used multiple threads that target the same function. Another very common case is that each thread is assigned to execute a different function. Let's see how the syntax changes in the following case.

Thread competition

A nice and simple example to see how two competing threads behave (concurrent programming) is the following code. Each thread is assigned a different function, **addA()** and **addB()**, which simulate a certain operation performed cyclically, and which takes **timeA** and **timeB** respectively at each iteration. The *two* threads will be launched together, and since in Python they cannot be executed in *parallel*, but only one at a time, during the execution of the program they will compete to end their cycle (**COUNT** equal to **5** iterations) as soon as possible. In order to monitor the execution sequence of the two threads, the two functions at each cycle will add the letters **A** and **B**, corresponding to the *two* threads, to a string of characters:

```
import threading
import time


sequence = ""
COUNT = 5
timeA = 5
timeB = 10


def addA():
  global sequence
  for i in range(COUNT):
    time.sleep(timeA)
    sequence = "%sA" %sequence
    print("Sequence: %s" %sequence)


def addB():
  global sequence
  for i in range(COUNT):
    time.sleep(timeB)
```

```
    sequence = "%sB" %sequence
    print("Sequence: %s" %sequence)


# the Main program
t1 = threading.Thread(target = addA)
t2 = threading.Thread(target = addB)
t1.start()
t2.start()
t1.join()
t2.join()
```

During the program, you will be able to see the sequence of execution. So, if you run the code you just wrote you will get a sequence similar to the following:

Sequence: A

Sequence: AA

Sequence: AAB

Sequence: AABA

Sequence: AABAA

Sequence: AABAAB

Sequence: AABAABA

Sequence: AABAABAB

Sequence: AABAABABB

Sequence: AABAABABBB

As we can see from the result, the *two threads* alternate with each other in execution in an arbitrary way. You will see that the sequence varies with the executions. You can also have fun changing the execution times of each thread by varying the values of the **timeA** and **timeB** variables. This will in turn affect the sequence of execution of the two threads that will be competing.

Using Thread subclasses

In the previous example, we used the definition of a thread through the **Thread()** constructor to which the name of the function is passed as an argument, through the **target** parameter:

```
t = threading.Thread(target = function_name)
```

In this case, we have separated the threads defined by the code defined within the functions into two distinct entities.

Another form of conceiving the code is to define a new thread as a **Thread** subclass, with its own methods and therefore some code to execute within it, without more calls to external functions. In this way, threads are *real objects*, consistent with object-oriented programming.

First, let's directly import the **Thread** class from the **threading** module:

```
from threading import Thread
```

Now we can define a new subclass of the **Thread** class, and we will override the **__init __ (self [, args])** method, adding any other definitions during the subclass initialization:

```
class myThread(Thread):

  def __init__(self):

    Thread.__init__(self)

    #add your code here
```

Then, we will override the **run(self [, args])** method to implement what the thread will have to execute when it starts with the **start()** call:

```
  def run(self):

    #code here
```

Subsequently, the instance of the new **myThread** class just defined is created, and the constructor is invoked with any arguments, if any. Finally, the thread is started by invoking the **start()** method on it which will execute the code implemented within the **run()** method:

```
t = myThread()

t.start()
```

Let's reconsider the previous example in which two different methods are passed to two instances of the same **Thread** class using the **target** option. Starting from the new considerations made, the two functions can be replaced by two distinct subclasses. Each of which will have the corresponding function code within the **run()** method.

So, the preceding code can be converted as follows:

```python
from threading import Thread
import time

sequence = ""
COUNT = 5
timeA = 5
timeB = 10

class ThreadA(Thread):
  def __init__(self):
    Thread.__init__(self)

  def run(self):
    global sequence
    for i in range(COUNT):
      time.sleep(timeA)
      sequence = "%sA" %sequence
      print("Sequence: %s" %sequence)

class ThreadB(Thread):
  def __init__(self):
    Thread.__init__(self)

  def run(self):
    global sequence
    for i in range(COUNT):
      time.sleep(timeB)
      sequence = "%sB" %sequence
      print("Sequence: %s" %sequence)
```

```
# the Main program
t1 = ThreadA()
t2 = ThreadB()
t1.start()
t2.start()
t1.join()
t2.join()
```

Synchronization mechanisms

As we saw in the previous section, threads are executed *concurrently*, and therefore operate simultaneously (but not in parallel). This gives rise to often unpredictable behavior which, if not controlled, can cause race condition problems, especially when competing for access to a shared resource. In this regard, the **threading** module provides a whole series of classes useful for implementing *thread synchronization* mechanisms. There are various types and each with its own peculiarities. In the course of this chapter, we will see them all, each of which will be implemented in a simple example, useful for better understanding how they work.

The synchronization objects provided by the **threading** module are:

- Lock
- RLock
- Semaphore
- Condition
- Event

Lock

The **Lock** is among all the classes provided by the **threading** module, the one with the lowest synchronization level. Lock can essentially assume *two* states:

- Locked
- Unlocked

and has two methods:

- **acquire()**
- **release()**

which have the function of modifying the status of the lock between *locked* and *unlocked*. When defining a lock using the **Lock()** constructor, it is in the *unlocked* state. When a thread invokes the **lock.acquire()** method, the lock switches to the *locked* state and blocks the execution of the thread, which will remain *on hold*. When another thread invokes the **lock.release()** method, the lock will return to the *unlocked* state, and the *waiting* thread will resume its execution (see *Figure 2.1*):

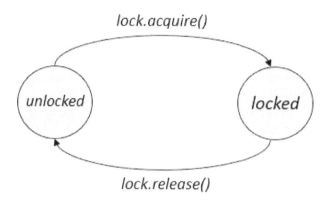

Figure 2.1: *The states of the Lock class*

If this *synchronization mechanism* is not well managed, it can lead to even more confusion in synchronization than not using it. In fact, there may be multiple threads that have invoked the **lock.acquire()** method, all waiting for at least one other thread to call **lock.release()** to change the status of the lock from *locked* to *unlocked*. In this case, what will be the *waiting* thread that will restart with the execution is unpredictable and can vary from implementation to implementation.

To illustrate how locks work, let's take an example with *two* threads each performing a different function. We will call the two functions **funcA()** and **funcB()**. From the first chapter, we saw that competing threads share process memory. So, in our example, we simply use a **shared** variable, which contains an *integer accessible* to both threads. The first thread, connected to **funcA()** will increase this value by **10**, while inversely the other thread, connected to **funcB()** will decrease the value by **10**. Both functions will perform this operation **10** times.

So, let's write the following code:

```python
import threading
import time


shared_data = 0


def funcA():
    global shared_data
    for i in range(10):
        local = shared_data
        local += 10
        time.sleep(1)
        shared_data = local
        print("Thread A wrote: %s" %shared_data)


def funcB():
    global shared_data
    for i in range(10):
        local = shared_data
        local -= 10
        time.sleep(1)
        shared_data = local
        print("Thread B wrote: %s" %shared_data)


t1 = threading.Thread(target = funcA)
t2 = threading.Thread(target = funcB)
t1.start()
t2.start()
t1.join()
t2.join()
```

This should be a great example of *inter-thread concurrency*. We run the code and get the following:

```
Thread A wrote: 10

Thread B wrote: -10

Thread A wrote: 20

Thread B wrote: -20

Thread B wrote: -30

Thread A wrote: 30

Thread A wrote: 40

Thread B wrote: 20

Thread A wrote: 50

Thread B wrote: 10

Thread A wrote: 60

Thread B wrote: 0

Thread A wrote: 70

Thread B wrote: -10

Thread B wrote: -20

Thread A wrote: 80

Thread B wrote: 70

Thread A wrote: 90

Thread B wrote: 60

Thread A wrote: 100
```

First, the iterations of **for** loops within the two functions are *separated* and *executed* separately. In this case, the threads execute *atomically* each **for** loop and each of these loops is in competition between the two functions. So, at each execution step, one of the for loops of the **funcA()** or the **funcB()** will prevail over the other, being executed *first* (threads cannot be executed in parallel in Python). However, this is the behavior we expected from multiple threads running simultaneously. So far, all correct.

The problem is in the value of the shared variable shared in the various steps. The value at the end of the execution should be **0**, instead in this execution, it is **100** (but it is a completely random value and differs from *execution to execution*). We are therefore, in a case of *race condition*. Furthermore, from the data we read we see that it did not happen just once, but it happens so frequently even in just 10 *cycles* and with only 2 *threads*.

It is therefore, clear that if we want this program to work correctly it will be necessary to use a *synchronization mechanism* that coordinates the *two* threads in accessing the **shared** variable, in order to avoid the phenomenon of the race condition. The **Lock** class provided by the **threading** module is the simplest case.

Then, we define an instance of the **Lock** class at the beginning of the program and insert calls to the **acquire()** and **release()** methods within the *two* threads, as in the following code:

```
import threading

import time


shared = 0

lock = threading.Lock()


def funcA():
  global shared
  for i in range(10):
    lock.acquire()
    local = shared
    local += 10
    time.sleep(1)
    shared = local
    print("Thread A wrote: %s" %shared)
    lock.release()


def funcB():
  global shared
  for i in range(10):
    lock.acquire()
    local = shared
```

```
    local -= 10
    time.sleep(1)
    shared = local
    print("Thread B wrote: %s" %shared)
    lock.release()


t1 = threading.Thread(target = funcA)
t2 = threading.Thread(target = funcB)
t1.start()
t2.start()
t1.join()
t2.join()
```

If we run the code this time we get a very different result:

```
Thread A wrote: 10
Thread A wrote: 20
Thread A wrote: 30
Thread A wrote: 40
Thread A wrote: 50
Thread A wrote: 60
Thread A wrote: 70
Thread A wrote: 80
Thread A wrote: 90
Thread A wrote: 100
Thread B wrote: 90
Thread B wrote: 80
Thread B wrote: 70
Thread B wrote: 60
Thread B wrote: 50
Thread B wrote: 40
Thread B wrote: 30
```

```
Thread B wrote: 20

Thread B wrote: 10

Thread B wrote: 0
```

As we can see, there are no more race condition problems. The **shared** variable is *read* and modified by only *one thread* at a time in a synchronized way, thus preventing incorrect values from coming out. However, it should be noted that by inserting this synchronization mechanism, the threads would seem to have lost their concurrent aspect. In fact, the threads do not exhibit concurrent patterns only within the synchronized code. From the result, we clearly see that first the **funcA()** will be executed entirely with all its **10** for loops, accessing only the **shared** variable, and bringing it up to the value of **100**. Then, the **funcB()** thread will act entirely by returning the value of shared to **0**.

Context management protocol with Lock

All objects within the **threading** module that use the **acquire()** and **release()** methods, such as the **Lock** objects, can be used in a context manager through the **with** statement (see Note as follows).

Note: In Python, the with statement creates a runtime context that allows you to execute a block of statements under the control of a context manager.

```
with expression:

    #code
```

The context manager consists in evaluating the expression relative to the block of code related to with (context). Therefore, the expression must return an object that implements a context management protocol which essentially consists of *two* methods:

- __enter__() which is called when entering the context.

- __exit__() which is called when exiting the context.

In addition to this, with statement has the further advantage of incorporating the functionality of the try ... finally construct.

This way you get a more readable and easily reusable code. Precisely for these numerous advantages, many classes of the standard library support the use of with statements as an alternative to traditional constructs.

In the case of locks, the **acquire()** method will be called when entering the block and the **release()** method will be called when *exiting*.

Hence the form:

```
lock.acquire()
try:
#code
finally:
        lock.release()
```

can be written in the following way:

```
with lock:
        #code
```

We then rewrite the previous code using the supported context manager protocol:

```
import threading
import time


shared_data = 0
lock = threading.Lock()


def funcA():
  global shared_data
  for i in range(10):
    with lock:
      local = shared_data
      local += 10
      time.sleep(1)
      shared_data = local
      print("Thread A wrote: %s" %shared_data)


def funcB():
  global shared_data
```

```
for i in range(10):
    with lock:
        local = shared_data
        local -= 10
        time.sleep(1)
        shared_data = local
        print("Thread B wrote: %s" %shared_data)


t1 = threading.Thread(target = funcA)
t2 = threading.Thread(target = funcB)
t1.start()
t2.start()
t1.join()
t2.join()
```

As we can see the code is much more *readable*. If we run the code, we won't find any difference in behavior, from the previous code.

The *Context Manager protocol* using the with statement is also supported by other objects in the **threading** module that we will see later in the chapter:

- RLock
- Condition
- Semaphore

All objects that, like **Lock**, use the **acquire()** and **release()** methods in their synchronization mechanism.

Another possible synchronization solution with Locks

Let's continue to analyze the previous code. As we have seen, we have added a *synchronization mechanism* that seems to totally (or at least almost) cancel the concurrent behavior of the two threads.

The mechanism we have created is the most intuitive one, adding the calls to the **acquire()** and **release()** methods in pairs within each thread, in order to delimit portions of blocks. Everything was pretty clear using context managers with **with** statement: we have *two* symmetrical code portions in both threads.

But we are not obliged to operate in this way. You can try and find more complex synchronization conditions. At your own *risk*. In fact, it is possible to insert calls to the **acquire()** and **release()** methods asymmetrically, in positions of the code that are not symmetrical to each other and sometimes using **acquire()** in one thread and **release()** in another. In this way, the blocks of code identifiable by the context manager are lost and a much more complex synchronization control is passed. In such cases, many problems could arise not only of race conditions but even of *deadlock*. Also, the **release()** method throws an *execution error* if called when the lock status is *unlocked*. However, just do not lose heart, do some tests and it may be that the synchronized and concurrent solution is possible.

For example, if we modify the code in the following way:

```python
import threading
import time


shared = 0
lock = threading.Lock()


def funcA():
  global shared
  for i in range(10):
    time.sleep(1)
    shared += 10
    print("Thread A wrote: %s" %shared)
    lock.acquire()


def funcB():
  global shared
  lock.acquire()
  for i in range(10):
    time.sleep(1)
    shared -= 10
```

```
        print("Thread B wrote: %s" %shared)
        lock.release()


t1 = threading.Thread(target = funcA)
t2 = threading.Thread(target = funcB)
t1.start()
t2.start()
t1.join()
t2.join()
```

There are a lot of changes. For example, the **funcA()** function no longer invokes the **release()** method while the **acquire()** method is invoked at the end of each iteration. In the **funcB()** function, on the other hand, the **acquire()** method is invoked at the beginning of the execution, outside the **for** loop. Furthermore, the functions no longer make use of *local variables*, but both directly modify the **shared** variable.

Running the modified code, we will get a result like the following:

```
Thread A wrote: 10
Thread B wrote: 0
Thread B wrote: -10
Thread A wrote: 0
Thread B wrote: -10
Thread A wrote: 0
Thread A wrote: 10
Thread B wrote: 0
Thread B wrote: -10
Thread A wrote: 0
Thread B wrote: -10
Thread A wrote: 0
Thread A wrote: 10
Thread B wrote: 0
Thread B wrote: -10
Thread A wrote: 0
```

```
Thread A wrote: 10
```

```
Thread B wrote: 0
```

```
Thread B wrote: -10
```

```
Thread A wrote: 0
```

As we can see, this time everything would seem to be working fine. We eventually got a final shared value of **0** and regained concurrent behavior between the two threads. In fact, the sequence of iterations between the **for** loops between the two threads returns to being random and concurrent. By running the program *several* times, we notice that the behavior remains correct, even if in these cases we will never have absolute certainty.

If we are not sure that the two threads are progressing alternately, but that one of the two remains *blocked* in its execution, while the other continues in its *execution*, we can (during the *debugging* phase) add some printed values to the previous code which confirms the execution progress of both threads. In our case, we can add the iteration number to the strings reporting the results of the counts for each thread. In this case, we will be able to ascertain the progress of the execution of the *two* threads at the same time:

```python
import threading
import time


shared = 0
lock = threading.Lock()


def funcA():
  global shared
  for i in range(10):
    time.sleep(1)
    shared += 10
    print("Thread A wrote: %s, %i" %(shared,i))
    lock.acquire()


def funcB():
  global shared
  lock.acquire()
```

```
  for i in range(10):
    time.sleep(1)
    shared -= 10
    print("Thread B wrote: %s, %i" %(shared,i))
    lock.release()


t1 = threading.Thread(target = funcA)
t2 = threading.Thread(target = funcB)
t1.start()
t2.start()
t1.join()
t2.join()
```

Running the code as soon as we modify, we will notice that both threads complete their execution by alternating between them:

```
Thread A wrote: 10, 0
Thread B wrote: 0, 0
Thread B wrote: -10, 1
Thread A wrote: 0, 1
Thread B wrote: -10, 2
Thread A wrote: 0, 2
Thread B wrote: -10, 3
Thread A wrote: 0, 3
Thread B wrote: -10, 4
Thread A wrote: 0, 4
Thread B wrote: -10, 5
Thread A wrote: 0, 5
Thread B wrote: -10, 6
Thread A wrote: 0, 6
Thread B wrote: -10, 7
Thread A wrote: 0, 7
Thread B wrote: -10, 8
```

```
Thread A wrote: 0, 8
```

```
Thread B wrote: -10, 9
```

```
Thread A wrote: 0, 9
```

The **Lock** mechanism in this case continues to work, even if executed in the code *asymmetrically* and without ever having the certainty that all executions will run exactly this way.

RLock

Another class used for thread synchronization is **RLock**, which is a **reentrant lock**. This class is very similar to the Lock class, but unlike this, it can be acquired multiple times by the same thread. Inside it, there is, in addition to the *locked-unlocked state*, also information on the owner thread and on the recursion level.

Like a *Lock*, an RLock can be acquired from a thread using the **acquire()** method. At this point RLock becomes *locked*, and the calling thread becomes one of the owners. Similarly, an RLock can be unlocked by calling the **release()** method. This time, however, unlike the Lock synchronization mechanism, the pairs of calls to the **acquire()** and **release()** methods are multiple, and can be nested together. Other threads that will invoke the **acquire()** method will be added to the list of owners. Only the final **release()** will be able to unlock the RLock, and make sure that another thread can *restart*.

So, moving on to an example, let's use three threads using a function where there are two nested for loops with access to the shared variable in both levels. Furthermore, we can differentiate the three threads by varying the execution time of each of them, in this way the concurrent behavior should be highlighted even more:

```
import threading
import time


shared = 0
rlock = threading.RLock()


def func(name, t):
  global shared
  for i in range(3):
    rlock.acquire()
```

```
    local = shared
    time.sleep(t)
    for j in range(2):
      rlock.acquire()
      local += 1
      time.sleep(2)
      shared = local
      print("Thread %s-%s wrote: %s" %(name, j, shared))
      rlock.release()
    shared = local + 1
    print("Thread %s wrote: %s" %(name, shared))
    rlock.release()


t1 = threading.Thread(target = func,args=('A',2,))
t2 = threading.Thread(target = func,args=('B',10,))
t3 = threading.Thread(target = func,args=('C',1,))
t1.start()
t2.start()
t3.start()
t1.join()
t2.join()
t3.join()
```

By running the previous code, we will get a result like the following:

```
Thread A-0 wrote: 1
Thread A-1 wrote: 2
Thread A wrote: 3
Thread A-0 wrote: 4
Thread A-1 wrote: 5
Thread A wrote: 6
Thread A-0 wrote: 7
```

```
Thread A-1 wrote: 8

Thread A wrote: 9

Thread B-0 wrote: 10

Thread B-1 wrote: 11

Thread B wrote: 12

Thread B-0 wrote: 13

Thread B-1 wrote: 14

Thread B wrote: 15

Thread B-0 wrote: 16

Thread B-1 wrote: 17

Thread B wrote: 18

Thread C-0 wrote: 19

Thread C-1 wrote: 20

Thread C wrote: 21

Thread C-0 wrote: 22

Thread C-1 wrote: 23

Thread C wrote: 24

Thread C-0 wrote: 25

Thread C-1 wrote: 26

Thread C wrote: 27
```

Also, in this case, as in the case of the Locks, the synchronization led to perfect management of the **shared** variable, but to a loss of the concurrent behavior of the threads. While without the use of the *RLock synchronization mechanism*, (that is, eliminating the calls to the **acquire()** and **release()** methods), the program would have given a result similar to the following:

```
Thread C-0 wrote: 1

Thread A-0 wrote: 1

Thread C-1 wrote: 2

Thread C wrote: 3

Thread A-1 wrote: 2

Thread A wrote: 3
```

```
Thread C-0 wrote: 4

Thread C-1 wrote: 5

Thread C wrote: 6

Thread A-0 wrote: 4

Thread B-0 wrote: 1

Thread A-1 wrote: 5

Thread A wrote: 6

Thread C-0 wrote: 7

Thread B-1 wrote: 2

Thread B wrote: 3

Thread C-1 wrote: 8

Thread C wrote: 9

Thread A-0 wrote: 7

Thread A-1 wrote: 8

Thread A wrote: 9

Thread B-0 wrote: 4

Thread B-1 wrote: 5

Thread B wrote: 6

Thread B-0 wrote: 7

Thread B-1 wrote: 8

Thread B wrote: 9
```

As you can see from the result, we have race condition phenomena that cause the **shared** variable to be valued with incorrect values.

Semaphore

Another synchronization mechanism available in the **threading** module is the one based on the semaphore. This primitive is the oldest form of synchronization in the history of computer science, having been invented by *Edsger W. Dijkstra* in 1962.

Its purpose is to synchronously manage the use of shared resources by multiple threads within the same process. To do this, each semaphore is associated with a shared resource, allowing access to all threads until the value of its internal counter is *negative*.

A semaphore is an object that, similar to Locks, works through calls to the **acquire()** and **release()** methods. Inside there is a counter that is *decremented* by one unit each time **acquire()** is called and *incremented* for each **release()** call.

So, if a thread needs to access a *shared* resource protected by a semaphore, it first invokes the **acquire()** method. The internal counter of the traffic light is decreased by one unit. If the value is *equal* to or *greater than zero*, then the thread will access the resource, otherwise, it will be blocked and will wait until another thread invokes a **release()** on that same resource. Only at that point, the thread will be able to continue with its execution, accessing the necessary resource.

Therefore, it is very important that for each thread that has invoked an **acquire()**, there is then, at the end of the operations on the shared resource, a call to the **release()** method, so that the other threads can also access the resources, avoiding so any *deadlocks*:

Figure 2.2: *The Producer–Consumer model*

For synchronization using Semaphore, we will use the *Producer-Consumer model* in the example code (see *Figure 2.2*). This programming model is based on *two* types of objects that act on a data flow. The **Producer** generates data, usually by acquiring it from an *external resource*, while the **Consumer** uses the data produced by the producer. The problem is that these two objects work independently, with different and variable speeds. Their numbers can also *vary*. For example, there can be only *one Producer* and *several Consumers*, or vice versa. This model is very well suited to threads (but also processes) and therefore it is a good idea to introduce it in these examples.

As an example of synchronization using Semaphore, we will define two **Thread** subclasses: **Consumer** and **Producer**. In their **run()** methods we will implement their code to execute. In the case of the **Producer**, we will implement a **request()** function that simulates the request for data from an external source, with a certain time taken through **time.sleep()**.

So, let's write the following code:

```python
from threading import Thread, Semaphore
import time
import random

semaphore = Semaphore(1)
shared = 1

class Consumer(Thread):
  def __init__(self):
    Thread.__init__(self)
    global semaphore

  def run(self):
    global shared
    semaphore.acquire()
    print("consumer has used this: %s" %shared)
    shared = 0
    semaphore.release()

class Producer(Thread):
  def __init__(self):
    Thread.__init__(self)
    global semaphore

  def request(self):
    time.sleep(1)
    return random.randint(0,100)
```

```python
def run(self):
    global shared
    semaphore.acquire()
    shared = self.request()
    print("producer has loaded this: %s" %shared)
    semaphore.release()


t1 = Producer()
t2 = Consumer()
t1.start()
t2.start()
t1.join()
t2.join()
```

By executing the code just written, we will get a result similar to the following:

producer has loaded this: 60

consumer has used this: 60

Since the semaphores synchronization mechanism also works via the **acquire()** and **release()** methods, semaphores also support the context management protocol. So, we can write the previous code as follows:

```python
from threading import Thread, Semaphore
import time
import random


semaphore = Semaphore(1)
shared = 1


class Consumer(Thread):
    def __init__(self):
        Thread.__init__(self)
        global semaphore
```

```
  def run(self):
    global shared
    with semaphore:
      print("consumer has used this: %s" %shared)
      shared = 0


class Producer(Thread):
  def __init__(self):
    Thread.__init__(self)
    global semaphore


  def request(self):
    time.sleep(1)
    return random.randint(0,100)


  def run(self):
    global shared
    with semaphore:
      shared = self.request()
      print("producer has loaded this: %s" %shared)


t1 = Producer()
t2 = Consumer()
t1.start()
t2.start()
t1.join()
t2.join()
```

Executing gives the same result.

producer has loaded this: 2

consumer has used this: 2

In this case, we have *two* threads, **Producer** and **Consumer**, which operate a single time; that is, they produce a value that is then consumed. But *what happens if instead we make the Producer thread produce more values (for example, 5) and we make the Consumer thread consume as many?*

We rewrite the code so that each thread performs the operation seen above five times:

```python
from threading import Thread, Semaphore

import time

import random


semaphore = Semaphore(1)

shared = 1

count = 5


class consumer(Thread):
  def __init__(self, count):
    Thread.__init__(self)
    global semaphore
    self.count = count


  def run(self):
    global shared
    for i in range(self.count):
      semaphore.acquire()
      print("consumer has used this: %s" %shared)
      shared = 0
      semaphore.release()


class producer(Thread):
  def __init__(self, count):
    Thread.__init__(self)
```

```
      self.count = count
      global semaphore


  def request(self):
    time.sleep(1)
    return random.randint(0,100)


  def run(self):
    global shared
    for i in range(self.count):
      semaphore.acquire()
      shared = self.request()
      print("producer has loaded this: %s" %shared)
      semaphore.release()


t1 = producer(count)
t2 = consumer(count)
t1.start()
t2.start()
t1.join()
t2.join()
```

Running the code, we get the following result:

```
producer has loaded this: 59
producer has loaded this: 85
producer has loaded this: 20
producer has loaded this: 4
producer has loaded this: 7
consumer has used this: 7
consumer has used this: 0
consumer has used this: 0
```

```
consumer has used this: 0
```

```
consumer has used this: 0
```

This is certainly not the behavior we want. In fact, the **Producer** thread continues to produce values that overwrite the shared resource, but the *consumer* is blocked and does not start until the *producer* has completed its work (five cycles). The **Consumer** thread, starting after the end of the five cycles of the **Producer**, consumes only the last value produced, losing the previous four.

Also, in this case, as happened with the *Lock* example, the *atomic* management of a block of the code of a thread by the semaphore is no longer good for our needs. By *atomic*, we mean precisely:

```
semaphore.acquire()
```

```
#code
```

```
semaphore.release()
```

or even:

```
with semaphore:
```

```
    #code
```

So, let's break down the **acquire()** and **release()** call mechanism between the *two* threads. The **Producer**, who will be the one who must access the *shared resource first*, will invoke the **acquire()** method before overwriting the data. While the **Consumer** thread after having *consumed* the shared resource, will invoke the **release()** method, releasing the *resource*:

```python
from threading import Thread, Semaphore

import time

import random


semaphore = Semaphore(1)

shared = 1

count = 5


def request():

  time.sleep(1)

  return random.randint(0,100)
```

```
class consumer(Thread):
  def __init__(self, count):
    Thread.__init__(self)
    global semaphore
    self.count = count

  def run(self):
    global shared
    for i in range(self.count):
      semaphore.acquire()
      print("consumer has used this: %s" %shared)
      shared = 0

class producer(Thread):
  def __init__(self, count):
    Thread.__init__(self)
    self.count = count
    global semaphore

  def run(self):
    global shared
    for i in range(self.count):
      shared = request()
      print("producer has loaded this: %s" %shared)
      semaphore.release()

t1 = producer(count)
t2 = consumer(count)
t1.start()
t2.start()
```

```
t1.join()
```

```
t2.join()
```

Executing gives the following result:

```
consumer has used this: 1
```

```
producer has loaded this: 0
```

```
consumer has used this: 0
```

```
producer has loaded this: 47
```

```
consumer has used this: 47
```

```
producer has loaded this: 25
```

```
consumer has used this: 25
```

```
producer has loaded this: 82
```

```
consumer has used this: 82
```

```
producer has loaded this: 23
```

As can be seen from the result, the synchronization is not yet perfect. We have the alternation of activities between the **Consumer** thread and the **Producer** thread. Except that the first to access the shared resource is the **Consumer**, and therefore the first consumed value is the starting default value **1**. While the one produced by the **Producer** at the end of the program is *not* consumed. To overcome this problem and correctly adjust the order of *execution*, simply set the initial internal value of the **semaphore** to **0** instead of **1**:

```
semaphore = Semaphore(0)
```

By running the program again, we will get the correct behavior this time:

```
producer has loaded this: 25
```

```
consumer has used this: 25
```

```
producer has loaded this: 45
```

```
consumer has used this: 45
```

```
producer has loaded this: 60
```

```
consumer has used this: 60
```

```
producer has loaded this: 9
```

```
consumer has used this: 9
```

```
producer has loaded this: 4
```

```
consumer has used this: 4
```

In this way, perfect synchronization is achieved. This is because, in our case, the *atomic* operation to be synchronized means the *production-consumption operation* of a single cycle, which involves *two* threads simultaneously:

```
Phase 1 synchronized: Producer (1 ciclo for) + Consumer (1 ciclo for)
```

```
Phase 2 synchronized: Producer (1 ciclo for) + Consumer (1 ciclo for)
```

```
Phase 3 synchronized: Producer (1 ciclo for) + Consumer (1 ciclo for)
```

```
Phase 4 synchronized: Producer (1 ciclo for) + Consumer (1 ciclo for)
```

```
Phase 5 synchronized: Producer (1 ciclo for) + Consumer (1 ciclo for)
```

While as we had set in the previous example, the synchronization scheme was *incorrect*:

```
Phase 1 synchronized: Producer ( 5 cicli for)
```

```
Phase 2 synchronized: Consumer ( 5 cicli for)
```

As we can see, when you want to insert a synchronization mechanism within your code, it is very important to first understand how the threads involved operate. Then extract from our conception of correct execution an *atomic* phase to be *repeated* and *synchronized*, which as we have seen is limited to a block of code present on a single thread but can include several threads at the same time. Then apply the right synchronization mechanism.

In the event that in the synchronized phase, there are more threads involved we must do without the context manager protocol with the **with** statement.

Condition

An alternative to **Semaphores** to use for thread synchronization is the **Condition** class. The **Condition** class has an *internal Lock*, which with **acquire()** and **release()** passes through the *locked* and *unlocked* states. But besides that, it also has other methods associated with it. The **wait()** method releases the lock but blocks the thread until another thread calls the **notify()** and **notify_all()** methods.

The **notify()** method wakes up only one of the threads waiting for the **condition** variable if any. While the **notify_all()** method wakes up all waiting threads.

Let's go back to the previous code used with the Semaphore and this time use the **Condition** as a thread synchronization system. We then modify the previously written code to get the following code at the end:

```
from threading import Thread, Condition
import time
import random


condition = Condition()
shared = 1
count = 5


class Consumer(Thread):
  def __init__(self, count):
    Thread.__init__(self)
    global condition
    self.count = count


  def run(self):
    global shared
    for i in range(self.count):
      condition.acquire()
      if shared == 0:
        condition.wait()
      print("consumer has used this: %s" %shared)
      shared = 0
      condition.notify()
      condition.release()

class Producer(Thread):
  def __init__(self, count):
    Thread.__init__(self)
    self.count = count
```

```
    global condition


  def request(self):
    time.sleep(1)
    return random.randint(0,100)


  def run(self):
    global shared
    for i in range(self.count):
      condition.acquire()
      shared = self.request()
      print("producer has loaded this: %s" %shared)
      condition.wait()
      if shared == 0:
        condition.notify()
      condition.release()


t1 = Producer(count)
t2 = Consumer(count)
t1.start()
t2.start()
t1.join()
t2.join()
```

If we run the code, we get a result similar to the following:

producer has loaded this: 43

consumer has used this: 43

producer has loaded this: 98

consumer has used this: 98

producer has loaded this: 51

consumer has used this: 51

```
producer has loaded this: 57
```

```
consumer has used this: 57
```

```
producer has loaded this: 40
```

```
consumer has used this: 40
```

Also, in this case, the synchronization system works like that of the Semaphore.

Event

In addition to the **Semaphore** and the **Condition**, there is another synchronization mechanism. The use of **Event** is one of the simplest conceptually. All this can be understood as a basic mechanism of communication between threads in which a thread signals a certain event to another thread waiting for it to happen.

An **Event** object manages an internal *Boolean* flag. There are also two methods that determine its value. The **set()** method sets the flag value to *True*, while the **clear()** method to *False*. *False* is the default value of the **Event** object when it is created. There is also a third **wait()** method that *blocks* the thread until the flag becomes *True*.

In other words, a thread, during its execution, freezes by calling the **wait()** method, waiting for an event to be able to continue. In another thread, when this event occurs, the **set()** method is called which *unlocks* the previous thread, which performs its operations, and then calls **clear()** to reset everything.

In our example of the two threads **Producer** and **Consumer**, we can replace the previous mechanisms with the *Event-based synchronization* mechanism.

Let's modify the code of the previous examples as follows:

```python
from threading import Thread, Event

import time

import random


event = Event()

shared = 1

count = 5


class Consumer(Thread):
  def __init__(self, count):
```

```python
        Thread.__init__(self)
        global event
        self.count = count


    def run(self):
        global shared
        for i in range(self.count):
            event.wait()
            print("consumer has used this: %s" %shared)
            shared = 0
            event.clear()


class Producer(Thread):
    def __init__(self, count):
        Thread.__init__(self)
        self.count = count
        global event


    def request(self):
        time.sleep(1)
        return random.randint(0,100)


    def run(self):
        global shared
        for i in range(self.count):
            shared = self.request()
            print("producer has loaded this: %s" %shared)
            event.set()


t1 = Producer(count)
```

```python
t2 = Consumer(count)
t1.start()
t2.start()
t1.join()
t2.join()
```

Running the code, we will get a result similar to the following:

```
producer has loaded this: 40
consumer has used this: 40
producer has loaded this: 100
consumer has used this: 100
producer has loaded this: 15
consumer has used this: 15
producer has loaded this: 27
consumer has used this: 27
producer has loaded this: 94
consumer has used this: 94
```

We can also see that in this case the synchronization between the two threads is *perfect*.

Queue

We continue to develop the previous example. So far, we have only used one **Producer** thread and one **Consumer** thread. But *what happens if we increase the number?*

We modify the previous program, this time making four threads work at the same time: two **Producer** and two **Consumer**:

```python
from threading import Thread, Event

import time

import random


event = Event()

shared = 1

count = 5
```

```python
class Consumer(Thread):
    def __init__(self, count):
        Thread.__init__(self)
        global event
        self.count = count


    def run(self):
        global shared
        for i in range(self.count):
            event.wait()
            print("consumer has used this: %s" %shared)
            shared = 0
            event.clear()


class Producer(Thread):
    def __init__(self, count):
        Thread.__init__(self)
        self.count = count
        global event


    def request(self):
        time.sleep(1)
        return random.randint(0,100)


    def run(self):
        global shared
        for i in range(self.count):
            shared = self.request()
            print("producer has loaded this: %s" %shared)
```

```
        event.set()


t1 = Producer(count)
t2 = Producer(count)
t3 = Consumer(count)
t4 = Consumer(count)
t1.start()
t2.start()
t3.start()
t4.start()
t1.join()
t2.join()
t3.join()
t4.join()
```

If we run the code, we will get a result similar to the following:

```
producer has loaded this: 92
consumer has used this: 92
consumer has used this: 0
producer has loaded this: 53
consumer has used this: 53
consumer has used this: 0
producer has loaded this: 62
consumer has used this: 62
producer has loaded this: 70
consumer has used this: 70
consumer has used this: 0
producer has loaded this: 7
consumer has used this: 7
producer has loaded this: 46
consumer has used this: 46
```

producer has loaded this: 30

producer has loaded this: 43

consumer has used this: 43

producer has loaded this: 36

producer has loaded this: 59

As we can see from the result, the behavior of the four threads is incorrect. It no longer has a synchronization in the use of the **shared** variable, with the following loss of many values produced by the two **Producer** threads, and with the **Consumers** that sometimes read **0**, without waiting for a new value to be generated.

How then to solve this further problem?

In these cases, the **Queue** comes to our aid.

By modifying the previous code, we remove the **shared** variable and replace it with a **Queue** that will be able to correctly manage the distribution between concurrent threads, whether it is a **Producer** thread or a **Consumer** thread:

```python
from threading import Thread

from queue import Queue

import time

import random


queue = Queue()

shared = 1

count = 5


class Consumer(Thread):
    def __init__(self, count):
        Thread.__init__(self)
        self.count = count


    def run(self):
        global queue
        for i in range(self.count):
```

```python
    local = queue.get()
    print("consumer has used this: %s" %local)
    queue.task_done()


class Producer(Thread):
  def __init__(self, count):
    Thread.__init__(self)
    self.count = count


  def request(self):
    time.sleep(1)
    return random.randint(0,100)


  def run(self):
    global queue
    for i in range(self.count):
      local = self.request()
      queue.put(local)
      print("producer has loaded this: %s" %local)


t1 = Producer(count)
t2 = Producer(count)
t3 = Consumer(count)
t4 = Consumer(count)
t1.start()
t2.start()
t3.start()
t4.start()
```

```
t1.join()
t2.join()
t3.join()
t4.join()
```

Running the code will give you the following result:

producer has loaded this: 31

producer has loaded this: 33

consumer has used this: 31

consumer has used this: 33

producer has loaded this: 11

consumer has used this: 11

producer has loaded this: 2

consumer has used this: 2

producer has loaded this: 27

consumer has used this: 27

producer has loaded this: 68

consumer has used this: 68

producer has loaded this: 92

consumer has used this: 92

producer has loaded this: 19

consumer has used this: 19

producer has loaded this: 87

consumer has used this: 87

producer has loaded this: 91

consumer has used this: 91

Now the behavior is *correct*.

Conclusion

In this chapter we have given comprehensive coverage of everything there is to learn about the tools provided by the **threadings** module. We have seen how it is possible to define a set of threads within a program in different ways, either by calling functions, using subclasses, or inserting them into a **ThreadPoolExecutor**. We also investigated the different possible thread synchronization mechanisms and how they differ from each other. In any case, we have seen the unpredictable nature of thread behavior and how easy it is to run into race condition problems. In the next chapter, we will move on to real parallel programming, which in Python is expressed exclusively with processes. We will talk about the multiprocessing module provided by the standard Python library.

Points to remember

- **Synchronization methods**: These are indispensable when you want to use memory shared between multiple threads.

- **Over-synchronization**: This suppresses the concurrent behavior of threads, executing them serially.

Questions

1. What is the difference between Lock and RLock classes?

2. What is the context manager protocol and what is it for?

3. Is there a synchronization mechanism better than others?

References

- https://realpython.com/python-with-statement/

- https://peps.python.org/pep-0343/

- https://en.wikipedia.org/wiki/Semaphore_(programming)

- https://www.meccanismocomplesso.org/i-thread-in-python-threading-parte-1/

- https://www.meccanismocomplesso.org/thread-in-python-lock-e-deadlock-parte-4/

- https://www.meccanismocomplesso.org/thread-in-python-il-modello-producer-consumer-parte-5/

## CHAPTER 3

Working with Multiprocessing and mpi4py Library

In this chapter, we will start working with parallel programming. In fact, in Python it is only the processes that can run simultaneously, bringing the real benefits of parallel computing. In Python, there are *two* main approaches by which processes can be implemented in parallel programming: the multiprocessing module of the standard library and the **mpi4py** library which extends the MPI *protocol* also for the Python language. Multiprocessing implements the shared memory programming paradigm, where processes within the program can access a common memory area. As with threads, this approach would create race conditions and synchronization problems. In this regard, we will introduce two communication channels between processes provided by the same multiprocessing module: **Queue** and **Pipe**. These will allow parallel processes to exchange data in perfect synchronization and without the problems of shared memory. The **mpi4py** library, on the other hand, is based on the message passing paradigm. In this model, there are no shared resources and all communications between processes take place through the exchange of processes.

Structure

In this chapter, we will cover the following topics:

- Multiprocessing module
- Process as class and subclass
- Channels of communication - Queue and Pipe
- Process pool
- ProcessPoolExecutor

- Mpi4py library
- Point-to-point communication
- Collective communication
- Topologies

Processes and the multiprocessing module

In Python, the real protagonists of parallel programming are the processes, the only ones that allow the real execution of the code simultaneously. This is because as we have seen in previous chapters, threads in Python cannot act in parallel and the most we can implement with them is concurrent behavior.

So, the programming of processes in Python is very important, so much so that we have a module completely dedicated to them in the standard library: **multiprocessing**.

This module offers all the possible operations for creating and managing processes within a program and does so in a very similar way to what the threading module does with threads. The instructions and constructs used in the implementation are almost identical:

- The **Process()** constructor allows the creation of a process.
- Calling the **start()** method starts the process activity.
- Calling the **join()** method causes the execution of the program (**Main** process) to wait until the execution of all the processes launched in parallel is completed.

The process life cycle is based on three states:

- Ready
- Running
- Waiting

Then the multiprocessing module structures the parallel programming in the following way. The main process is one that starts with the execution of the program. Within it, a number of processes will be defined using the **Process()** constructor. At this point the processes just defined are in the *Ready* state. Then at a certain point, the part of the program is started for execution in parallel. All defined processes (children processes) will be activated together by calling the **start()** method for each of them. The *main* process, in this case also the parent process, will continue its execution asynchronously, and will not wait for the execution of the children process (see *Figure 3.1*):

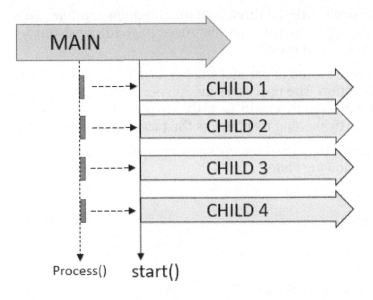

Figure 3.1: *Asynchronous mode without join()*

If instead, we want a synchronization mechanism, and we want the main process to wait for the result of its children processes, we will call the **join()** method for each process (see *Figure 3.2*):

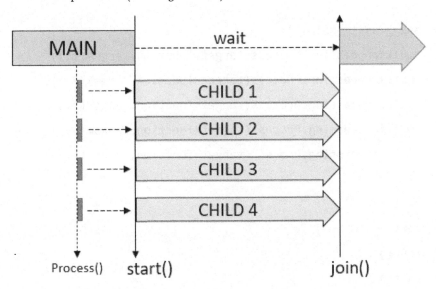

Figure 3.2: *Synchronous mode with join()*

Like how we dealt with the threads of the threading module, we write the code with the processes. As you can see, there is good consistency in API design between threads and processes.

Each process activated in parallel will perform certain operations specified by the *target* function. The processes may all perform the same operation or each of the different operations. In fact, the *target* function is specified for every single process by passing its name as the target argument in the constructor.

To better understand the concepts just explained, let us make an example by writing the following code:

```python
import multiprocessing

import time


def function(i):
    print ("start Process %i" %i)
    time.sleep(2)
    print ("end Process %i" %i)
    return


if __name__ == '__main__':
    p1 = multiprocessing.Process(target=function, args=(1,))
    p2 = multiprocessing.Process(target=function, args=(2,))
    p3 = multiprocessing.Process(target=function, args=(3,))
    p4 = multiprocessing.Process(target=function, args=(4,))
    p5 = multiprocessing.Process(target=function, args=(5,))
    p1.start()
    p2.start()
    p3.start()
    p4.start()
    p5.start()
    p1.join()
    p2.join()
    p3.join()
```

```
p4.join()

p5.join()

print("END Program")
```

As we can see in the code, five processes are defined in parallel, through the **Process()** constructor. They will all perform the same target function that we have called function here for simplicity. If the function needs some arguments in this regard, you can also pass them to the **Process()** constructor as a tuple to the **args** argument. In the code, we pass a number that we need to identify the process running within the function. All these processes will be activated with the **start()** method and then synchronized with the main processes through the **join()** method.

Running the code, we will get a result similar to the following:

start Process 1

start Process 2

start Process 3

start Process 4

start Process 5

end Process 1

end Process 2

end Process 4

end Process 3

end Process 5

END Program

The result is very similar to those obtained with threads and the threading module, but in this case, the five processes will have worked in parallel.

The way to implement the code in parallel as we did in the previous case is very *readable*, with all the instructions expressed individually and explicitly. Having to use five processes in parallel, we have defined five lines for the constructors, five lines to activate them with the start method, and five lines to synchronize them with the main process with the **join()** method. But if the number of processes was to become many more, implementing the code in this way could become very problematic.

There are many more efficient constructs, which take advantage of iterations and other mechanisms to generalize all the previous steps. An example of modifying the preceding code could be as follows:

```python
import multiprocessing
import time


def function(i):
  print ("start Process %i" %i)
  time.sleep(2)
  print ("end Process %i" %i)
  return


if __name__ == '__main__':
  processes = []
  n_procs = 5


  for i in range(n_procs):
    p = multiprocessing.Process(target=function, args=(i,))
    processes.append(p)
    p.start()


  for i in range(n_procs):
    processes[i].join()


  print("END Program")
```

If you run the modified code, you will see that the result obtained will not change at all.

Using process IDs

In the previous case, we used the passage of the arguments within the **Process()** constructor to communicate the process number through the iterator **i**. There is also another way to identify running processes among themselves, that is, by means of their **Process ID (PID)**. It is a very simple operation, we import the **os** module of the standard library which provides us with the **getpid()** function which allows us to obtain the PID of each running process.

We apply the following changes to the previous code, replacing the numbers with the process ID, as in the following code:

```python
import multiprocessing

import os

import time


def function():
    pid = os.getpid()
    print ("start Process %s" %pid)
    time.sleep(2)
    print ("end Process %s" %pid)
    return


if __name__ == '__main__':
    processes = []
    n_procs = 5

    for I in range(n_procs):
        p = multiprocessing.Process(target=function)
        processes.append(p)
        p.start()

    for i in range(n_procs):
        processes[i].join()


    print("END Program")
```

You can see that the **Process()** constructor no longer needs to use **args** as an argument, as the function itself will handle it. Inside it, there is in fact the call to the **getpid()** function which will return the PID of the process in which it will be executed. We will get five different PIDs from the same function, without having to use arguments passed from the main process.

If we run the code, we will get a result similar to the following:

```
start Process 20644

start Process 20000

start Process 16240

start Process 1988

start Process 24388

end Process 20644

end Process 20000

end Process 16240

end Process 1988

end Process 24388

END Program
```

As we can see from the result, this time instead of progressive numbers, we have the PIDs that allow us to identify different processes running in parallel. These PIDs are the same as those recognized by the operating system. It will therefore be possible to monitor their progress also from other tools or applications that monitor the consumption of resources or manage active processes, outside the scope of the Python interpreter.

Process pool

A further evolution of the programming pattern to manage multiple processes together is to use a **process pool**, expressed in Python by **multiprocessing. Pool** class.

A **pool** is that object responsible for a certain number of processes. Through it you will have control of their status, from creation to use, and whether or not some of them should be paused to save computational resources. So **multiprocessing.Pool** is nothing more than an interface for the ad hoc execution of a specific task, making use of a set of processes, without having to specify how many and which processes will have to perform this task. This allows us to greatly simplify the code and make it much more readable.

Let us take the previous code and convert it this time using **multiprocessing. Pool**:

```python
import multiprocessing
import time


def function(i):
  process = multiprocessing.current_process()
  print ("start Process %i(pid:%s)" %(i,process.pid))
  time.sleep(2)
  print ("end Process %i(pid:%s)" %(i,process.pid))
  return


if __name__ == '__main__':
  pool = multiprocessing.Pool()
  print("Processes started: %s" %pool._processes)
  for i in range(pool._processes):
    results = pool.apply(function, args=(i,))
  pool.close()


  print("END Program")
```

There are many changes within the code that we need to account for. First, we used the constructor of the class to define a process pool:

```python
pool = multiprocessing.pool.Pool()
```

This will create a process pool that will use a number of worker processes that match the number of logical CPU cores in your system. This number is accessible in code via pool._processes. Then **pool.apply()** is used to make the pool execute a given task represented by the **function()** function, passing it the number of the process generated via **args** as an argument. Once all the tasks required in the code have been performed, the pool will be closed using the **pool.close()** function.

As for the **function()** function, we have added the PID of the process, so that it can be recognized unambiguously. To obtain this value, first, the running process is obtained with **current_process()** and then the **pid** attribute is invoked on this.

Running the code just written we will get a result similar to the following:

```
Processes started: 12
start Process 0(pid:18196)
end Process 0(pid:18196)
start Process 1(pid:5300)
end Process 1(pid:5300)
start Process 2(pid:11984)
end Process 2(pid:11984)
start Process 3(pid:23436)
end Process 3(pid:23436)
start Process 4(pid:16224)
end Process 4(pid:16224)
start Process 5(pid:3784)
end Process 5(pid:3784)
start Process 6(pid:9196)
end Process 6(pid:9196)
start Process 7(pid:6248)
end Process 7(pid:6248)
start Process 8(pid:9272)
end Process 8(pid:9272)
start Process 9(pid:4168)
end Process 9(pid:4168)
start Process 10(pid:22676)
end Process 10(pid:22676)
start Process 11(pid:16500)
end Process 11(pid:16500)
END Program
```

As we can see from the result, the *first twelve workers* are created corresponding to the number of cores present on the computer from which the code is executed (this value can change from *computer* to *computer*). And then each of them executes the called function, following the steps dictated by **for** iteration. As is evident from the result, the execution of each task takes place sequentially. We'll see later how to make the most of the process pools by running them in parallel using the **map()** function.

Let's make a small change to better understand how the process pool works. During the invocation of **Pool()**, it is also possible to determine a fixed number of processes inside the pool regardless of the cores present in the CPU. In the constructor, the number of processes that will become part of the pool is defined, using the **processes** parameter:

```
pool = multiprocessing.Pool(processes=4)
```

We make the appropriate changes to the previous code, replacing the definition of **Pool()** and leaving the **for** loop with twelve calls to the function. Within **function()**, we replace the term **Process** with the more correct term **Task**:

```
import multiprocessing

import time


def function(i):
  process = multiprocessing.current_process()
  print ("start Task %i(pid:%s)" %(i,process.pid))
  time.sleep(2)
  print ("end Task %i(pid:%s)" %(i,process.pid))
  return


if __name__ == '__main__':
  pool = multiprocessing.Pool(processes=4)
  print("Processes started: %s" %pool._processes)
  for i in range(12):
    results = pool.apply(function, args=(i,))
  pool.close()


  print("END Program")
```

So, in this case, we will have twelve tasks to be performed by only **4** processes. By executing the newly modified code we will have a result similar to the following:

```
Processes started: 4

start Task 0(pid:5284)

end Task 0(pid:5284)

start Task 1(pid:2220)

end Task 1(pid:2220)

start Task 2(pid:15236)

end Task 2(pid:15236)

start Task 3(pid:4692)

end Task 3(pid:4692)

start Task 4(pid:5284)

end Task 4(pid:5284)

start Task 5(pid:2220)

end Task 5(pid:2220)

start Task 6(pid:15236)

end Task 6(pid:15236)

start Task 7(pid:4692)

end Task 7(pid:4692)

start Task 8(pid:5284)

end Task 8(pid:5284)

start Task 9(pid:2220)

end Task 9(pid:2220)

start Task 10(pid:15236)

end Task 10(pid:15236)

start Task 11(pid:4692)

end Task 11(pid:4692)

END Program
```

As we can see from the result, all twelve tasks are executed *sequentially* as in the previous case, but this time the four processes (workers) will take turns activating and deactivating themselves to execute all the tasks.

Defining processes as subclasses

So far, we have seen how to define in code the processes that will work in parallel via the **Process()** constructor. This was then assigned a target function containing the code to execute in *parallel*. Another way to implement the scheme of processes in parallel is to define the latter as subclasses of **Process()**. Within these, their functionality will then be specified by overriding the **__init__()** and **run()** methods. In this case, the code to run in parallel will be inserted into the **run()** method of the class.

Let's get a better understanding of this concept in a practical way, taking the following code as an example:

```python
from multiprocessing import Process

import time

import random


class ChildProcess(Process):
  def __init__(self, count):
    Process.__init__(self)
    self.count = count


  def run(self):
    print ("start Process %s" %self.count)
    time.sleep(2)
    print ("end Process %s" %self.count)


if __name__ == '__main__':
  processes = []
  n_procs = 5


  for i in range(n_procs):
    p = ChildProcess(i)
    processes.append(p)
```

```
    p.start()

  for i in range(n_procs):
    processes[i].join()
```

As we can see from the code, we define a subclass of **Process()** which we have called **ChildProcess()**. Within the class, we have *two* overridden methods. In **__init __()**, we will define the attributes of the subclass to be added, as in this case, the **count** argument is passed to the constructor. While in the **run()** method, we will insert the code that was present in the target function.

Running the code, we will get a result similar to the following:

start Process 0

start Process 1

start Process 2

start Process 3

start Process 4

end Process 0

end Process 1

end Process 2

end Process 4

end Process 3

Channels of communication between processes

Processes, unlike *threads*, generally do not share a memory space, and therefore need a different mechanism to be able to communicate with each other and exchange data. The multiprocessing module, however, is based on a *shared memory paradigm*, and therefore would allow the sharing of resources between processes. Since this practice would lead to the same problems as threads with race condition phenomena and lack of synchronization between processes, it is highly not recommended to use it. The multiprocessing module provides like the *threading* module the same tools for process synchronization, such as **semaphores**, **locks**, **events**, and so on, but it is not recommended to follow this approach. Unlike threads, to work with a set of processes in parallel, the multiprocessing module provides communication channels to be used as secure and synchronized data exchange mechanisms. There are two different modes of communication channels:

- Queues
- Pipes

These channels are defined within the code through the **Queue** and **Pipe** classes provided by the multiprocessing module itself. Both are equipped with **Queue()** and **Pipe()** constructors, and a whole series of methods that manage the exchange of data between processes, and their internal synchronization mechanisms. These communication channels, once defined at the main process level, are excellent tools for exchanging data in a perfectly synchronized manner. In fact, thanks to them, the processes will be able to send and receive data in a *safe* and *synchronized* way, without the risk of race conditions. Furthermore, if the data sent is more than requested, these will not be overwritten, but accumulated within these objects, providing buffering of data.

Queues

The **Queues** that we will use as a communication channel between the processes are implemented by the *multiprocessing* module. In Python, there are also queues belonging to the queue module (which we have already used with threads). But in reality, the internal implementations are different, and **multiprocessing.Queue** uses a different data transfer mechanism, specific to working with processes. That is, they make use of the *message passing paradigm* used exclusively for processes and avoid using synchronization mechanisms to add to the queues.

Queue is a data structure that implements a **First IN-First OUT (FIFO)** queue. Processes will be able to add data to the queue through the **put()** method or they will be able to receive data from it through the **get()** method. The order of the data entered is maintained within the queue, and the data sent to the processes that request them will then follow the order of entry.

The data can be accumulated within the queue, and these can be both simple numerical data and even complex objects. The queue has *no size limit* and therefore there are no data overflow problems. However, you can define a capacity limit, passing as an argument of the **Queue()** constructor, a value of **maxsize** that represents the maximum number of objects contained:

```
queue = multiprocessing.Queue(maxsize=100)
```

Still, in the context of the capacity of a queue, it is sometimes important during execution to know the current number of objects contained within it. For this purpose, there is a **qsize()** method which returns this number:

```
size = queue.qsize()
```

Still, in the context of managing a queue when you want to affix conditions to the program flow, it might be useful to know if a queue is empty or full. The **empty()** method returns a Boolean that has the value *True* when the queue is *empty*, while the **full()** method returns *True* if the queue is *full*:

```
if queue.empty():

    ...


if queue.full():

    ...
```

In order to better understand how a queue works, we can use the *Consumer-Producer paradigm*, which is very useful in these cases of sending and receiving data. The *producer* will be any process that will provide data as a result of its execution and the consumer will be any process that will need that data in order to complete its execution. To make this mechanism work, created by at least two processes, an exchange of data will therefore be necessary. Since the processes do not have a common memory area, they will exchange their data through the queue. The *Consumer* will send the produced data to the queue, while the *consumer* will request them from the *Producer*. *Consumers* and *Producers* are always *asynchronous*, they usually do not depend except for the data flow that happens via the Queue. Since the times of the consumer and producer rarely coincide, there may be cases in which the *producer* produces *consumer* data faster, and these can be accumulated in an orderly manner within the queue, without being overwritten. The *consumer* will thus have plenty of time to use this produced data in an orderly manner.

The following code implements a simple *Producer-Consumer paradigm* which is based on two parallel processes that make use of a Queue to exchange data:

```
from multiprocessing import Process, Queue

import time

import random


class Consumer(Process):
  def __init__(self, count, queue):
    Process.__init__(self)
    self.count = count
```

```
    self.queue = queue


  def run(self):
    for i in range(self.count):
      local = self.queue.get()
      time.sleep(2)
      print("consumer has used this: %s" %local)


class Producer(Process):
  def __init__(self, count, queue):
    Process.__init__(self)
    self.count = count
    self.queue = queue


  def request(self):
    time.sleep(1)
    return random.randint(0,100)


  def run(self):
    for i in range(self.count):
      local = self.request()
      self.queue.put(local)
      print("producer has loaded this: %s" %local)


if __name__ == '__main__':
  queue = Queue()
  count = 5
  p1 = Producer(count, queue)
  p2 = Consumer(count, queue)
  p1.start()
```

```
p2.start()
p1.join()
p2.join()
```

Running the code will produce a result similar to the following:

```
producer has loaded this: 55

producer has loaded this: 30

consumer has used this: 55

producer has loaded this: 60

producer has loaded this: 14

consumer has used this: 30

producer has loaded this: 97

consumer has used this: 60

consumer has used this: 14

consumer has used this: 97
```

As we can see, the values generated by the producer process are accumulated within the Queue and subsequently used by the consumer process in perfect synchrony, without loss or overwriting of values.

Pipes

The other class that performs the functions of the communication channel between processes is the **Pipe**. The pipe implements *two-way communication* between the two processes, designed to send and receive data between them. Like the Queue class, it has its own **Pipe()** constructor which will create two different **multiprocessing.connection.Connection** objects when it is declared. So normally when you declare the **Pipe()** constructor, you put the two instances of the connections separately:

```
conn1, conn2 = multiprocessing.Pipe()
```

One of these connections will be used to send the data and the other to receive them. By default, the first connection (**conn1**) is used only to receive data, while the second connection (**conn2**) is used only to send data.

In addition to the *bidirectional mode*, a Pipe can also be created in *duplex mode*, in which each of the two connections can be used to both send and receive data. In this case, we will have to set the duplex argument passed in the constructor to **True**:

```
conn1, conn2 = multiprocessing.Pipe(duplex=True)
```

In both modes, the processes, through the two generated *Connection* objects, will be able to send data through the **send()** method, and receive them through the **recv()** method:

```
conn2.send(object)
```

```
object = conn1.recv()
```

As for the queues, there is no limit to the size of the objects to be sent; the only condition is that they are *pickable*. When sent, they will be picked, and then upon being received, they will automatically be unpicked.

As with the Queue, the **Pipe** class also provides a set of methods that can be used to manage the connections created in their use. For example, the state of the Pipe can be controlled by the **poll()** function. This function returns a *Boolean: True* if there is data in the connection waiting to be received by a process. This method is very useful in conditions to manage the flow of execution of a program:

```
if conn1.poll():
```

Let's see the concepts just exposed through an example code, like the following one:

```
from multiprocessing import Process, Pipe

import time

import random


class Consumer(Process):
  def __init__(self, count, conn):
    Process.__init__(self)
    self.count = count
    self.conn = conn


  def run(self):
    for i in range(self.count):
      local = self.conn.recv()
      time.sleep(2)
```

```python
      print("consumer has used this: %s" %local)


class Producer(Process):
  def __init__(self, count, conn):
    Process.__init__(self)
    self.count = count
    self.conn = conn


  def request(self):
    time.sleep(1)
    return random.randint(0,100)


  def run(self):
    for i in range(self.count):
      local = self.request()
      self.conn.send(local)
      print("producer has loaded this: %s" %local)


if __name__ == '__main__':
  recver, sender = Pipe()
  count = 5
  p1 = Producer(count, sender)
  p2 = Consumer(count, recver)
  p1.start()
  p2.start()
  p1.join()
  p2.join()
  recver.close()
  sender.close()
```

Also, in this case, we used the *Producer-Consumer paradigm* and kept as much as possible the code used with the Queue previously. This is to help the reader make appropriate comparisons between the two modes. Running the code, you will get a result similar to the following:

```
producer has loaded this: 0

producer has loaded this: 76

consumer has used this: 0

producer has loaded this: 28

producer has loaded this: 90

consumer has used this: 76

producer has loaded this: 75

consumer has used this: 28

consumer has used this: 90

consumer has used this: 75
```

At the end of using the Pipe, we called the **close()** method for each of the two connections. This operation is very important in order to release all the resources used by the Pipe.

The most important, and perhaps most limiting, aspect of Pipes is that it works exclusively between two endpoints, therefore between only two processes. If you have to work with several processes at the same time, you will need to establish a Pipe for each pair of processes. It is clear that when the processes that work in parallel become many, the management of Pipes will become *problematic*.

Pipe versus Queue

We have just seen that as communication channels, the multiprocessing module provides both *Pipes* and *Queues* as a solution. So, *which of the two to choose to exchange data between processes in parallel?*

At first glance, given the limited use of Pipes between only two processes, it would seem that a queue is always the best solution. But that's not always *true*.

Pipe is a much simpler class than a queue. They are implemented at a low level, and it is this feature that makes them more efficient and potentially faster for exchanging data between two processes. Therefore, if this type of connection can be used between pairs of processes, it is preferable to a Queue. If, on the other hand, the data exchange is consistent and the number of processes involved in this exchange is large, the use of the Queue is only possible.

Mapping of a function through a process pool

Another very important aspect of parallel programming is the mapping of a function. In fact, it is possible to extend the functionality of **map()** in Python between multiple processes in parallel. This function is very useful when you want to apply a function on an **iterable** object. In fact, the **map()** function applies the function to each element of the object and returns, as a result, an array of elements of *equal size*, each with the result of the function on each element.

To better understand how the **map()** function works, there is nothing better than a direct example. Let's consider the following code:

```python
import time

import math

import numpy as np


def func(value):
    result = math.sqrt(value)
    print("The value %s and the elaboration is %s" %(value, result) )
    return result


if __name__ == '__main__':
    data = np.array([10,3,6,1])
    results = map(func, data)
    for result in results:
        print("This is the result: %s" %result)
```

In the code, we have chosen a **NumPy** array of four elements on which we will apply the function **func()**. As a result of the function, we will get an array of four elements, each with the return value of the function applied to the corresponding element.

Running the code will produce a result similar to the following:

```
The value 10 and the elaboration is 3.1622776601683795

This is the result: 3.1622776601683795

The value 3 and the elaboration is 1.7320508075688772
```

This is the result: 1.7320508075688772

The value 6 and the elaboration is 2.449489742783178

This is the result: 2.449489742783178

The value 1 and the elaboration is 1.0

This is the result: 1.0

This **iterable** object mapping mechanism can be extended in parallel programming. The efficiency could grow enormously if the calculation of the function on each element could take place in parallel. For example, each element could be assigned to a process whose target is just the function passed in **map()**. In this case, all elements would be calculated at the same time. For an array of n elements, a normal program would take $n * t$ time, where t is the execution time of the function. In the parallel case, the same array of n elements would be passed to n processes, and the execution time would be limited to t (if there are n cores or n processors in the system). So, the increase in efficiency is clear.

For parallel mapping of a function, the multiprocessing module provides the **multiprocessing.pool.Pool** class. This class provides two methods for this:

- map()
- map_async()

In the case of parallel programming, there are *two* methods due to the different synchronization possible. They both work almost the same way except that the **map()** function should be used when we need to block program execution until all target functions in *parallel* have completed their work. While the **map_async()** function should be used when it will not block the entire execution of the program.

The **map()** method receives two arguments, the **target** function, and the **iterable** object:

```
results = pool.map(target, iterable):
```

As the name implies, the **pool** class will create a pool of processes equal to the number of elements of the **iterable** and will pass the **target** function to these processes.

But to better understand these concepts and how they work, it is necessary to move on to practical examples:

```
import time

import math

import numpy as np
```

```python
from multiprocessing.pool import Pool


def func(value):
    result = math.sqrt(value)
    print("The value %s and the elaboration is %s" %(value, result) )
    time.sleep(value)
    return result


if __name__ == '__main__':
    with Pool() as pool:
        data = np.array([10,3,6,1])
        results = pool.map(func, data)
        print("The main process is going on...")
        for result in results:
            print("This is the result: %s" %result)
    print("END Program")
```

Running this program, we get a result similar to the following:

```
The value 10 and the elaboration is 3.1622776601683795

The value 3 and the elaboration is 1.7320508075688772

The value 6 and the elaboration is 2.449489742783178

The value 1 and the elaboration is 1.0

The main process is going on...

This is the result: 3.1622776601683795

This is the result: 1.7320508075688772

This is the result: 2.449489742783178

This is the result: 1.0

END Program
```

As for the **map_async()** function, we can modify the previous code by making the appropriate substitutions as in the following code:

```python
import time
import math
import numpy as np
from multiprocessing.pool import Pool


def func(value):
    result = math.sqrt(value)
    print("The value %s and the elaboration is %s" %(value, result) )
    time.sleep(value)
    return result


if __name__ == '__main__':
    with Pool() as pool:
        data = np.array([10,3,6,1])
        results = pool.map_async(func, data)
        print("Main Process is going on...")
        for result in results.get():
            print("This is the result: %s" %result)
    print("END Program")
```

Running the program, we get a result similar to the following:

Main Process is going on...

The value 10 and the elaboration is 3.1622776601683795

The value 3 and the elaboration is 1.7320508075688772

The value 6 and the elaboration is 2.449489742783178

The value 1 and the elaboration is 1.0

This is the result: 3.1622776601683795

This is the result: 1.7320508075688772

This is the result: 2.449489742783178

This is the result: 1.0

END Program

As we can see from the two different results, we got the behavior we expected. Using the **map()** method you have a synchronization mechanism that interrupts the flow of execution of the **main** process. This does not restart until all parallel processes launched by **map()** finish their execution. In fact, the text **Main process is going on...** appears only after all *child* processes have finished their task and returned their results to results. While using **map_async()**, the execution of the **main** process goes on and does not wait for the complete evaluation of results. The text **Main process is going on...** appears at the beginning of the text.

Mapping in parallel with chunksize

The **map()** function will apply a function to each element in an **iterable**. If the **iterable** has a large number of elements, it may be very inefficient to call as many processes to execute them.

A more efficient approach is to divide the elements of the **iterable** into portions of a certain number of elements, each to be assigned to a process. This can be achieved by passing the **chunksize** argument to the **map()** function.

Let's modify the example code we used earlier for the **map()** method, increasing the number of elements in the **np.array()**. We will then set portions of four elements of the array for each process, passing the **chunksize** argument equal to **4** to the **map()** method:

```python
import time

import math

import numpy as np

from multiprocessing.pool import Pool


def func(value):
    result = math.sqrt(value)
    print("The value %s and the elaboration is %s" %(value, result) )
    time.sleep(value)
    return result


if __name__ == '__main__':
    with Pool() as pool:
        data = np.array([10,3,6,1,4,5,2,9,7,3,4,6])
```

```
        results = pool.map(func, data, chunksize=4)
        print("The main process is going on...")
        for result in results:
            print("This is the result: %s" %result)
    print("END Program")
```

Running the code, you will get a result similar to the following:

```
The value 10 and the elaboration is 3.1622776601683795
The value 4 and the elaboration is 2.0
The value 7 and the elaboration is 2.6457513110645907
The value 5 and the elaboration is 2.23606797749979
The value 3 and the elaboration is 1.7320508075688772
The value 2 and the elaboration is 1.4142135623730951
The value 3 and the elaboration is 1.7320508075688772
The value 4 and the elaboration is 2.0
The value 9 and the elaboration is 3.0
The value 6 and the elaboration is 2.449489742783178
The value 6 and the elaboration is 2.449489742783178
The value 1 and the elaboration is 1.0
The main process is going on...
This is the result: 3.1622776601683795
This is the result: 1.7320508075688772
This is the result: 2.449489742783178
This is the result: 1.0
This is the result: 2.0
This is the result: 2.23606797749979
This is the result: 1.4142135623730951
This is the result: 3.0
This is the result: 2.6457513110645907
This is the result: 1.7320508075688772
This is the result: 2.0
```

```
This is the result: 2.449489742783178
END Program
```

In addition to the **map()** function, the **Pool** class provides a whole series of methods with similar behavior, such as **imap()** and **apply()**, all also in the asynchronous versions.

The ProcessPoolExecutor

We have a similar mechanism to that of process pools with another class, the **ProcessPoolExecutor** distributed by the **concurrent.future** module. This class also provides a pool of reusable processes to perform specific operations, including **map()**.

Also, in this case, you specify the name of the **target** function to execute and the **iterable** on which the function will be applied. Once all the assigned tasks have been completed, the **ProcessPoolExecutor** must be closed in order to release all the resources used. The **shutdown()** function is used for closing.

But even in this case, there are much simpler and more efficient constructs. In fact, the **ProcessPoolExecutor** is compatible with the context manager and the **with** declaration:

```
with ProcessPoolExecutor() as executor:
```

In this case, when execution exits the context manager block, the **shutdown()** function is called automatically. The context manager is equivalent to the following wording:

```
try:
    executor = ProcessPoolExecutor()
finally:
    executor.shutdown()
```

It is therefore clear that the use of a context manager is very convenient in these cases. The **ProcessPoolExecutor** as a pool is very useful for running the **map()** function in *parallel*. We can see it, for example, in the following code:

```
import time
import math
import numpy as np
from concurrent.futures import ProcessPoolExecutor


def func(value):
```

```
    result = math.sqrt(value)
    print("The value %s and the elaboration is %s" %(value, result) )
    time.sleep(value)
    return result


if __name__ == '__main__':
    with ProcessPoolExecutor(10) as executor:
        data = np.array([10,3,6,1])
        for result in executor.map(func, data):
            print("This is the result: %s" %result)
    print("END Program")
```

Running the code will produce a result similar to the following:

```
The value 10 and the elaboration is 3.1622776601683795

The value 3 and the elaboration is 1.7320508075688772

The value 6 and the elaboration is 2.449489742783178

The value 1 and the elaboration is 1.0

This is the result: 3.1622776601683795

This is the result: 1.7320508075688772

This is the result: 2.449489742783178

This is the result: 1.0

END Program
```

Previously, we saw the **map()** method of **Pool()** which offered the possibility of using portions of multiple elements to be assigned to each process thanks to the **chunksize** argument. Well, even in the case of the **ProcessPoolExecutor**, the **map()** method takes the same argument.

We then modify the previous code by extending the number of elements in the **np.array()** and adding the **chunksize** argument equal to **4**. Also, to recognize which process treats the different elements of the **np.array** we import the **os** module, which uses the **getpid()** to get the ID of the various processes:

```
import time

import math

import os
```

```python
import numpy as np
from concurrent.futures import ProcessPoolExecutor


def func(value):
    result = math.sqrt(value)
    pid = os.getpid()
    print("[Pid:%s] The value %s and the elaboration is %s" %(pid, value,
result) )
    time.sleep(value)
    return result


if __name__ == '__main__':
    with ProcessPoolExecutor(10) as executor:
        data = np.array([10,3,6,1,4,5,2,9,7,3,4,6])
        for result in executor.map(func, data, chunksize=4):
            print("This is the result: %s" %result)
    print("END Program")
```

Running the code will produce a result similar to the following:

```
[Pid:14716] The value 10 and the elaboration is 3.1622776601683795
[Pid:22496] The value 4 and the elaboration is 2.0
[Pid:6508] The value 7 and the elaboration is 2.6457513110645907
[Pid:22496] The value 5 and the elaboration is 2.23606797749979
[Pid:6508] The value 3 and the elaboration is 1.7320508075688772
[Pid:22496] The value 2 and the elaboration is 1.4142135623730951
[Pid:14716] The value 3 and the elaboration is 1.7320508075688772
[Pid:6508] The value 4 and the elaboration is 2.0
[Pid:22496] The value 9 and the elaboration is 3.0
[Pid:14716] The value 6 and the elaboration is 2.449489742783178
[Pid:6508] The value 6 and the elaboration is 2.449489742783178
[Pid:14716] The value 1 and the elaboration is 1.0
This is the result: 3.1622776601683795
```

```
This is the result: 1.7320508075688772

This is the result: 2.449489742783178

This is the result: 1.0

This is the result: 2.0

This is the result: 2.23606797749979

This is the result: 1.4142135623730951

This is the result: 3.0

This is the result: 2.6457513110645907

This is the result: 1.7320508075688772

This is the result: 2.0

This is the result: 2.449489742783178

END Program
```

The mpi4py library

A completely different approach to parallel programming in Python using processes is with the use of the **Message Passage Interface (MPI)**. This is a *communication protocol*, practically a standard, with regard to parallel programming, particularly in systems with multiple nodes (multiple processors). This protocol has been implemented in many programming languages such as Fortran and C.

Python also has a number of MPI modules useful for parallel programming. The most interesting of these is the **mpi4py** library. This was developed based on the MPI-1/2 *specification* and provides an object-oriented interface based on MPI-2 C ++ *bindings*.

This library is based on general concepts very different from those we have seen with the multiprocessing module and with the standard Python library in general. These concepts are in fact based on standards developed specifically for multiprocessor and distributed architectures, as well as clusters. It is therefore clear that the execution methods and the code constructs are very different from those seen in the first part of the chapter.

But, *why use MPI modules instead of the multiprocessing module?* This is due to many factors. The first is because MPI has practically become a standard of parallel programming for many programming languages, including Python, and is adaptable to the most varied architectures. At the same time, it can also be used on simple systems with a single multi-core computer, where the efficiency of the calculation is not so evident, but it is useful for practicing and developing programs in parallel that can be adapted to very complex architectures.

First, you need to install the **mpi4py** library. For Anaconda, just run the command:

```
conda install mpi4py
```

while if you are using Python, you will use **pip**:

```
pip install mpi4py
```

For the execution of programs in Python, instead of the classic **python** command, you will have to use the following wording from the shell:

```
mpiexec -n x python mpi4py _name.py
```

The **mpiexec** command is typically used to be able to directly start multiple processes in parallel, where **x** will be the number of processes in parallel.

To see how the library works, let's start with the simplest program you can run with **mpiexec**:

```
from mpi4py import MPI

comm = MPI.COMM_WORLD

rank = comm.rank

print("The process %d is started" %rank)
```

To execute the code, we will have to use the **mpiexec** command. If we want to start **2** processes in parallel:

```
$ mpiexec -n 2 python mpi01.py
```

We will get the output of the two processes:

```
The process 0 is started

The process 1 is started
```

If, on the other hand, we want to start **6** in parallel, it will be sufficient to modify the value of the parameter **n** passed on the command line:

```
$ mpiexec -n 6 python mpi01a.py
```

This time, obtaining a result similar to the following:

```
The process 2 is started

The process 5 is started

The process 1 is started

The process 4 is started
```

```
The process 3 is started
```

```
The process 0 is started
```

As we can see from the outputs, the rank order of the processes is not *ordered* but is a random result that varies from execution to execution. Analyzing the code, the **comm** parameter expresses the communicator and defines the group of processes that can communicate through the *message passing mechanism*:

```
comm = MPI.COMM_WORLD
```

While the rank is an identification number of the process within the group of communicating processes. That is, all the processes launched by the **mpiexec** command become part of this communication group and each of them is identified by a number, the *rank*.

Parallelism of the processes

As we have seen for the *multiprocessing* module, the processes allow the execution of code in parallel. We can perform the same tests with the **mpi4py** library, and this time we will perform some benchmarking by measuring the execution times. For this purpose, we launch a program:

```
import time

from mpi4py import MPI

comm = MPI.COMM_WORLD

rank = comm.rank

print("The process %d is started" %rank)

time.sleep(10)

print("The process %d is ended" %rank)
```

To measure the time taken with the **mpiexec** command we cannot use the **time** module, but we can use the **time** command on Linux, or on Windows PowerShell. By running, we get a result similar to the following:

```
> Measure-Command { mpiexec -n 4 python mpi01b.py | Out-Host }
```

```
The process 2 is started
```

```
The process 2 is ended
```

```
The process 3 is started
```

```
The process 3 is ended
```

```
The process 1 is started
```

```
The process 1 is ended
```

```
The process 0 is started
The process 0 is ended
```

```
Days               : 0
Hours              : 0
Minutes            : 0
Seconds            : 10
Milliseconds       : 298
Ticks              : 102985516
TotalDays          : 0,000119196199074074
TotalHours         : 0,00286070877777778
TotalMinutes       : 0,171642526666667
TotalSeconds       : 10,2985516
TotalMilliseconds  : 10298,5516
```

As we can see, the execution takes about **10** seconds, the time we expected for the execution of each process. The sequential version of the previous program results in the following code:

```python
import time


for i in range(4):
        print("The process %d is started" %i)
        time.sleep(10)
        print("The process %d is ended" %i)
```

We measure the time taken to run the previous program again via PowerShell with the **Measure-Command** command (although we could have used the **time** module):

```
> Measure-Command { python mpi01c.py }
```

```
Days               : 0
Hours              : 0
```

```
Minutes            : 0
Seconds            : 40
Milliseconds       : 99
Ticks              : 400994538
TotalDays          : 0,000464114048611111
TotalHours         : 0,0111387371666667
TotalMinutes       : 0,66832423
TotalSeconds       : 40,0994538
TotalMilliseconds  : 40099,4538
```

As we can see, it takes **40** seconds as we would expect from a sequential execution (four executions of **10** seconds each), compared to about **10** seconds for four executions (four processes) in parallel. We, therefore, have a significant increase in efficiency.

Efficiency of parallelism based on the number of processors/cores

As for the efficiency of *parallelism* based on the number of processors or cores, different time measurements can be made by varying the number of parallel processes. We use the following code:

```
import time

from mpi4py import MPI

comm = MPI.COMM_WORLD

rank = comm.rank

print("The process %d is started" %rank)

n = 0

for i in range(100000000):

    n += i

print("The process %d is ended" %rank)
```

We execute the code with **mpiexec** by varying the number of processors. Measurements are obtained as shown in *Table* 3.1. In the first column, we have the number of processes launched in parallel. In the second column, we have the measured times related to the number of processes:

N	t	s
1	10,7	10,7
2	13,8	6,9
4	16,0	4
6	19,9	3,317
8	27,6	3,45
12	39,6	3,3

Table 3.1: *Execution times depending on the number of processes*

But what interests us is the ratio s = t / N, that is, the execution time for the task to be performed for each process. As you can see, this value progressively decreases as the number of processes increases. However, as we can see, the value tends to a threshold beyond which it does not drop further, of about 3.3s. This is much more visible in the following figure (see *Figure 3.3*):

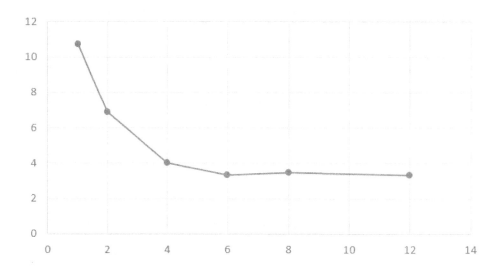

Figure 3.3: *Time taken based on the number of processes*

From *Figure 3.3*, it can be seen that over six processes, the time taken for each task remains almost the same. This happens because in my system I have six cores and beyond it is not possible to work in parallel.

Main applications of mpi4py

The **mpi4py** library is therefore based on the message passing according to MPI standards. Its applications in the world of parallel programming can be divided into three different groups:

- Point-to-point communication
- Collective communication
- Topologies

In the second half of the chapter, we will look at all three applications through a series of examples.

Point-to-point communication implementation

Point-to-point operations consist of an exchange of messages between two processes. In a perfect world, each sending operation should be perfectly synchronized with the respective receiving operation. Obviously, this is not the case, and the MPI implementation must be able to preserve the data sent even when the sending process and the receiving process are not synchronized. Typically, a buffer is used, which is transparent to the developer and entirely managed by the **mpi4py** library.

The **mpi4py** module enables point-to-point communication through *two* functions:

- **comm.send(data, receiver_process)**
- **comm.recv(sender_process)**

The **send()** function sends data to the receiving process through its rank in the communication group. The **recv()** function receives data from the sending process, which is also identified by its communication group rank number:

```
from mpi4py import MPI

comm = MPI.COMM_WORLD

rank = comm.rank

print("Process %s started" %rank)

if rank==0:

    msg ="This is my message"

    receiver = 1
```

```
    comm.send(msg,dest=receiver)
    print("Process 0 sent: %s " %msg + "to %d" %receiver)
if rank==1:
    source=0
    msg=comm.recv(source)
    print("Process 1 received is: %s" %msg + "from %d" %source)
```

You run the preceding code in parallel by running the following shell command:

```
$ mpiexec -n 9 python programma01.py
```

And you get a result similar to the following:

The **send()** and **recv()** methods are blocking, that is, they block the calling process until the buffered data can be safely used.

Collective communications

The most commonly used collective communications are the following:

- Barrier synchronization
- Broadcasting data
- Gathering data
- Scattering data
- Reduction operation

Collective communication using data broadcast

During parallel programming, we often find ourselves in a situation where it is necessary to share the value of a certain variable at runtime among several processes or to distribute different operations on variables to which each process provides a partial solution. To solve this kind of situation, tree communication groups are used (for example, *process 0* sends data to *processes 1 and 2*, which in turn will send it to *processes 3,4,5,6*).

A method of communication that involves all the processes that belong to a communicator is called **collective communication**. Consequently, collective communication is based on more than two processes. In this case, we can call it *broadcast*, where a single process sends the same data to the processes (see *Figure 3.4*):

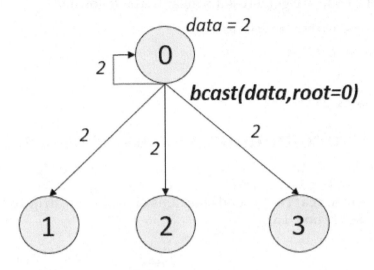

Figure 3.4: *Broadcasting*

Reads the data defined in *process* 0 defined as *root* and then distributes it among all processes, including the *root* process itself:

```
from mpi4py import MPI

import random

comm = MPI.COMM_WORLD

rank = comm.rank

if rank == 0:

    data=random.randint(1, 10)

else:

    data=None

data = comm.bcast(data, root=0)

if rank == 1:

    print("The square of %d is %d" %(data,data*data))

if rank == 2:

    print("Half of %d is %d" %(data,data/2))

if rank == 3:

    print("Double of %d is %d" %(data,data*2))
```

Running the code, we get a result similar to the following:

```
$mpiexec -n 4 python mpi04a.py

The square of 6 is 36

Half of 6 is 3

Double of 6 is 12
```

Collective communication using data scattering

The scattering functionality is very similar to that of broadcast, but with one difference. While **comm.bcast()** sends the same type of data to all listening processes, **comm.scatter()** sends portions of data in an array to the different processes (see *Figure 3.5*):

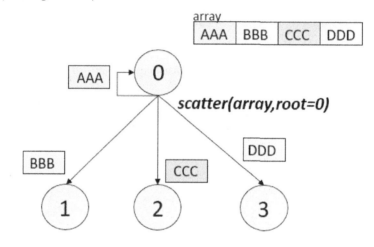

Figure 3.5: *Scattering*

The **comm.scatter()** function takes the elements of the array and distributes them among the processes based on their rank, so the first element will be sent to *process 0*, the second element to *process 1*, and so on:

```
from mpi4py import MPI

comm = MPI.COMM_WORLD

rank = comm.rank

if rank == 0:

    array = ['AAA','BBB','CCC','DDD']

else:
```

```
    array = None
data = comm.scatter(array,root=0)
print("Process %d is working on %s element" %(rank,data))
```

Running the code, we will get a result similar to the following:

```
$mpiexec -n 4 python mpi05a.py
Process 0 is working on AAA element
Process 1 is working on BBB element
Process 2 is working on CCC element
Process 3 is working on DDD element
```

Collective communication using data gathering

The gathering function performs the inverse operation of scattering. In this case, all the processes involved in the calculation send their portions of data to a receiving *root* process which will collect them all together (see *Figure 3.6*):

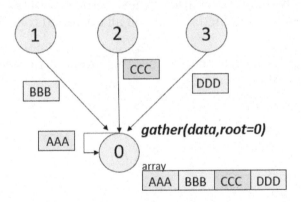

Figure 3.6: Gathering

```
from mpi4py import MPI
comm = MPI.COMM_WORLD
rank = comm.rank
if rank == 0:
    data = 'AAA'
if rank == 1:
```

```
    data = 'BBB'
if rank == 2:
    data = 'CCC'
if rank == 3:
    data = 'DDD'
array = comm.gather(data, root=0)
if rank == 0:
    print("The new array is %s " %array)
```

By running the code, you will get a code similar to the following:

```
$mpiexec -n 4 python mpi06a.py
```

```
The new array is ['AAA', 'BBB', 'CCC', 'DDD']
```

This method of passing messages can be very useful for carrying out parallel computing. Many algorithms rely on calculations that can be broken down into *smaller identical chunks*. By assigning each of them to a parallel process, you will effectively reduce execution times. At the end of the calculation, many partial results will be obtained which will all be added together to give a final result.

Let's take a simple example to see how this concept fits well with collective communication with gathering:

```
from mpi4py import MPI
comm = MPI.COMM_WORLD
rank = comm.rank
size = comm.size
data = 2*rank + 1
print("Process %d calculated this value: %d" %(rank,data))
array = comm.gather(data, root=0)
if rank == 0:
    result = 0
    for i in range(0, size):
        result += array[i]
    print("The result of the parallel computation is %d" %result)
```

Running this code on four processes, we will get a result similar to the following:

```
$mpiexec -n 4 python mpi06b.py

Process 3 calculated this value: 7

Process 1 calculated this value: 3

Process 2 calculated this value: 5

Process 0 calculated this value: 1

The result of the parallel computation is 16
```

As can be seen from the result, we have divided the calculation into four equal portions. In these cases, in the calculation present in the code, it often happens to exploit the number of ranks of every single process for iterations, and to index the computation portions. The individual results are then added together to produce the final result. By varying the number of parallel processes, it is possible to extend the iteration of the calculation to more extended values.

For example, by extending the parallel computation to eight processes we will obtain the following result:

```
$mpiexec -n 8 python mpi06b.py

Process 5 calculated this value: 11

Process 7 calculated this value: 15

Process 3 calculated this value: 7

Process 6 calculated this value: 13

Process 1 calculated this value: 3

Process 2 calculated this value: 5

Process 4 calculated this value: 9

Process 0 calculated this value: 1

The result of the parallel computation is 64
```

Collective communication using the AlltoAll mode

Another way of collective communication is using the **AlltoAll mode**. In this case, there is behavior by the processes similar to gathering and scattering at the same time. In this communication group, each process sends and receives portions of an array of data from other processes belonging to the group (see *Figure 3.7*):

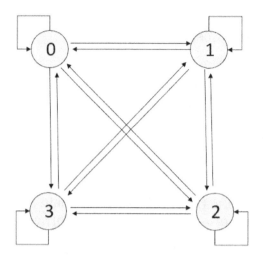

Figure 3.7: *AllToAll*

```
from mpi4py import MPI
comm = MPI.COMM_WORLD
rank = comm.rank
if rank==0:
    output = ['0A','0B','0C','0D']
if rank==1:
    output = ['1A','1B','1C','1D']
if rank==2:
    output = ['2A','2B','2C','2D']
if rank==3:
    output = ['3A','3B','3C','3D']


input = comm.alltoall(output)
print("Process %s received %s" %(rank,input))
```

Running the code, you will get a result similar to the following:

```
$mpiexec -n 4 python mpi07a.py
Process 0 received ['0A', '1A', '2A', '3A']
```

```
Process 2 received ['0C', '1C', '2C', '3C']
Process 3 received ['0D', '1D', '2D', '3D']
Process 1 received ['0B', '1B', '2B', '3B']
```

As we can see from the result:

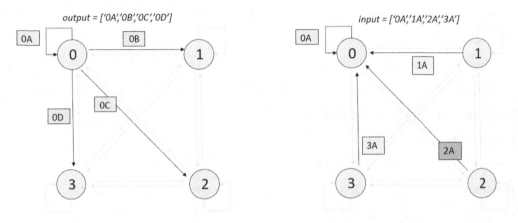

Figure 3.8: *AllToAll for process 0*

Reduction operation

The reduction operation, performed by **comm.reduce()**, takes an array of input elements from each process and returns an array of output elements to the root process. The output items contain the reduced result:

```
from mpi4py import MPI

import numpy as np


comm = MPI.COMM_WORLD

rank = comm.rank


if rank == 0:
  output = np.array([0,0,0,0])
if rank == 1:
  output = np.array([1,1,1,1])
if rank == 2:
  output = np.array([2,2,2,2])
```

```
if rank == 3:
  output = np.array([3,3,3,3])


print("Process %d. Sending %s" %(rank,output))
input = comm.reduce(output, root=0, op=MPI.SUM)
if rank == 0:
   print("The result of the parallel computation is %s" %(input))
```

By running the preceding code, you will get a result similar to the following:

```
$mpiexec -n 4 python mpi08a.py

Process 3. Sending [3 3 3 3]

Process 2. Sending [2 2 2 2]

Process 1. Sending [1 1 1 1]

Process 0. Sending [0 0 0 0]

The result of the parallel computation is [6 6 6 6]
```

The operations available in the reduction are different, *Table* 3.2 shows a complete list:

SUM	Sum of the elements.
PROD	Multiplication of the elements.
MAX	The maximum value of the elements.
MAXLOC	The maximum value and the rank of the related process.
MIN	The minimum value of the elements.
MINLOC	The minimum value and rank of the related process.
LAND	Logical AND across the elements.
LOR	Logical OR across the elements.
BAND	Bitwise AND across the elements.
BOR	Bitwise OR across the elements.

Table 3.2: *List of reduction operations*

Optimization of communications through topologies

An interesting feature provided by MPI is the possibility to intervene in virtual topologies. All communication between processes occurs through communication groups. So far using **MPI_COMM_WORLD**, all processes are assigned to a group and each of them is assigned a rank number starting from 0 up to n-1, where n is the number of processes launched in parallel execution.

The **mpi4py** library allows us to define a virtual topology for this communicator. That is, the way in which ranks are assigned can be redefined. By defining a virtual topology, each node (process) will only be able to communicate with neighboring nodes in the virtual topology. In this way, we will improve the performance given the reduction in execution times. In fact, in complex cases, as the ranks are randomly assigned to the various processes, the messages could pass through many of them before reaching the correct destination, that is the process for which this message was intended.

MPI provides two ways of building a topology:

- Cartesian
- Adjacency matrix

The first creates a **Cartesian** topology, while the second requires an adjacency matrix of the graph we want to create.

In this example, we will use only the Cartesian topologies, through which it is possible to build many topologies widely used as *rings* and *toroids*:

```
from mpi4py import MPI

comm = MPI.COMM_WORLD

rank = comm.rank


comm_3D = comm.Create_cart(dims = [3,3,3],
                           periods=[False,False,False],
                           reorder=False)
xyz = comm_3D.Get_coords(rank)
print ("In this 3D topology, process %s has coordinates %s " %(rank,xyz))
```

Running the code will give you the following result:

```
$mpiexec -n 27 python mpi09.py
```

In this 3D topology, process 0 has coordinates [0, 0, 0]

In this 3D topology, process 1 has coordinates [0, 0, 1]

In this 3D topology, process 4 has coordinates [0, 1, 1]

In this 3D topology, process 6 has coordinates [0, 2, 0]

In this 3D topology, process 7 has coordinates [0, 2, 1]

In this 3D topology, process 8 has coordinates [0, 2, 2]

In this 3D topology, process 12 has coordinates [1, 1, 0]

In this 3D topology, process 10 has coordinates [1, 0, 1]

In this 3D topology, process 9 has coordinates [1, 0, 0]

In this 3D topology, process 11 has coordinates [1, 0, 2]

In this 3D topology, process 13 has coordinates [1, 1, 1]

In this 3D topology, process 14 has coordinates [1, 1, 2]

In this 3D topology, process 15 has coordinates [1, 2, 0]

In this 3D topology, process 16 has coordinates [1, 2, 1]

In this 3D topology, process 17 has coordinates [1, 2, 2]

In this 3D topology, process 20 has coordinates [2, 0, 2]

In this 3D topology, process 5 has coordinates [0, 1, 2]

In this 3D topology, process 2 has coordinates [0, 0, 2]

In this 3D topology, process 18 has coordinates [2, 0, 0]

In this 3D topology, process 24 has coordinates [2, 2, 0]

In this 3D topology, process 26 has coordinates [2, 2, 2]

In this 3D topology, process 21 has coordinates [2, 1, 0]

In this 3D topology, process 3 has coordinates [0, 1, 0]

In this 3D topology, process 22 has coordinates [2, 1, 1]

In this 3D topology, process 19 has coordinates [2, 0, 1]

In this 3D topology, process 25 has coordinates [2, 2, 1]

In this 3D topology, process 23 has coordinates [2, 1, 2]

This result allows us to graphically place the typology as in the following figure (see *Figure 3.9*):

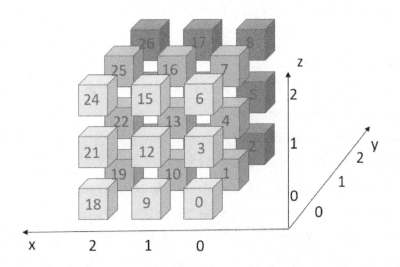

Figure 3.9: *Cartesian ranking on 3D topology*

Given one of the processes, it is possible to know which processes are adjacent to it, using the following function:

```
shift(direction,displacement)
```

This function returns *two* integers, which correspond to the ranks of the two adjacent processes on one of the Cartesian axes. The direction argument indicates in which direction we want to know the neighbors, corresponding to the Cartesian axes. The direction range is *[0, n-1]* where *n* is the size of the Cartesian mesh. So, in our case **0** will be **Z**, **1** will be **X**, and **2** will be **Y** (based on the previous figure). The other argument indicates when we need to move.

```
displacement (> 0: upwards shift, < 0: downwards shift) (integer)
```

However, in our case, since we want to know the adjacent processes, this value will always be **1**. Continuing with our example, if we want to know the neighbors of *process 12*, we can add new lines to the code:

```
from mpi4py import MPI

comm = MPI.COMM_WORLD

rank = comm.rank
```

```
comm_3D = comm.Create_cart(dims = [3,3,3],
                           periods =[False,False,False],
                           reorder=False)
xyz = comm_3D.Get_coords(rank)


if rank==12:
  print ("In this 3D topology, process %s has coordinates %s " %(rank,xyz))
  right,left = comm_3D.Shift(0,1)
  up,down = comm_3D.Shift(1,1)
  forward,backward = comm_3D.Shift(2,1)
  print("Neighbors (left-right): %s %s" %(left,right))
  print("Neighbors (up-down): %s %s" %(up,down))
  print("Neighbors (forward-backward): %s %s" %(forward,backward))
```

Running the code will produce a result similar to the following:

$mpiexec -n 27 python mpi09b.py

In this 3D topology, process 12 has coordinates [1, 1, 0]

Neighbors (left-right): 21 3

Neighbors (up-down): 9 15

Neighbors (forward-backward): -1 13

So, if during our parallel calculations, we need to exchange information only between topologically adjacent processes, we can directly insert their rank into the code, without using collective forms of communication, with nested ifs to make selections between the various processes, to select only the ones you want.

So, we can use the methods directly:

- **comm.send(data, neighbor)**
- **comm.recv(neighbor)**

to send and receive messages between adjacent processes directly and efficiently.

Conclusion

Completed this chapter, you have in hand all the basic tools to carry out programming in parallel. The concepts related to the *parent-children process mechanisms* on which the multiprocessing module works have been highlighted and treated with a series of examples. You have also acquired the ability to extend the powerful features of the **map()** function to parallel systems, significantly increasing the efficiency of your programs. At the same time, we have seen the **mpi4py** library which is based on the MPI standard, and allows you to launch a certain set of parent processes in parallel, and which uses the message passing paradigm for data exchange. In the next chapters, however, we will go into detail on more advanced concepts of parallel programming, with a series of libraries that further extend its potential.

References

- https://mpi4py.readthedocs.io/en/stable/

- https://docs.python.org/3/library/multiprocessing.html

- https://github.com/PowerShell/PowerShell/releases/tag/v7.2.6

- https://superfastpython.com/multiprocessing-pipe-in-python/

## CHAPTER 4

Asynchronous Programming with AsyncIO

In the second chapter of the book, we looked at concurrent programming based on threads and the threading module in particular. The limitations imposed by the GIL pose major problems to overcome if we want to work with threads in Python. This feature of Python, therefore, imposes thread concurrency, an inevitable limitation compared to parallel programming. Thus, in Python, a concurrent programming approach becomes indispensable as regards the management of tasks involving I / O communications where unpredictable waiting times have to be managed in conjunction with other tasks. In this chapter, we return to this type of programming but using a completely alternative approach: the **asynchronous model** and the **asyncio library**.

Structure

In this chapter, we will cover the following topics:

- Asynchronous and synchronous programming
- AsyncIO library
- async/await syntax
- Coroutines
- Tasks
- Future
- Event loop
- async for
- Queues

Asynchronous and synchronous programming

In the world of programming, there are *two* opposing models:

- Synchronous model (also referred to as **sync**)
- Asynchronous model (also referred to as **async**)

Asynchronous programming, which is the subject of this chapter of the book, is based on a model based on multiple entities acting concurrently. These entities may be threads, processes, or whatever else, which will have the ability to act simultaneously, and be executed in any order, independently of each other. The asynchronous model is a *non-blocking* architecture, that is, in programs created with this model there are no execution interruptions, even if one or more operations within it are waiting for some event and service.

Specifically, with asynchronous programming, it is possible to manage multiple operations at the same time, each with its specific task and independently from the other. Their execution does not depend on that of the others, and they all simultaneously try to complete their task (competition). In addition, the execution of each component of the program can be controlled, so as to activate it only when it is convenient or when it is possible to do so. This allows you to manage multiple requests at the same time, making the most of both resources and execution times. As an example, this is the behavior required by server applications that is referenced by multiple clients. Each of them will request the server for a service through a message, and then the server will manage which message to process and when to send the responses to the client. This behavior might not be required but is preferred owing to the waiting times for data on the network.

On the other hand, **synchronous programming** is the one we are most familiar with. It is based on a model, often with a single executing entity (single thread in a single process), where the code is nothing more than a sequence of operations to be performed. In fact, *synchronous server-side applications* usually use one thread per request. The execution of these operations is mutually dependent. Only when an operation is completed, the execution will go to the next operation. The synchronous model is a blocking architecture, that is, programs created with this model have a rigid flow of execution, and if an operation is blocked waiting for a response, the entire program will crash.

Pros and cons of asynchronous and synchronous programming

Asynchronous programming, if well designed for correct and consistent execution, is more *fluid*, and dynamically more responsive to external events such as a user or an external service that provides data or whatever. This type of programming is mainly based on the exploitation of the competition (even if they are not the same thing) and therefore the programs that use them can be *quick, more performing*, and also more *powerful*, considerably eliminating waiting times within the code execution, waiting for responses from external services.

The most obvious example of this programming is the one used to create **graphical user interfaces (GUI)**. Here the user sees fluid behavior with no waiting times, between button presses, text interaction, and drop-down menus that appear and disappear, thanks to the different event handlers that seem to work simultaneously (but often *don't*).

Synchronous programming, on the other hand, follows a predetermined execution, where the tasks are often sequential, and never concurrent, where each task waits for the previous one to be executed. Even if there are tasks in the program in parallel, they all perform the same function, and all are expected to execute in order to continue with the execution of the program. This programming is used when a task to be executed requires the result of the previous task, and so on going on with the program.

The advantage of *synchronous programming* is that this type of programming rarely causes problems in *run-time*. The behavior of the program is easily predictable and its implementation generates codes that are easy to create and read. On the contrary, *asynchronous programming* can be very *complex*, both in the implementation of the code and in its correct reading. Such a program can give rise to unpredictable and anomalous behaviors, difficult to predict in the development phase and even more difficult to fix. Asynchronous programming is therefore very demanding in maintenance.

Concurrent programming and asynchronous model

The concepts underlying concurrent programming have already been covered quite in depth in the previous chapters. Unlike parallel programming, this mode is capable of working on both *single-processor* and *multi-processor systems*. As we compared asynchronous to synchronous models, now let's compare it to concurrent programming.

The *asynchronous model* is a more restricted model than that used for threads since it is limited to working exclusively on a single thread running on a single-core CPU and not on multiple threads at the same time. Most asynchronous models use background worker threads for operations which are just not published in most documentation. In the thread model, the different tasks are distributed among the various threads that simultaneously (but not in parallel) compete for the execution timeline and the same shared resources. In the asynchronous model, on the other hand, the tasks all belong to the same thread, and they must alternate in the single flow of execution, asynchronously. The execution of each task can be suspended at any time, to make room for other pending tasks, to then be resumed when others are pending, and so on, until all operations are completed (as it is shown in *Figure 4.1*):

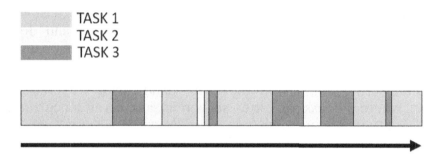

Figure 4.1: *The asynchronous execution*

The asynchronous model, in Python, has proved to be much more *efficient* and secure than the one used with threads, and in recent years it has taken more and more place in programming, so much so that it completely replaces the threading module in concurrent programming, whenever it is necessary to manage *IO-bound tasks*. Furthermore, it is perfect for working in complete synergy with parallel programming, since the latter, on the other hand, responds efficiently mainly with regard to the management of *CPU-bound tasks*. The complementarity of the two programs therefore often makes it necessary to use both programs.

AsyncIO library

In Python, the asynchronous model is implementable with the **AsyncIO** library. Although other alternatives are currently being developed, the AsyncIO library still remains the reference for concurrent programming asynchronously.

In this chapter we will introduce the concepts behind the asynchronous model, using only the AsyncIO library, where we find these concepts in the form of components. In this way, you will be able to become familiar with the asynchronous model through direct examples.

The main components of the module are:

- **Coroutine**
- **Task**
- **Future**
- **Event loop**

async/await syntax

The **AsyncIO** library has undergone many changes in recent years, and many programming patterns have been used. It is often possible to find on the internet code with obsolete structures linked to old words and patterns (decorators such as **@asyncio.coroutine**, and so on). The current syntax is one based on the **async-await** keywords.

Let's take a very simple example of how to implement code with the **asyncio** library following this syntax:

```
import asyncio


async def main():
    print('Awaiting for ...')
    await asyncio.sleep(1)
    print('... AsyncIO!')


asyncio.run(main())
```

As we can see, the code presents what we think is the definition of a function we called **main()**, with a prefix that is the **async** keyword. Well, in this case, we have not defined a function, but a coroutine, a specific entity of the asynchronous programming model.

Then inside the code, we find a call to **asyncio.sleep()** (this is not a function either, but a co-routine) preceded by the **await** keyword. This indicates that the called *object* will be included in the scheduling for concurrent execution. Its execution, entering this mechanism, will be subject to interruptions, pending the execution of other similar objects, and then resume its execution once the latter have finished their task.

The **asyncio.sleep()** co-routine works in the same way as the **time.sleep()** function, delaying the execution of a certain number of seconds passed as a parameter. Except, being a coroutine, it operates correctly in an asynchronous execution context.

In the AsyncIO library, objects such as co-routines, tasks, and futures are classified as *awaitable* objects. All these objects, once defined and created within the code, can later be scheduled for concurrent execution, using the await prefix.

The reason why it was decided in Python to add the **async-await** syntax is to eliminate any form of ambiguity in the code. As we have seen, **async** allows us to quickly distinguish co-routines from functions, and await allows us to quickly recognize calls that must be scheduled asynchronously.

Coroutines

The heart of the asynchronous model is the coroutines. A **coroutine** is a specialized version of a generator function in Python.

Note:
Generator functions

In Python, a generator function is a function that returns an iterator.

```
def generator():
```

  yield "A"

  yield "B"

  yield "C"

Instead of return, the generators use the yield statement. In this way, the generator returns one element at a time of the iteration if it is called with the next() function.

```
iterator = generator()
print("First call: %s" %next(iterator))
print("Second call: %s" %next(iterator))
print("Third call: %s" %next(iterator))
```

By running the code, you get:

```
First call: A
Second call: B
Third call: C
```

As can be seen from the result, at each call we will have a different result, that is, the corresponding value in the iteration sequence defined by yield in the generator function.

A coroutine is a function that can suspend its execution before reaching a return, and pass control to another coroutine, for some time.

In AsyncIO, we can define a function as a coroutine through the **async** keyword. In the previous example, the coroutine is the **main()** function, whose definition is anticipated by **async**:

```
async def main():
    print('Awaiting for ...')
    await asyncio.sleep(1)
    print('... AsyncIO!')
```

If you try to make a call to the coroutine by itself, like any other function:

```
>>> main()
```

You will see that you will not get any results: in fact, it has not been performed.

In fact, coroutines are not simple functions, and to be performed, the AsyncIO library provides three different ways:

- The first is precisely that of the example. The **asyncio.run()** function accepts as an argument a coroutine that will be considered the entry point of program execution. To execute the previous coroutine, we can run the following instruction:

  ```
  >>> asyncio.run(main())
  ```

- Another way in which a coroutine can be performed is through another coroutine. For example, let's define a second coroutine always with **async** as a prefix:

  ```
  async def other():
      print("I am a coroutine")
  ```

  In the **main()** coroutine, the call to the new coroutine to execute is placed after await:

  ```
  import asyncio


  async def other():
      print("I am a coroutine")
  ```

```
async def main():

    print('Awaiting for ...')

    await asyncio.sleep(1)

    await other()

    print('... AsyncIO!')
```

```
asyncio.run(main())
```

Executing gives the following result:

Awaiting for ...

I am a coroutine

... AsyncIO!

- There is also a third method that makes use of AsyncIO's **task** class. By calling the **asyncio.create_task()** function, we create a new object of the **Task** class that executes the coroutine concurrently:

```
import asyncio


async def other():

  print("I am a coroutine")


async def main():

    task = asyncio.create_task(other())

    print('Awaiting for ...')

    await asyncio.sleep(1)

    await task

    print('... AsyncIO!')
```

```
asyncio.run(main())
```

If we execute the code, we will get the same preceding result. The latter case anticipates the tasks, the topic that we will see in the next section.

Task

The **Tasks** in AsyncIO allow you to schedule the coroutines to work in a competitive way. Coroutines can be wrapped in objects of the **Task** class through the **asyncio.create_task()** function as we saw in the previous code. The Tasks thus created are then called with **await** in the **main()** coroutine and executed in a competitive manner. Let's look at this with a practical example. We modify the previous code in order to create a coroutine that accepts *two* parameters: **id** is an integer value that we will use as the identifier of the coroutine, and another integer that will indicate the *execution time* of the coroutine that we will simulate using the function:

```python
asyncio.sleep().

import asyncio


async def other(id,t):
  await asyncio.sleep(t)
  print("I am a coroutine %s" %id)


async def main():
    task1 = asyncio.create_task(other(1,10))
    task2 = asyncio.create_task(other(2,4))
    task3 = asyncio.create_task(other(3,1))
    await task1
    await task2
    await task3


asyncio.run(main())
```

Running the code will produce a result similar to the following:

```
I am a coroutine 3
I am a coroutine 2
I am a coroutine 1
```

As we can see from the result, the three coroutines were performed concurrently and since **coroutine 3** is the one that takes the least time, it is also the one that will finish the execution first, without having to wait for the results of the others.

If we had used the coroutines without the tasks, we would not have achieved any concurrent behavior. We write the previous code version using coroutines only as shown as follows:

```python
import asyncio


async def other(id,t):
  await asyncio.sleep(t)
  print("I am a coroutine %s" %id)


async def main():
    t1 = time.perf_counter()
    await other(10,1)
    await other(4,2)
    await other(3,3)
    t2 = time.perf_counter()
    elapsed_time = t2 - t1
    print("Elapsed time %s" %elapsed_time)


asyncio.run(main())
```

Executing will result in a result similar to the following:

I am a coroutine 1

I am a coroutine 2

I am a coroutine 3

Elapsed time 17.021660084999894

As we can see from the result, the behavior is not *concurrent*, since the coroutines finish their task in the same sequence in which they were launched, even if the first coroutine takes much longer than the others. The *total time taken* is the sum of the execution time of the *three coroutines* (10 + 4 + 3 = 17).

If we measure the execution time of the code version with the tasks we get:

```
I am a coroutine 3

I am a coroutine 2

I am a coroutine 1

Elapsed time 10.006599820999327
```

As we can see, the execution time is almost that used by the slowest coroutine. In fact, the advantage of concurrent programming is to take advantage of the *dead times of execution*, putting the slow coroutines on hold, and in the meantime letting the faster ones run. This code is a splendid example of this behavior.

We will continue with the tasks by making changes to the previous code. Tasks created within the program can have an identifying name. This can be assigned at the time of their creation, through the *optional* **name** parameter:

```
asyncio.create_task(coroutine,name="..")
```

Or later through the **set_name()** method:

```
task.set_name('...')
```

In the coroutine, **other()** we used an input parameter to identify the task in which it is wrapped. This can be avoided since it is possible to trace the current task within the coroutine without having to pass external parameters. The **asyncio.current_task()** function returns the current task. Since, we only need the task name, we can call the **get_name()** method. Then the previous code can be modified in the following way:

```
import asyncio


async def other(t):
  await asyncio.sleep(t)
  id =  asyncio.current_task().get_name()
  print("I am a coroutine %s" %id)


async def main():
    task1 = asyncio.create_task(other(10),name="1")
    task2 = asyncio.create_task(other(4),name="2")
    task3 = asyncio.create_task(other(3),name="3")
```

```
    await task1

    await task2

    await task3


asyncio.run(main())
```

By running we get the same previous result:

I am a coroutine 3

I am a coroutine 2

I am a coroutine 1

As can be seen from the result, using tasks instead of coroutines shows evidence of concurrent behavior. In fact, the first to be performed will be the *third coroutine* which takes only 2 *seconds* to run. The first coroutine, taking more time (10 *seconds*), will finish last.

Gathering of the awaitables for concurrent execution

A more explicit way to launch a set of *awaitable* objects such as coroutine, task, and future concurrently is with the **asyncio.gather()** function. This function accepts a sequence of awaitables as parameters. If there are coroutines in the sequence, they will be automatically scheduled as tasks. The order of execution, even if concurrent, follows the order of the sequence. When all the *awaitable* objects are completed, the **asyncio.gather()** function will return an aggregated list of values, whose order follows that of the sequence of awaitable passed as a parameter:

```
import asyncio

async def coroutine(t,id):

    await asyncio.sleep(t)

    print("I am the coroutine %s" %id)

    return t+2


async def main():

    results = await asyncio.gather(
```

```
        coroutine(10,"A"),
        coroutine(4,"B"),
        coroutine(2,"C"),
    )
    print("The results are: %s" %results)
```

```
asyncio.run(main())
```

Running the code produces a result similar to the following:

I am the coroutine C

I am the coroutine B

I am the coroutine A

The results are: [12, 6, 4]

As we can see from the result we have obtained a concurrent behavior while using the coroutines instead of the tasks. In reality, these passed to the **asyncio.gather()** function converted them implicitly, making the code much more *readable* and *intuitive*. Here's what the corresponding code would have looked like if we'd used tasks:

```
async def main():
    task1 = asyncio.create_task(coroutine(10,"A"))
    task2 = asyncio.create_task(coroutine(4,"B"))
    task3 = asyncio.create_task(coroutine(2,"C"))
    r1 = await task1
    r2 = await task2
    r3 = await task3
    results = [ r1, r2, r3]
    print("The results are: %s" %results)
```

```
asyncio.run(main())
```

Future

Another concept related to asynchronous programming is the use of futures, implemented in the **asyncio** module by the **Future** class. A **future** conceptually represents a result (including an exception) that is not yet available at the time it is processed.

Let's consider the following code:

```
import asyncio


async def get_result(result):
    await asyncio.sleep(5)
    result = '...an awaited result'


async def main():
    my_result = ' '
    task1 = asyncio.create_task(get_result(my_result))
    await task1


    print("I'm waiting for ...")
    print(my_result)


asyncio.run(main())
```

Running the code will produce a result similar to the following:

I'm waiting for ...

As we can see from the result, no result was printed out: *the program finished its execution without waiting for the result.*

It is in similar cases that a **Future** is used. By making the appropriate substitutions in the previous code, we will obtain a code similar to the following:

```
import asyncio


async def get_result(future):
    await asyncio.sleep(5)
```

```
        future.set_result('...a future result')

async def main():
    my_future = asyncio.Future()
    task1 = asyncio.create_task(get_result(my_future))
    await task1


    print("I'm waiting for ...")
    print(await my_future)
    print('Before continuing with my execution')


asyncio.run(main())
```

By running the program this time, we will get the following result:

```
I'm waiting for ...

...a future result

Before continuing with my execution
```

As we can see from the result, this time the program waited for the result to be generated (5 *seconds*) and then printed all the outputs.

By introducing a **future** with **await**, the program will have to wait for the **get_result()** coroutine to produce the result (the **future** itself), and to continue with its execution.

The mechanism of a **Future** is therefore based on callback functions, (such as **get_result()** in the previous example) whose task is to process any result and assign it to the instance of the **Future()** class using the **set_result()** method.

> **Note:**
>
> **Callback functions**
>
> A callback is a function that is passed as an argument to another function.
>
> ```
> def callbackFunc():
>     #It Does something
> ```

```
def mainFunc(callbackFunc):

    ...

    callbackFunc()

    ...
```

The instance of the **Future** class is generated through its constructor:

```
future = asyncio.Future()
```

The new instance is thus passed as an argument in the callback function which must value it. When the result contained in the future is to be used, it will be inserted into the code with the await prefix, so that it enters the **AsyncIO** scheduling mechanism. In this way, all program execution will be adjusted according to the *awaitable* objects, which will all be taken into account according to their execution times, asynchronously. The program, therefore, will wait all the time necessary for the valorization of the future, in the meantime executing everything possible in a *concurrent* manner, and then continue the *flow of execution.*

A **Future** is therefore also an *awaitable* object. A **future** is a result of a process (the callback function) whose execution status is *unknown*, but which requires attention until its completion (in the future). So, when calling a **future** with **await**, it is already assumed that at that point in the program, that result will not yet be available. In this case, the following cases may occur:

- The process that **future** represents has finished and a result has already been entered for future. In this case, the **await** statement immediately returns that value.

- The process that **future** represents has *failed*, returning an *exception*. In this case, the **await** statement immediately throws the exception.

- The process that **future** represents is still running and the **future** is not valued. In this case, all the other tasks await the end of the process and the valorization of the **future**. As soon as the status of the **future** is completed, then the **await** statement will return the result or raise an exception, depending on the case, and the execution of the program will go on.

The distinction between a **Coroutine** and a **Future** is very important. A **coroutine** code will *not* execute while it is waiting. A **future** represents something that is running anyway, and it simply allows your code to wait for it to finish, check if it is done, and then deliver the result it produced.

> **Note:** `Asyncio.futures` and `concurrent.futures`. Despite the similarity, one must be very careful not to confuse these two types of `Future` classes. The futures of the concurrent module are based on a multi-threaded construct, while those of `asyncio` are strongly single-threaded. So, although semantically they perform the same tasks, they work completely differently and cannot be interchanged with each other.

Event loop

From the point of view of programming models, as far as events are concerned, we have *three* entities at play:

- Event source
- Event handler
- Event loop

In a calculation system, an **event source** is defined as the entity that generates events. The latter is managed by another entity, defined as an **event handler**. The **event loop** acts as a link between the *event sources* and the *event handler* (refer to *Figure 4.2*):

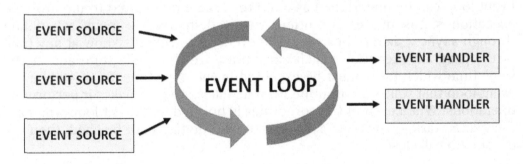

Figure 4.2: *The event loop*

In fact, **events** are generated *randomly* and *asynchronously* and therefore very rarely there is direct correspondence between event generation and event management. There is always a *period of time (asynchronicity)* between the *two* operations and it may also be that in this time further events are generated to be managed.

From the programming point of view, the AsyncIO library implements the *event loop* through the **Loop** class with a whole series of methods that allow it to be managed:

- **asyncio.new_event_loop()**: Creates and returns a new event loop.
- **asyncio.get_event_loop()**: Returns the event loop of the current context.
- **asyncio.set_event_loop()**: Sets the event loop for the current context.
- **Loop.call_later()**: Schedules a callback to be called after the given delay number of seconds.
- **Loop.call_soon()**: Schedules a callback to be called at the next iteration of the event loop.
- **Loop.run_until_complete()**: Runs until the coroutine (passed as argument) has been completed.
- **Loop.run_forever()**: Runs the event loop until **stop()** is called.
- **Loop.stop()**: Stops the event loop.
- **Loop.close()**: Closes the event loop.

The event loop is an *intrinsic object* in the asynchronous execution mechanism of **asyncio** and is implicitly activated when the command is launched:

```
asyncio.run(main())
```

Event loop can be understood as a **while True** loop created to monitor the execution status of the coroutines involved in asynchronous scheduling through **async / await** construct. The event loop will thus know at any time of the program execution which coroutines are in an *idle* state and at the same time which tasks must be executed in the meantime. So, it will be the event loop that wakes a coroutine from its *idle* state and makes it perform its operations. When each of the coroutines is finished, the event loop will mark the related task as *complete*. Finally, when all the tasks are finished, then the event loop will close.

Therefore, the event loop can be considered the great director of asynchronous operation of the AsyncIO library. Normally, the event loop starts, carries out its operations, and closes, all implicitly. In fact, we have not seen any reference to it in the previous examples with the coroutines, tasks, and futures.

However, it is also possible to manage the event loop in the code explicitly. The typical pattern is:

```
loop = asyncio.get_event_loop()

try:

    loop.run_until_complete(main())

finally:
```

```
        loop.close()
```

Which is perfectly equivalent to just the **asyncio.run(main())** command, as you can see directly in the following code:

```
import asyncio


async def main():
  print('Starting...')
  await asyncio.sleep(10)
  print('...Ending')


#asyncio.run(main())
loop = asyncio.get_event_loop()
try:
    loop.run_until_complete(main())
finally:
    loop.close()
```

In the code, we see how the **asyncio.get_event_loop()** function is used first in order to assign the current event loop to a loop reference variable. In this way, it will be possible to explicitly control the workflow of the event loop. Within a **try-finally** construct, we then launch the scheduling and execution of the **main()** coroutine and at the same time, all the *awaitables* called within it. Upon completion of all scheduled asynchronous operations, or in the eventual launch of exceptions, the event loop must be closed, to release the resources, using the **loop.close()** method.

This is the simplest and most straightforward case, but many more complex cases can be implemented where there is a need for greater control over its operation. There are a whole series of methods that regulate its flow or allow its monitoring. For example, the methods **loop.is_running()** and **loop.is_closed()** allow you to check the execution status of the event loop.

But it must be said that in many cases, it will never be necessary to make the event loop explicit in our code.

Asynchronous iterations with and without async for

async for allows you to iterate over an asynchronous iterator, the purpose of which is to be able to make asynchronous calls at each step of the iteration. An extension of this concept is the asynchronous generator, a coroutine in which it is possible to use **await** and **yield** together:

```python
async def gen(n):
  for i in range(n):
    await asyncio.sleep(1)
    yield i
```

This asynchronous generator can be used as an asynchronous iterator in an **async for** as in the case of the following code:

```python
import asyncio


async def gen(n):
  for i in range(n):
    await asyncio.sleep(1)
    yield i
async def main():
    async for i in gen(10):
      print(i)


asyncio.run(main())
```

Running the code gives the following result:

```
0
1
2
3
4
5
6
```

7

8

9

However, as we can see from the result, the use of asynchronous generators fails to make the iteration concurrent. The results of the various steps are shown in the same iteration order. Async for therefore does not allow at the moment to be able to implement concurrent execution. All it provides is the ability to leave the event loop in control for some other running coroutine.

If, on the other hand, we want to obtain an iteration in which the various steps compete with each other, we will use another way. The **asyncio.as_completed()** function accepts, similar to what we saw with **asyncio.gather()**, a sequence of *awaitable*. This function returns an iterator of coroutines that will act in competition with each other.

We can see this with a simple example implemented through the following code:

```python
import asyncio


async def f(i):
    print('start iteration step %s' %i)
    await asyncio.sleep(1)
    print('end iteration step %s' %i)
    return i


async def main():
  for j in asyncio.as_completed([f(i) for i in range(10)]):
      result = await j
      print('result received: %s' %result)


asyncio.run(main())
```

As we can see from the code, we pass a sequence of ten coroutines **f(i)** ranging from **f(0)** to **f(9)** to the **asyncio.as_completed()** function. This will return an iterator whose steps will represent the coroutines in the order of completion (not of the incoming sequence). The coroutine of the sequence that will end *first* will be the first iteration step, and its result will be the one collected first and printed in the output. Then it will be the turn of the one that will end immediately after and so on, until the last one.

By executing the preceding code, you get a result that perfectly reflects the behavior just described:

```
start iteration step 2
start iteration step 0
start iteration step 6
start iteration step 9
start iteration step 3
start iteration step 7
start iteration step 4
start iteration step 8
start iteration step 5
start iteration step 1
end iteration step 2
end iteration step 0
end iteration step 6
end iteration step 9
end iteration step 3
end iteration step 7
end iteration step 4
end iteration step 8
end iteration step 5
end iteration step 1
result received: 2
result received: 0
result received: 6
result received: 9
result received: 3
result received: 7
result received: 4
```

```
result received: 8
```

As we can see, the execution of the various steps of the iteration no longer follows the *sequential* order of the iteration, but each step competes in its execution, trying to finish its task as soon as possible.

Queue in the asynchronous model

The **AsyncIO** library provides many tools to better implement the asynchronous model, and like the *threading* and *multiprocessing* module, it can make use of **queues** for proper management of shared memory. In this case, it will no longer be threads competing for this resource, but the coroutines. In fact, there is the **asyncio.Queue** class that allows you to implement the *producer-consumer* model also in asynchronous programming in a very similar way to the queue seen in the two previous chapters.

Creating a shared space organized as regards asynchronous programming is no longer linked to a race condition problem as was the case with threads. Let us remember once again that AsyncIO works on a *single thread* and therefore you shouldn't have to deal with the thread-safety problems of the Python language.

In the case of **asyncio**, a queue carries out the task of connecting between *coroutine producer* and *coroutine consumer* which may not know of their reciprocal existence and may not be included in the same scheduling scheme. So, there will be a group of coroutine producers who will add items to a queue, one at a time, *asynchronously*. The *consumer coroutine* group will not have to wait for the completion of all the *producer coroutines* but will receive a *signal* that they can in turn operate, taking the items already processed within the queue.

So, let's create an example code in which we establish the number of *producers* and *consumers* through *two* variables that will be passed as arguments to the **main()** coroutine:

```python
import asyncio

import random


async def producer(name, queue):

    n = random.randint(0, 10)

    await asyncio.sleep(n)

    await queue.put(n)

    print("Producer %s adds %s to the queue" %(name,n))
```

```
async def consumer(name, queue):

    while True:

        n = await queue.get()

        await asyncio.sleep(n)

        print("Consumer %s receives %s from the queue" %(name,n))

        queue.task_done()


async def main(nproducers, nconsumers):

    q = asyncio.Queue()

        producers = [asyncio.create_task(producer(n, q)) for n in
range(nproducers)]

        consumers = [asyncio.create_task(consumer(n, q)) for n in
range(nconsumers)]


    await asyncio.gather(*producers)

    await q.join()

    for c in consumers:

        c.cancel()



asyncio.run(main(4,2))
```

As we can see from the code, we have chosen *four producers* and *two consumers* as an example. All coroutine producers will insert a random integer from 0 to 9 sec into the column, and in doing so they will take as many seconds as this random value, *thanks* to the **asyncio.sleep()** function. All coroutine producers will be launched in competition with each other using the **asyncio. gather()** function. A queue object will be instantiated and the values generated by the producers will be added to it according to the runtime via the **queue. put()** method. As you can see from the code, this method is also a coroutine anticipated by the **await** prefix. The *consumer coroutines* will then be created and scheduled separately for the producers. In fact, they are not present in the **asyncio.gather()** method, but are implicitly activated with the queue, at each call **queue.get()** with which the coroutines obtain the values contained within it. This relationship between the *consumers* and the *queue* allows for the perfect functioning of the whole *producer-consumer system* since the queue will take care of activating the consumers available when there are items inside.

If we execute the code, we will get a result consistent with what has been said similar to the following:

```
Producer 1 adds 0 to the queue

Consumer 0 receives 0 from the queue

Producer 2 adds 1 to the queue

Consumer 1 receives 1 from the queue

Producer 3 adds 8 to the queue

Producer 0 adds 9 to the queue

Consumer 0 receives 8 from the queue

Consumer 1 receives 9 from the queue
```

Alternatives to the AsyncIO library

In recent years, *thanks* also to the success of asynchronous programming that does not use threads, other interesting libraries have developed that can be taken as valid alternatives to the AsyncIO library.

- **Curio** (https://curio.readthedocs.io/) is a library that makes use of coroutines, tasks, and queues, and also has an **async / await** syntax. It is therefore recommended for those who already know **asyncio** and the concepts that structure the implementation of the *asynchronous model*.

- **Trio** (https://trio.readthedocs.io/) is an even more ambitious project since it is manifestly presented as a direct alternative to the **asyncio** library, defining itself as simpler, and more in step with the continuous innovations added to the Python language. A young, exciting project that deserves special attention.

Conclusion

In this chapter, we have gone into depth with the concept of asynchronous programming and the different cases in which this becomes concurrent. You will certainly have understood the subtle consequences of different types of execution and how these in turn differ from the results of parallel programming. You will have understood that where parallel programming loses its advantages, being closely linked to *CPU-bound operations, asynchronous programming*, or even more so *concurrent programming*, instead give their best, allowing you to effectively manage IO-bound. All these concepts have been implementable *thanks* to the AsyncIO library with which you will have become familiar by now and the basic tools. In the next chapter, we will deal with distributed programming, where we will apply the concepts learned in systems that are no longer limited to a single machine but in systems that involve multiple processors distributed on often different machines and located in different places.

References

- https://docs.python.org/3/library/asyncio.html
- https://realpython.com/async-io-python/
- https://trio.readthedocs.io/en/stable/
- https://curio.readthedocs.io/en/latest/

## CHAPTER 5

Realizing Parallelism with Distributed Systems

Distributed systems fall within the scope of parallel and concurrent programming and can prove to be a valid solution; thanks to their performance levels. So, it is imperative to be familiar with these types of systems, and the related solutions that Python offers in this regard. In this chapter, we will cover several possible solutions. We will first talk about **Celery** which is now the reference point in Python for the realization of distributed systems. This library represents a valid tool for the construction of this type of system and is an excellent example to understand the possible architectures, the elements that compose it, and the various mechanisms underlying them. With a series of examples, we will see how to use this library to perform multiple concurrent operations, called **tasks**, and how these are distributed and executed in parallel on a *Celery-based system*. In addition, we will subsequently move on to other alternative solutions, starting from a very similar one such as **Dramatiq** to a simpler one, but which conceptually differs from these, such as **SCOOP**.

Structure

In this chapter we will cover the following topics:

- Distributed systems
- Client-server model
- Celery framework
- Messaging
- Task
- Worker

- Dramatiq
- Docker
- SCOOP

Distributed systems and programming

A **distributed system** is any system in which the application elements that compose it run on different machines and work in synergy for the same purpose. These elements, being on different machines, and possibly even geographically distant, can communicate with each other through the exchange of messages that are passed through a connection network.

The presence of entities that perform their tasks independently and simultaneously is a further extension of the threads and processes that we have seen in previous chapters. Thus, distributed systems, in addition to carrying out their useful operations in the key of the *client-server model*, are perfectly capable of carrying out a series of operations in concurrency or even in parallel. It is therefore clear that distributed systems can be perfectly inserted in the context of parallel programming, and most of the concepts dealt with are also perfectly valid for these systems.

So, we can extend the parallel programming in the client-server model (*Figure 5.1*) where a *client* requests a series of tasks from the *server*, which takes care of searching in the distributed system, an equal series of computation entities, called worker, capable of performing these tasks in parallel:

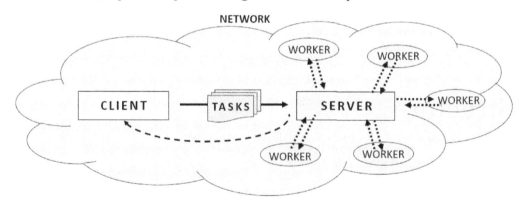

Figure 5.1: Distributed system in parallel programming

The *server* will collect the results produced asynchronously and send them to the requesting client. This type of programming can be defined as distributed programming which is the topic of this chapter.

Pros and cons of distributed systems

These systems allow for excellent performance thanks to factors such as:

- Scalability
- Concurrency
- Flexibility
- Robustness (fault tolerance)

All factors are essentially due to the distributed nature of these systems:

- **Scalability**: This is guaranteed by the possibility of increasing the number of elements present in the system as the request for resources by the problem to be solved increases. From the theoretical point of view, in distributed systems, there is no limit to this increase. If the problem grows, it will be sufficient to add other machines inside other copies of the elements of the system that will take over the competing calculation. It is clear that distributed systems focus on horizontal rather than vertical scalability.

- **Concurrency**: This is another feature implicit in the architecture of these systems. In fact, in carrying out a series of tasks, a distributed system is able to assign each of them to an independent processing unit, which will act simultaneously with the other units. All tasks will therefore be carried out in competition, and often also in parallel.

- **Flexibility**: Flexibility of a distributed system is due to the fact that it is composed of numerous elements, each of which plays a certain role, distributed on some machine connected to the system. Well, these machines can be heterogeneous in nature, and the components of the system can be considered as real independent applications, which can be replaced with other compatible applications that play the same role. When building a distributed system, there is therefore a possibility of choosing the application that will play the role of a particular component. Our choice can be motivated by a different operating system, by the functionality of the application itself or by particular characteristics that we want to enter into our system. All this allows us to create a distributed system that is always different according to our needs.

- **Robustness or fault tolerance of the system**: This is also guaranteed by the redundancy of elements distributed in the system. The fact of having copies of elements on different machines guarantees the possibility of continuing the work carried out even following the failure of an application, or of an entire machine. These kinds of systems are able to manage in a transparent and rapid way the movement of a task from an application in failure to a free one on hold. From the customer's point of view, even after a failure, there will be no discontinuity in the execution of the requested services.

Not all is gold, and despite the great qualities of distributed systems, it must be taken into account that there is also a price to pay.

The fact that distributed systems are based on a large number of elements, possibly distributed on different machines, requires a communication mechanism between the various elements: **messaging**. The components of distributed systems make use of messages in order to communicate with each other and exchange information. So, each time it will be necessary to create a message and send it over the network to the right recipient, who will have to receive it and unpack it to search for the information inside. It is clear that such a system also requires a system that manages it and all this requires a large consumption of resources.

Another problem due to the fact that distributed systems are composed of many different elements also requires a certain difficulty in their *maintenance*. In fact, there are many applications that can perform these tasks, and all of them should be implemented in order to be supported on all systems and perform all possible functionalities. Well, this is indeed impossible. So, when building a distributed system, it may happen that our choice was not perfect and some elements do not perfectly support all the required features. Incompatibilities may arise, especially if you have version updates of some elements compared to others.

Furthermore, as the elements of the system grow, the complexity of operation also increases. So, in case of problems or management, it becomes increasingly difficult to check its perfect functioning.

The last thing to take into account is the *dependence* of the network infrastructure of a distributed system on the network with which it is connected. This infrastructure is essential for the efficiency of a distributed system. Network failures, bad configurations, or other problems are often an indication of imperfect network management. This task is often out of the developer's purview.

Celery

Celery is a framework developed in Python, whose purpose is to create distributed systems based on this language.

Therefore, Celery, through a series of *components and tools*, allows you to build a distributed system suitable for different needs in an easy way and within everyone's reach. Its particular characteristics allow us to build systems of increasing complexity, starting from a distributed system enclosed in a single machine, up to systems networks comprising countless machines also based on different technologies. This possibility is largely given to us, thanks to the great portability of Python which allows it to run on different architectures and operating systems.

Going into detail, the characteristics of a Celery distributed system can be expressed in three key points:

- Portability
- High availability
- Scaling

In this system, even if its architecture is mainly controlled by Celery, the various components that compose it can belong to other technologies and be added, replaced, and modified, without major problems (*pluggable* components). In this way, there is great portability of the system to the various needs and technologies used. This approach is also perfectly suited to distributed systems since each of these components could generally reside in a different machine, physically separated and even geographically distant, connected to the system via a network connection.

Another advantage of this type of architecture is the fact that the components that perform services for clients (such as **brokers** and **workers**) can be present in a variable number and distributed on different machines. In this way, continuous operability is guaranteed even if some machines may encounter hardware or software problems, thus giving the system the characteristic of high availability. Furthermore, the number of such components is variable according to the request, and from a theoretical point of view, this number has no upper limit. It is easy to add additional machines to the system via network connections and thus share the consumption of resources, keeping it unchanged for each component. Therefore, as the problem grows, it is possible to add additional components, distributing resources efficiently, and ensuring horizontal scaling.

Architecture of Celery systems

In a *Celery-based distributed system*, many different components come into play, each of which plays a specific role in the mechanism of distributed computing (see *Figure 5.2*). The main components are:

- Broker
- Task queue
- Clients

- Workers
- Result backend (*optional*)

These components exchange values and information with each other through a *message mechanism.* In order for this to work, it must be supported by a message transport application, which in the context of a Celery system is defined as a **Broker**. There are several message transport applications compatible with Celery systems, and each of them uses a different *communication protocol:*

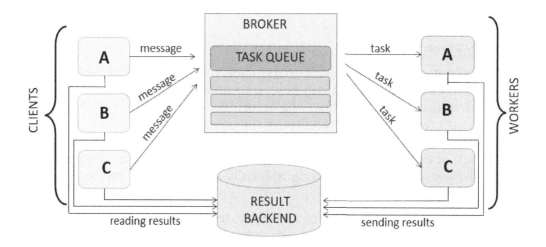

Figure 5.2: *Celery architecture*

CLIENTS are processes that, in carrying out their tasks, require certain services made available by the distributed system. These requests are made through messages, containing an indication of the task to be performed. These messages are sent to the *broker* who will then manage them. At the end of the processing of the task, the *client* will find the result of the request in the result backend, usually a database. A schematic of this architecture is shown in *Figure* 5.2.

WORKERS are processes present, either on the same machine or on other machines distributed on the network and connected to the Celery system. These processes have been specifically designed to perform the tasks that are dispatched to them by the broker. Once started, the workers wait, and once they receive the task assigned to them, they execute it, and finally send the result to the result backend.

Generally, these workers may be able to perform various tasks. This only increases the efficiency of the system. Given that if a worker does not receive a specific task, instead of waiting, it can perform other types of tasks present in the task queue.

In the context of the components that make up Celery's distributed architecture, the broker, and the task queues within it play a central role. The broker performs *two* basic tasks:

- The first is to receive messages sent by various customers by entering the related tasks within the task queue.

- The other task will then be to dispatch the various tasks queued to the corresponding waiting workers.

The task queues accumulate the tasks requested by the various clients. In this way, if at a certain request for service by a *client*, a worker is not immediately available, the task will remain in the task queue, waiting to be processed. The broker will take care of distributing the various tasks to the various waiting workers. In this way, it will be possible to manage the execution of tasks in an *asynchronous* and *concurrent* manner.

The result backend has the task of collecting the results produced by the different workers during the execution of the tasks. These results will then be available, by reading, to clients. Also, in this phase, the returned values enter a sort of asynchronous mechanism, which allows the accumulation of results without the need to manage the single result immediately after its return. These mechanisms are necessary in a distributed system, where the various components act independently from each other, asynchronously, carrying out their activities of request, processing, and management of the result in unpredictable times, in which waiting times are necessary.

Tasks

As we have seen in the previous sections, *Celery systems* (and *distributed systems* in general) are based on the distribution of tasks to be performed efficiently among the various components. In particular, the concept of task is used in these cases. Any task to be performed that needs to be distributed in the system must be encapsulated in a task. A **task** can also be identified as a unit of work that can be distributed in this type of system. This last definition is very useful to us because it can be traced back to concurrent and parallel programming, in which any task can generally be divided into small *atomic* parts, that is, which can be performed separately and independently, also defined as a task.

And here is the point of contact between the two technologies, that of distributed systems and of concurrent programming. Once we have broken down our problem into tasks, each one executable independently; in a distributed system, these can be sent to a broker and executed concurrently by the different workers distributed on the network. The results then produced will be collected in the result backend, and recomposed by the client program to obtain the final result. We have already encountered similar behavior when dealing with *threading threads* and *asynchronous co-routines*. In this case, however, we have workers, a conceptual entity under which many different realities are identified, such as **processes**, **threads**, **events**, and **eventlets**. All are managed transparently or through appropriate settings.

Setting up a Celery system

Having defined, in a concise but complete way, the theoretical part of the components of a system distributed on Celery, let's now move on to its practical implementation, installing, and setting all the components away.

Installing Anaconda

A *practical tip*: when you want to build test systems, like the examples in this book, it is good practice to create a virtual environment on which to install the different Python packages and modules. This in case of errors, or when it will no longer be necessary, can be removed without problems, without ever creating conflicts between the basic versions of Python installed in our application system and all the *dependencies*, *deletions*, and *manual installations*, made during our test environment installations.

We can use the **Anaconda** development platform which helps greatly in managing virtual environments and package installations. For those not yet familiar with it, this platform can be downloaded for *free* from the web (**https:// www.anaconda.com/products/distribution**). The web page will already suggest you the most updated and stable distribution for your operating system as shown in *Figure 5.3*:

Figure 5.3: *Anaconda distribution web page*

Once installed, to create a virtual environment go to the **Environments** panel (see *Figure 5.4*):

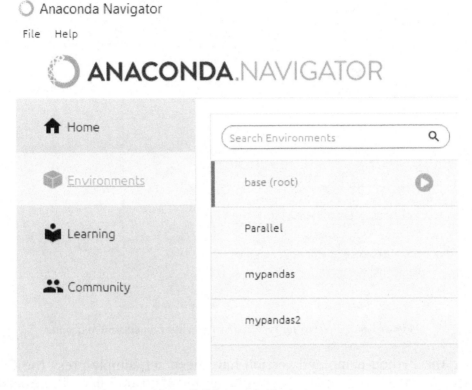

Figure 5.4: *Anaconda Navigator*

Then click on the **Create** button at the bottom center as shown in the following *Figure 5.5*:

Figure 5.5: *Create a virtual environment button in Anaconda Navigator*

Pressing this button will open a dialog box where you can enter the name of the virtual environment you want to use and choose the version of Python on which it will be based, as shown in *Figure 5.6*:

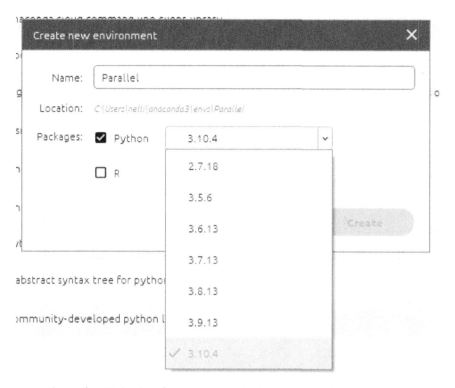

Figure 5.6: *Dialog box for creating virtual environments on Anaconda*

Once the Python name and version have been set, simply press the **Create** button to create the virtual environment and then find it on the **Anaconda Navigator** panel. At this point, you can activate the virtual environment by simply clicking on the name that will appear in the list in the center. In my case, I chose to call the virtual environment **Parallel**. When the virtual environment is active, a *green icon (PLAY)* will appear on the side, as shown in *Figure 5.7*. On the right side of the panel, the list of all Python packages installed in the virtual environment will appear. Those with the *Anaconda icon (green circle)* will be installed through the distribution itself, while those with the Python icon will have been installed externally through the **pip** command:

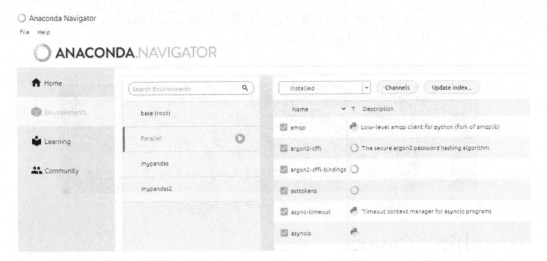

Figure 5.7: *A virtual environment with its packages in Anaconda Navigator*

Anaconda is a very useful and very flexible platform. It provides a whole series of development applications that allows you to work in many ways. By going to the **Home** panel, all the applications available for the virtual environment we have just created will appear (see *Figure 5.8*):

Figure 5.8: *Anaconda Navigator home page*

As we can see, there are many applications available, including the very useful **Jupyter Notebook** and **CMD.exe** Prompt. On the latter, clicking on the **Launch** button will open a command console completely set up to work with the virtual environment, as shown in *Figure 5.9*:

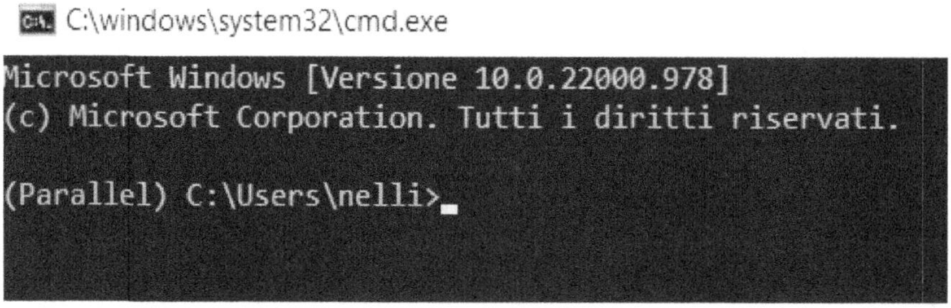

Figure 5.9: *Virtual environment command console*

Installing Celery

In the newly opened command console, we will install the Celery library using PIP.

```
pip install celery
```

Note: The `celery` package is present in the Anaconda distribution but is not complete (at least in my version). Then, I download Celery directly from PIP which also provides all other related packages which will give me the applications I need for the examples in this book.

Installing Docker

Another application that I prefer to use when I want to test distributed environments such as the ones we will present in this chapter, is **Docker Desktop**. This application allows you to isolate, in the form of packages called **containers**, applications that offer services of some kind such as servers, databases, and so on. Its usefulness in development environments is enormous since these applications enclosed in containers can be *activated*, *deactivated*, *deleted*, and *cloned* in a very simple way. Excellent if you want to test a distributed environment in which there are many active *listening* services such as Celery. Given the complexity of Python versions and package dependencies, Docker allows you to change and test versions of various server applications quickly, without having to perform complicated installations and configurations. Furthermore, again in the case of Celery, there are different applications that play the same role and can be evaluated in *real-time* directly in the Celery distributed system. By installing them all together as containers and then activating and testing them one after the other, while the rest of the system remains unchanged.

To install Docker Desktop, simply go to the official application page (**https://www.docker.com/**). On the loaded web page, you will be prompted to download the latest stable version suitable for your operating system, as shown in *Figure 5.10*:

Figure 5.10: *Docker web page*

Once Docker Desktop is installed, it will be possible to install a whole series of ready-made containers of the various applications in the various distributed versions, simply through the command line:

```
docker run -d appname:version
```

Installing a message transport (Broker)

After installing Celery, the key component to install is the **Broker**. There are several message transport applications available that are compatible with Celery, however not all of them fully support all the mechanisms of Celery brokers. The most complete and compatible message transport applications in terms of functionality are:

- RabbitMQ
- Redis

Both applications are easily installed on systems:

1. To install the **Redis** application on the server machine, if you are using Linux:

   ```
   $ sudo apt-get install redis-server
   ```

2. Then you start the server by entering from the command line:

   ```
   $ redis-server
   ```

3. In my case, since I use a single machine (*client-server*) I prefer to use the Docker application in which to install and start all the services, as well as Redis:

```
$ docker run -d -p 6379:6379 redis
```

4. Then you install both the specific Celery module to use Redis within it:

```
pip install celery[redis]
```

5. If, on the other hand, we prefer to use the **RabbitMQ** application, it can be installed:

```
$ sudo apt-get install rabbitmq-server
```

6. To install RabbitMQ on Docker:

```
docker run -d –p 5672:5672 rabbitmq:3.9
```

At the end of the Docker Desktop, we will have active services: **RabbitMQ** and **Redis**, as shown in *Figure 5.11*:

Figure 5.11: *Docker Desktop*

Also, in this case, it is necessary to install the Celery module created specifically to use RabbitMQ inside it:

```
pip install celery[librabbitmq]
```

Installing the result backend

There are also many different applications available for a component such as a result backend. Among the result backends well supported by Celery, we can find:

- RabbitMQ
- Redis
- MongoDB
- Memcached

For simplicity's sake, we will use RabbitMQ and Redis as a result backend as well. So, it is not necessary, in the case of our book, to make further installations.

Setting up a Celery system

Celery does not require *special configurations* to function, at least in the most general cases. Only a few settings are made programmatically. In fact, you can define the components that will become part of the Celery system, at the time of Celery instantiation:

1. To create an instance of Celery, which by convention we will call **app** (but can be called in any way), we use the **Celery()** constructor. This accepts as arguments the module that will contain the tasks that the system will provide to the clients (**tasks.py**), and the various URLs, and protocols of the components belonging to the system.

   For example, if we want to use the RabbitMQ server application as a Broker, we will write:

   ```
   from celery import Celery

   app    =    Celery('tasks',    broker='pyamqp://guest@localhost//',
   backend='rpc://')
   ```

   As you can see, the RabbitMQ server works on the **pyamqp** protocol and is available at the local host address (that is, on the same machine as ours) as a *guest* user.

2. While if we want to use the Redis application as a Broker, we will write:

   ```
   from celery import Celery

   app       =       Celery('tasks',       broker='redis://localhost//',
   backend='redis://localhost')
   ```

   These code snippets will have to be inserted into the **tasks.py** file.

3. Now that the appropriate configurations have been made, we can start the Celery service:

   ```
   $ celery -A tasks worker --loglevel=INFO
   ```

   By running this command, we will get an output similar to the following:

   ```
   -------------- celery@LAPTOP-1STIRGLU v5.2.7 (dawn-chorus)
   ```

```
--- ***** -----

-- ******* ---- Windows-10-10.0.22000-SP0 2022-09-22 14:40:30

- *** --- * ---

- ** ---------- [config]

- ** ---------- .> app:         tasks:0x2c647cdad40

- ** ---------- .> transport:   amqp://guest:**@localhost:5672//

- ** ---------- .> results:     rpc://

- *** --- * --- .> concurrency: 12 (prefork)

-- ******* ---- .> task events: OFF (enable -E to monitor tasks in
this worker)

--- ***** -----

 ------------- [queues]

             .> celery           exchange=celery(direct) key=celery
```

```
[tasks]

  . tasks.add
```

```
[2022-09-22 14:40:30,583: INFO/MainProcess] Connected to amqp://
guest:**@127.0.0.1:5672//

[2022-09-22 14:40:30,604: INFO/MainProcess] mingle: searching for
neighbors

[2022-09-22 14:40:31,535: INFO/SpawnPoolWorker-1] child process
28788 calling self.run()

[2022-09-22 14:40:31,535: INFO/SpawnPoolWorker-2] child process
27892 calling self.run()

[2022-09-22 14:40:31,550: INFO/SpawnPoolWorker-3] child process
19868 calling self.run()

[2022-09-22 14:40:31,566: INFO/SpawnPoolWorker-4] child process
19072 calling self.run()

[2022-09-22 14:40:31,566: INFO/SpawnPoolWorker-8] child process
31208 calling self.run()
```

```
[2022-09-22 14:40:31,566: INFO/SpawnPoolWorker-7] child process
30672 calling self.run()

[2022-09-22 14:40:31,582: INFO/SpawnPoolWorker-5] child process
30480 calling self.run()

[2022-09-22 14:40:31,582: INFO/SpawnPoolWorker-6] child process
6328 calling self.run()

[2022-09-22 14:40:31,582: INFO/SpawnPoolWorker-9] child process
14124 calling self.run()

[2022-09-22 14:40:31,598: INFO/SpawnPoolWorker-11] child process
28616 calling self.run()

[2022-09-22 14:40:31,598: INFO/SpawnPoolWorker-10] child process
26540 calling self.run()

[2022-09-22 14:40:31,613: INFO/SpawnPoolWorker-12] child process
4888 calling self.run()

[2022-09-22 14:40:31,726: INFO/MainProcess] mingle: all alone

[2022-09-22 14:40:31,779: INFO/MainProcess] celery@LAPTOP-1STIRGLU
ready.
```

4. As you can see, the server started generating twelve worker processes by default. This number depends on the characteristics of the machine you are running Celery on. In my case, there are twelve cores and therefore twelve workers were created. The Broker will remain *active* waiting for the calls to the tasks to be assigned to the workers.

   If you are working on Windows you have to write:

   ```
   $ celery -A tasks worker --pool=solo --loglevel=INFO
   ```

   But in this case, you will work with a single thread and there will be no more competition phenomena. In this case, we will need to set up the workers using **eventlet**. Let's install them:

   ```
   pip install eventlet
   ```

   ```
   celery -A tasks worker --pool=eventlet --loglevel=INFO
   ```

   At the end of using Celery, to shut down, press CTRL + C. The following messages will appear on the Celery console:

   ```
   worker: Hitting Ctrl+C again will terminate all running tasks!
   ```

   ```
   worker: Warm shutdown (MainProcess)
   ```

5. Once all processes are finished, the prompt will be returned to you.

6. For a complete list of command line options:

```
$ celery worker -help
```

But there are also many other commands available, to know them you can write them on the command line:

```
$ celery -help
```

Defining tasks

Now that we have a simple but sufficient *Celery-based distributed system* in place, we can start defining tasks and testing examples.

In Celery, on the server side, where the tasks.py module file is present, you can implement the tasks that the system will make available to clients. To identify a task in the code, the **@app.task** decorator is used, where app is the Celery instance, used within the **tasks.py** file:

```
@app.task

def my_task():

    return "This is a task"
```

Calling tasks

Tasks are the services available from the distributed system that clients can request. So, in the *customer code*, we can make the request for a service that is the call to a task, at any time. To do this, Celery provides us with *two* different methods:

- **delay()**
- **apply_async()**

Both methods send the task to the broker via a message, what changes between them is the type of passable arguments. The **delay()** method takes arguments placed separately:

```
task.delay(arg1, arg2, kwarg1='x', kwarg2='y')
```

While **apply_async()** wraps them in a list and a dictionary:

```
task.apply_async(args=[arg1,  arg2], kwargs={'kwarg1':  'x',  'kwarg2': 'y'})
```

When we make a call to a task, we will have an **AsyncResult** value as a *return* value. This object will allow us to check the status of the task, from the client side.

Example task

In the module file on the server **tasks.py**, we define a task like the following:

```
@app.task

def add(x, y):

    return x + y
```

On the client side, we will open a Python session at the level of the same directory where **tasks.py** is present, this simplifies things considerably. After opening the session, we first import the task created within **tasks.py** and then call it, simply using the **delay()** method:

```
>>> from tasks import add
```

```
>>> add.delay(4,4)
```

When the client code is executed, the task will be encapsulated in the message and sent to the *listening broker*. Once processed by a worker, you can see the output on the console of the machine where the worker is present:

[2022-09-22 15:30:46,024: INFO/MainProcess] Task tasks.add[4966d730-5334-4089-8395-cb04f40de3c9] received

[2022-09-22 15:30:46,041: INFO/MainProcess] Task tasks.add[4966d730-5334-4089-8395-cb04f40de3c9] succeeded in 0.01600000000325963s: 8

As we can, *two* lines are shown in the output. The first shows that the broker has received the message, and the second shows that the task has been successfully executed, reporting the execution time and the returned result.

If instead, we wanted to use **apply_async()**, we would have had to pass the *two* arguments required by the task within a list:

```
>>> add.apply_async([4,4])
```

If instead, we have set Celery that makes use of the result backend, we can also get this value on the client side in the following way:

```
>>> ares = add.delay(4,4)
```

```
>>> ares.get()
```

```
8
```

Calling the task returns an **AsyncResult** object. With the **get()** method, we will ask the object to read the result from the result backend. This value will only be available when the task has been processed and therefore it will take some time. Since the **get()** call must be *asynchronous*, it would be necessary to check the state of the called task *first*. For example, through the **ready()**

method it is possible to know if the task has been completed or not:

```
>>> ares.ready()
```

```
True
```

This will return a Boolean: **True** if the task has been completed, otherwise **False**. Another fundamental information is to know if the task was successful or failed by raising an exception, with the methods **successful()** and **failed()** respectively. These also return Boolean values. All these methods, and others similar, are useful for managing program execution control depending on the status of the task:

```
>>> ares.successful()
```

```
True
```

```
>>> ares.failed()
```

```
False
```

Signatures and primitives

We have seen how to call tasks within a client program. But the possibilities offered by Celery do not end there. In fact, the library also provides a series of tools that allow you to build complex workflows on a number of tasks at the same time, in a very simplified way in the code.

First of all, Celery makes use of a concept such as **signatures**, which allow you to simplify the call of a task such as:

```
>>> s1 = add.signature((2,2), countdown=10)
```

In this case, we have stored the call to the task in a signature, which will allow us to use it within the code without rewriting everything, but simply using the signature just defined:

```
>>> s1.delay()
```

There is also a default signature **s()** which simply replaces the call to **delay()**:

```
>>> add.delay(4,5)
```

Simply with this signature:

```
>>> add.s(4,5)
```

This can make a programmer's life a lot easier. In fact, these signatures are essential to be used as arguments in a series of functions made available by the Celery library:

- **group()**

- `chain()`

- `chord()`

These functions are based on *primitives*, which are nothing more than signatures with complex call structures and which, precisely because of their shape, generate particular workflows within distributed systems.

For example, the **group()** method takes as an argument a list of tasks that will be executed at the same time. The returned value is a particular value that allows it to be inspected as a group, obtaining at the end a list with the elements that follow the order of the called tasks:

```
>>> from celery import group
>>> g = group(add.s(i,i) for i in range(10))()
>>> g.get()
[0, 2, 4, 6, 8, 10, 12, 14, 16, 18]
```

From the server console, we will see the following output:

```
[2022-09-22 16:24:24,645: INFO/MainProcess] Task tasks.add[4dfadc20-7deb-459c-8dc5-9db5ea377263] succeeded in 0.031000000017229468s: 2

[2022-09-22 16:24:24,670: INFO/MainProcess] Task tasks.add[fb8fa5fc-7c9f-4659-8168-26133100f17b] succeeded in 0.01600000000325963s: 6

[2022-09-22 16:24:24,695: INFO/MainProcess] Task tasks.add[1b9b73e9-a8f4-43d5-aacc-791a19789a1c] succeeded in 0.030999999590218907s: 4

[2022-09-22 16:24:24,721: INFO/MainProcess] Task tasks.add[f2764fb6-ed38-4f8c-927a-0b4c4810a03f] succeeded in 0.031000000017229468s: 14

[2022-09-22 16:24:24,746: INFO/MainProcess] Task tasks.add[9e6d6b83-1b3f-4b9f-963f-2a94bea21b93] succeeded in 0.01600000000325963s: 18

[2022-09-22 16:24:24,771: INFO/MainProcess] Task tasks.add[c4b3b795-329b-4f88-8409-4f425ad986a7] succeeded in 0.031000000017229468s: 8

[2022-09-22 16:24:24,796: INFO/MainProcess] Task tasks.add[72bc2b1c-189b-4d56-921d-decbc17cc29f] succeeded in 0.01600000000325963s: 16

[2022-09-22 16:24:24,825: INFO/MainProcess] Task tasks.add[30d86bf8-2f46-4e50-b2df-1a9b051c283a] succeeded in 0.01600000000325963s: 12

[2022-09-22 16:24:24,850: INFO/MainProcess] Task tasks.add[bdbc022a-2e01-4cf9-870a-3ae0cf20ea9e] succeeded in 0.031000000017229468s: 10
```

As we can see, the **10** tasks sent were performed at different times, not executing the order of the iteration used in the call. We can see that the execution times are also different between the various tasks. However, the results of the individual operations were collected and sorted according to this order.

Another very useful method is **chain()** which allows several tasks to be linked together in a chain so that the result of *one task* is used as the argument of the *second task*, and so on:

```
>>> from tasks import add, mul

>>> from celery import chain

>>> c = chain(add.s(4,4) | mul.s(8))()

>>> c.get()
```

While from the server console, we will get the following output:

```
[2022-09-22 16:41:52,501: INFO/MainProcess] Task tasks.add[9bad176a-937d-4742-8698-469b0918fe69] received

[2022-09-22 16:41:52,539: INFO/MainProcess] Task tasks.add[9bad176a-937d-4742-8698-469b0918fe69] succeeded in 0.031000000017229468s: 8

[2022-09-22 16:41:52,540: INFO/MainProcess] Task tasks.mul[21339f93-56f3-45c1-a09a-09b24b36999a] received

[2022-09-22 16:41:52,565: INFO/MainProcess] Task tasks.mul[21339f93-56f3-45c1-a09a-09b24b36999a] succeeded in 0.030999999959021807s: 64
```

From here we can see that exactly what we described has happened. The message from the *first task* in the chain is received and executed immediately thereafter. Its result is then passed as an argument to the *second task* and sent back as a message to the *broker*. This is in turn performed and the result is returned to the client.

Another method is **chord()** which uses a group of tasks in a callback:

```
>>> from tasks import add, mul, xsum

>>> from celery import chord

>>> c = chord((add.s(i,i) for i in range(10)), xsum.s())()

>>> c.get()
90
```

Note: If you try to get a chord with RPC you will get an error message, as this feature is not implemented in this type of Result Backend:

```
NotImplementedError: The "rpc" result backend does not support chords!
```

Note that a group chained with a task is also upgraded to be a chord, as this pattern requires synchronization.

Result backends that support chords: Redis, Database, Memcached, and more.

In this case, you must therefore use Redis as a Result Backend. Replace the settings and restart the Celery server.

In the Celery server console, you will get the following output:

```
[2022-09-22 16:59:09,209: INFO/MainProcess] Task tasks.add[c4a4c71c-3c4b-
45ce-aef2-842cfe024330] received

[2022-09-22 16:59:09,242: INFO/MainProcess] Task tasks.add[a03d2f04-347b-
47da-b052-087ef34f478f] received

[2022-09-22 16:59:09,279: INFO/MainProcess] Task tasks.add[e3af658d-d41f-
4714-87e1-1af6a63c2401] received

[2022-09-22 16:59:09,309: INFO/MainProcess] Task tasks.add[920cbf97-7a20-
4c57-8024-22f69fbdccea] received

[2022-09-22 16:59:09,335: INFO/MainProcess] Task tasks.add[c4a4c71c-3c4b-
45ce-aef2-842cfe024330] succeeded in 0.125s: 0

[2022-09-22 16:59:09,344: INFO/MainProcess] Task tasks.add[a03d2f04-347b-
47da-b052-087ef34f478f] succeeded in 0.10899999999674037s: 2

[2022-09-22 16:59:09,349: INFO/MainProcess] Task tasks.add[2bc571ef-794a-
4581-8cbe-3a8cf6dea136] received

[2022-09-22 16:59:09,379: INFO/MainProcess] Task tasks.add[e3af658d-d41f-
4714-87e1-1af6a63c2401] succeeded in 0.09399999998277053s: 4

[2022-09-22 16:59:09,382: INFO/MainProcess] Task tasks.add[2e5bc833-b47e-
40a7-85e9-74fc152eeb16] received

[2022-09-22 16:59:09,398: INFO/MainProcess] Task tasks.add[920cbf97-7a20-
4c57-8024-22f69fbdccea] succeeded in 0.0940000000409782s: 6

[2022-09-22 16:59:09,419: INFO/MainProcess] Task tasks.add[004d45e8-1b93-
4377-9695-fe000432be75] received

[2022-09-22 16:59:09,448: INFO/MainProcess] Task tasks.add[2bc571ef-794a-
4581-8cbe-3a8cf6dea136] succeeded in 0.09399999998277053s: 8

[2022-09-22 16:59:09,451: INFO/MainProcess] Task tasks.add[ff29e563-cc91-
44f9-a3cb-b2a1895444e3] received
```

```
[2022-09-22 16:59:09,484: INFO/MainProcess] Task tasks.add[2e5bc833-b47e-
40a7-85e9-74fc152eeb16] succeeded in 0.10899999999674037s: 10

[2022-09-22 16:59:09,488: INFO/MainProcess] Task tasks.add[760cf014-8613-
44f5-bbc3-77abcf6a7901] received

[2022-09-22 16:59:09,507: INFO/MainProcess] Task tasks.add[004d45e8-1b93-
4377-9695-fe000432be75] succeeded in 0.09399999998277053s: 12

[2022-09-22 16:59:09,521: INFO/MainProcess] Task tasks.add[2938bca7-6566-
4c47-8d0d-c8e94045ea52] received

[2022-09-22 16:59:09,538: INFO/MainProcess] Task tasks.add[ff29e563-cc91-
44f9-a3cb-b2a1895444e3] succeeded in 0.07800000003771856s: 14

[2022-09-22 16:59:09,560: INFO/MainProcess] Task tasks.add[760cf014-8613-
44f5-bbc3-77abcf6a7901] succeeded in 0.061999999976251274s: 16

[2022-09-22 16:59:09,575: INFO/MainProcess] Task tasks.xsum[3329ba27-
eb79-47b2-9618-7e71a8cad91e] received

[2022-09-22 16:59:09,616: INFO/MainProcess] Task tasks.add[2938bca7-6566-
4c47-8d0d-c8e94045ea52] succeeded in 0.09399999998277053s: 18

[2022-09-22 16:59:09,622: INFO/MainProcess] Task tasks.xsum[3329ba27-
eb79-47b2-9618-7e71a8cad91e] succeeded in 0.0470000000204891s: 90
```

The **chunks()** method allows us to split an *iterable* into *smaller chunks*. In this way, if we have 100 *objects*, these can be divided into 10 *tasks* of 10 *objects* each:

```
>>> from tasks import add

>>> from celery import chunks

>>> z = zip(range(10),range(10))

>>> list(z)

[(0, 0), (1, 1), (2, 2), (3, 3), (4, 4), (5, 5), (6, 6), (7, 7), (8, 8),
(9, 9)]

>>> ch = add.chunks(z,10)()

>>> ch.get()

[[0, 2, 4, 6, 8, 10, 12, 14, 16, 18]]
```

Dramatiq library as an alternative to Celery

Although Celery is currently the reference library for those who want to set up distributed systems in Python, there are also other valid alternatives that are gradually gaining momentum. Perhaps the one that differs the least from Celery's basics is the **Dramatiq** library. The many similarities to Celery make it a suitable candidate for those already familiar with Celery, as they both share many characteristics. Both are based on *asynchronous tasks* and rely on applications such as **Redis** or **RabbitMQ**

One of Celery's *flaws*, at least in the opinion of some developers, is that it is quite *complex*, while Dramatiq has been designed to be much simpler and more intuitive.

Installing Dramatiq

Before starting with some examples, let's install the latest release of **Dramatiq** (currently *version* 1.13) on our virtual environment or on one dedicated to it. We open the command console and insert:

```
pip install dramatiq
```

For our examples, we will use the Redis application with Dramatiq; therefore, we need to install the necessary dependencies to be able to use it. To do this we will also write the following command:

```
pip install dramatiq[redis]
```

But if you want to use RabbitMQ you can write instead:

```
pip install dramatiq[rabbitmq]
```

At this point, all that remains is to *activate* the Redis (or RabbitMQ) container that we had loaded into Docker Desktop, as shown in *Figure* 5.12:

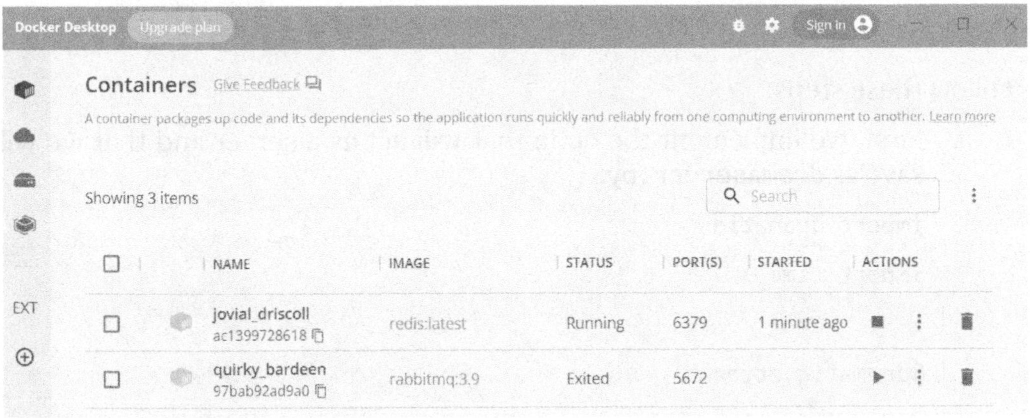

Figure 5.12: *The Redis container is activated in Docker Desktop*

Getting started with Dramatiq

Now that we have Dramatiq and all other necessary dependencies installed, we can start working with this library.

In Dramatiq the tasks are replaced by the actors, which are nothing more than the functions containing the code to be executed by the workers that will be created by Redis, which also in this architecture will work in a similar way to what it does in Celery. Redis will take care of encapsulating the activity of the *actors (task)* in messages that will be dispatched to the various waiting workers (see *Figure 5.13*):

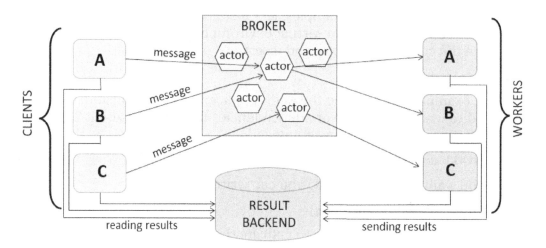

Figure 5.13: *The Dramatiq architecture*

Follow these steps:

1. First, we implement the code that will act as a server and that we will save as **dramaserver.py**:

```python
import dramatiq
import time


@dramatiq.actor
def wait(t,n):
    time.sleep(t)
    print("I am the actor %s and I will wait for %s secs" %(n,t))
```

As we can see from the code, we first import the necessary libraries, including **dramatiq**. Then we will define the functions that will perform the activities of the workers, recognizable in the code through the **@ dramatiq.actor** decorator. In our example, we will define as actor a **wait()** function that does nothing but waits for a certain period of seconds, and then print a message about the expected seconds in output.

2. Now that we have defined a very simple example of a file server in which the services *performed (actors)* by the distributed Dramatiq system are described, we can activate the latter simply by running the following command from the virtual environment console:

dramatiq dramaserver

As you can see, you enter the name of the file server, to make active the actors defined within them. Once the command has been launched, the following text will appear in the output:

```
[2022-09-27 16:46:00,775] [PID 18332] [MainThread] [dramatiq.
MainProcess] [INFO] Dramatiq '1.13.0' is booting up.

[2022-09-27 16:46:00,685] [PID 7452] [MainThread] [dramatiq.
WorkerProcess(0)] [INFO] Worker process is ready for action.

[2022-09-27 16:46:00,580] [PID 25400] [MainThread] [dramatiq.
WorkerProcess(1)] [INFO] Worker process is ready for action.

[2022-09-27 16:46:00,685] [PID 25192] [MainThread] [dramatiq.
WorkerProcess(2)] [INFO] Worker process is ready for action.

[2022-09-27 16:46:00,705] [PID 6828] [MainThread] [dramatiq.
WorkerProcess(3)] [INFO] Worker process is ready for action.

[2022-09-27 16:46:00,705] [PID 17300] [MainThread] [dramatiq.
WorkerProcess(4)] [INFO] Worker process is ready for action.

[2022-09-27 16:46:00,700] [PID 18248] [MainThread] [dramatiq.
WorkerProcess(5)] [INFO] Worker process is ready for action.

[2022-09-27 16:46:00,666] [PID 10216] [MainThread] [dramatiq.
WorkerProcess(6)] [INFO] Worker process is ready for action.

[2022-09-27 16:46:00,661] [PID 9372] [MainThread] [dramatiq.
WorkerProcess(7)] [INFO] Worker process is ready for action.

[2022-09-27 16:46:00,736] [PID 25952] [MainThread] [dramatiq.
WorkerProcess(8)] [INFO] Worker process is ready for action.

[2022-09-27 16:46:00,705] [PID 20300] [MainThread] [dramatiq.
WorkerProcess(9)] [INFO] Worker process is ready for action.
```

```
[2022-09-27 16:46:00,721] [PID 15876] [MainThread] [dramatiq.
WorkerProcess(10)] [INFO] Worker process is ready for action.

[2022-09-27 16:46:00,770] [PID 6644] [MainThread] [dramatiq.
WorkerProcess(11)] [INFO] Worker process is ready for action.

[2022-09-27 16:46:01,270] [PID 6640] [MainThread] [dramatiq.
ForkProcess(0)]    [INFO]    Fork    process    'dramatiq.middleware.
prometheus:_run_exposition_server' is ready for action.
```

As we can see, twelve workers have been created in the Dramatiq distributed system, corresponding to twelve different processes (the PIDs are indicated in the text) that will wait to receive messages from Redis containing the actors to be executed.

Note: On Windows to shut down the server, press the X button at the top right. The window will not close and all active services on Dramatiq will close.

3. At this point, we implement the client of the client side, which we will save as **dramaclient.py**:

```
import dramatiq

import time

from dramaserver import wait


[wait.send(10,i) for i in range(10)]

print("End Program")
```

4. We just have to open another virtual environment console and run the *customer code*:

python dramaclient.py

5. By executing the code, on the console, you will immediately get the text of the end of the program, and the prompt ready for a new command:

End Program

While from the server console, after about 10 *seconds*, we will obtain an output similar to the following at the same time:

```
I am the actor 10 and I will wait for 0 secs

I am the actor 10 and I will wait for 7 secs

I am the actor 10 and I will wait for 3 secs

I am the actor 10 and I will wait for 9 secs
```

```
I am the actor 10 and I will wait for 1 secs

I am the actor 10 and I will wait for 6 secs

I am the actor 10 and I will wait for 4 secs

I am the actor 10 and I will wait for 2 secs

I am the actor 10 and I will wait for 5 secs

I am the actor 10 and I will wait for 8 secs
```

In the previous code, we used a for inline command to launch multiple actors at the same time. But this way can only be used in limited cases, where the actors are all the same and one of the parameters is often the value of the iterator itself. A more general way to launch multiple actors in parallel together is through **grouping**.

6. Let's rewrite the previous client code as follows:

```
import dramatiq

import time

from dramaserver import wait

from dramatiq import group


g = group([

    wait.message(10,'A'),

    wait.message(5,'B'),

    wait.message(4,'C'),

    wait.message(7,'D'),

]).run()


print("End Program")
```

7. As we can see, a **group()** function is used which accepts a list of calls to *actors*, which can also be different from each other. But this time the actors will call the **message()** method to send the parameters to use.

By executing, a result similar to the following is obtained on the output of the server console:

```
I am the actor C and I will wait for 4 secs

I am the actor B and I will wait for 5 secs
```

```
I am the actor D and I will wait for 7 secs

I am the actor A and I will wait for 10 secs
```

This time the execution times are different and therefore the lines will appear in the order of execution at different times.

Management of results

So far we have managed actors who did not produce results, that is, *return values*. These actually require special management with Dramatiq. These too will have to be enclosed in messages and collected in a result backend very similar to what we had seen with Celery. Here, too, you can choose whether to use Redis or RabbitMQ as an application for the result backend.

To add all the necessary settings and activate the broker and result backend services we will have to make changes and additions to the previous codes, this time completing the complete picture of an implementation distributed through Dramatiq.

As for the code that manages the server side, we will apply the changes to the code as follows.

```python
import dramatiq

import time


from dramatiq.brokers.redis import RedisBroker

#from dramatiq.brokers.rabbitmq import RabbitmqBroker

from dramatiq.results import Results

from dramatiq.results.backends import RedisBackend


broker = RedisBroker(host="localhost")

#broker = RabbitmqBroker(host="localhost")

dramatiq.set_broker(broker)

result_backend = RedisBackend(host="localhost")

broker.add_middleware(Results(backend=result_backend))


@dramatiq.actor(store_results=True)

def wait(t,n):
```

```
    time.sleep(t)

    print("I am the actor %s and I will wait for %s secs" %(n,t))

    return "I waited for {0} secs".format(t)
```

As we can see in the code a lot of additions have been made. In the first part, all the classes responsible for the *Broker* and *Result Backend* services will have to be imported this time. In our example, we have decided to use Redis for both features. However, I have left comments on the classes corresponding to RabbitMQ, in order to leave indications for those wishing to use this other application. Since the example takes place locally on the same computer, I entered local host as the host for both services. If you were to operate on the network, replace these values with the corresponding IP address. As for the actor, we added a return value which is still a *string*. In this case, our purpose will be to display this string from the *client side* on the console.

The *client-side code* also needs some modifications:

```
import dramatiq

import time

from dramaserver import wait

from dramatiq import group


from dramatiq.brokers.redis import RedisBroker

from dramatiq.results import Results

from dramatiq.results.backends import RedisBackend


broker = RedisBroker(host="localhost")

dramatiq.set_broker(broker)

result_backend = RedisBackend(host="localhost")

broker.add_middleware(Results(backend=result_backend))


g = group([

    wait.message(10,'A'),

    wait.message(5,'B'),

    wait.message(4,'C'),

    wait.message(7,'D'),
```

```
]).run()
```

```
for res in g.get_results(block=True, timeout=12000):
    print(res)
```

```
print("End Program")
```

As we can see, also on the client code it will be necessary to import the same classes of the *Broker* and *Result Backend* services that we used for the client side. This is generally also useful to make the client understand where the services that make up the Dramatiq distributed system are present by specifying the different IPs.

As for the actors, gathered in a group this time keep their results in memory in the result backend for a certain period of time. With the **get_results()** method, you can retrieve them from the group. The dwell time of the results in the result backend by default is **10** seconds, and since in our example we work on these times, it will be better to extend the timeout to **12** seconds (12000 *ms*).

By running the two codes in the Dramatiq system that we made we will get it on the client-side console:

I waited for 10 secs

I waited for 5 secs

I waited for 4 secs

I waited for 7 secs

End Program

And on the server-side console:

I am the actor C and I will wait for 4 secs

I am the actor B and I will wait for 5 secs

I am the actor D and I will wait for 7 secs

I am the actor A and I will wait for 10 secs

SCOOP library

Another library available online for distributed computing using Python is **Scalable Concurrent Operation in Python (SCOOP)**. This project is still in *beta* (currently in version 0.7) and consists of a single module, called **scoop**, whose task is to distribute concurrent tasks, here called **Futures**, to worker processes distributed on different machines connected in a network:

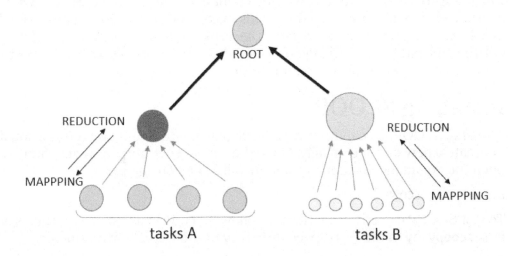

Figure 5.14: SCOOP *multi-layer mechanism*

The SCOOP developers have set themselves the main purpose of keeping the management of *distributed* and *parallel* programming as simple and transparent as possible. SCOOP is able to manage different tasks at multiple processing levels, passing through mapping and reduction mechanisms (see *Figure* 5.14). The module will then deal with the physical considerations regarding the possibility of how to distribute the tasks based on the physical potential of the machines connected to the system and the parallelization methods to be applied in the various cases.

As for the elements that make up the architecture, SCOOP is much simpler than distributed systems such as Celery, since it only has **WORKERS** (all the same) and a **BROKER**, as shown in *Figure* 5.15:

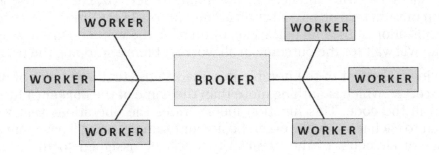

Figure 5.15: SCOOP *architecture*

The central element of the communication system is the **Broker** who interacts with all the independent workers to dispatch messages between them. **Futures** are created in worker elements instead of the broker with a centralized serialization procedure. This makes the architecture more *reliable* and *improves performance*. In fact, the broker's main workload consists of networking and I / O exchange between the various processes present in the workers with a relatively low response time.

Installing SCOOP

To install SCOOP, we can use the same virtual environment created previously or create a new one specifically. Once the virtual environment is activated, we open the command line console and install SCOOP using **pip**:

```
pip install SCOOP
```

To test SCOOP directly, we write the following code in a text editor, then save it as **scoopy.py** in the workspace directory of the virtual environment:

```
from scoop import futures

def worker(value):

    print("I am the Worker %s" %value)



if __name__ == "__main__":

    list(futures.map(worker, range(4)))
```

Before running the code, let's take a quick look. From the **scoop** module, you import futures which is nothing more than the pool of tasks to be addressed to the workers by the broker. The broker builds the tasks through the **map()** method which, like that of the standard library, accepts an *iterable* as a second argument, in this case, **range(4)**, which is nothing more than a sequence of four elements with integers in ascending order: **(0,1,2,3)**. The **map()** function must in turn be passed as an argument to a **list()** function, to have a synchronization at the end of the execution of all the workers. In this way, the program will wait for the outcome of all workers before stopping the program.

Every single element of the iterable is passed to the first argument of **map()**, that is *worker*, which is nothing more than the name of the **worker()** function defined in the code. This function incorporates the operations that will be assigned to each individual worker. So, in our example, we will have four tasks (number of elements of the *iterable*) that will be assigned to the available workers, each of which will print a string in which it will add its identification number, which corresponds precisely to the value of the iterable.

To run the code that uses SCOOP, you need to specify the **-m** scoop option in the Python code execution command. So, let's write:

```
python -m scoopy.py
```

Executing the code will result in console output similar to the following:

```
[2022-09-26 15:01:08,933] launcher  INFO    SCOOP 0.7 2.0 on win32 using
Python 3.10.4 | packaged by conda-forge | (main, Mar 30 2022, 08:38:02)
[MSC v.1916 64 bit (AMD64)], API: 1013

[2022-09-26 15:01:08,933] launcher  INFO    Deploying 12 worker(s) over
1 host(s).

[2022-09-26 15:01:08,933] launcher  INFO    Worker distribution:

[2022-09-26 15:01:08,933] launcher  INFO       127.0.0.1:       11 + origin

Launching 12 worker(s) using an unknown shell.

I am the Worker 0

I am the Worker 1

I am the Worker 3

I am the Worker 2

[2022-09-26 15:01:09,934] launcher  (127.0.0.1:64064) INFO    Root process
is done.

[2022-09-26 15:01:09,934] launcher  (127.0.0.1:64064) INFO    Finished
cleaning spawned subprocesses.
```

As we can see from the execution result, SCOOP automatically created twelve workers on my computer (*11 + origin*). This value is automatically set by SCOOP according to the characteristics of the machine where the program is being executed. The four tasks are performed concurrently, as we can see from the output printed by the individual **worker()** functions that highlight a random order of execution.

Let's make the previous example more complex by adding a mathematical calculation with a result to the function called which we will call **func()**:

```
from scoop import futures

import math

import numpy as np


def func(value):

    result = math.sqrt(value)
```

```
    print("The value %s and the elaboration is %s" %(value, result))
    return result


if __name__ == "__main__":
    data = np.array([10,3,6,1,4,8,25,9])
    results = list(futures.map(func, data))
    for result in results:
        print("This is the result: %s" %result)
```

As we can see from the code, now the **func()** function processed by the workers, in addition to writing a string as output, will return the result to the broker which will then be passed to the return value of the **map()** function, which through **list()** will be saved in a **results** variable. We also replaced the ordered sequence **range(4)** with a NumPy array of eight elements. At the end of the program, the results will then be printed in the output.

Let's save the code in a file and call it for example **scoopy2.py**. In the previous example, we had seen that SCOOP had created twelve workers automatically. This number can be set per command line by adding the **-n** option to the **python** command. For example, if we wanted to make use of **4** workers, you will have to run the following command from the virtual environment console:

```
python -m scoop -n 4 scoopy2.py
```

Running the code will produce a result similar to the following:

```
[2022-09-26 15:12:25,473] launcher  INFO     SCOOP 0.7 2.0 on win32 using
Python 3.10.4 | packaged by conda-forge | (main, Mar 30 2022, 08:38:02)
[MSC v.1916 64 bit (AMD64)], API: 1013

[2022-09-26 15:12:25,473] launcher  INFO     Deploying 4 worker(s) over 1
host(s).

[2022-09-26 15:12:25,489] launcher  INFO     Worker distribution:

[2022-09-26 15:12:25,489] launcher  INFO        127.0.0.1:       3 + origin

Launching 4 worker(s) using an unknown shell.

The value 10 and the elaboration is 3.1622776601683795

The value 3 and the elaboration is 1.7320508075688772

The value 6 and the elaboration is 2.449489742783178

The value 1 and the elaboration is 1.0
```

```
The value 4 and the elaboration is 2.0

The value 8 and the elaboration is 2.8284271247461903

The value 25 and the elaboration is 5.0

The value 9 and the elaboration is 3.0

This is the result: 3.1622776601683795

This is the result: 1.7320508075688772

This is the result: 2.449489742783178

This is the result: 1.0

This is the result: 2.0

This is the result: 2.8284271247461903

This is the result: 5.0

This is the result: 3.0

[2022-09-26 15:12:26,474] launcher  (127.0.0.1:64354) INFO    Root process
is done.

[2022-09-26 15:12:26,474] launcher  (127.0.0.1:64354) INFO      Finished
cleaning spawned subprocesses.
```

As we can see from the result, we still have a random order of execution of the various tasks. But in the results output, it should be noted that **list(map())** will return all the results in the same order in which they were defined in the **NumPy** array. In this phase, there is therefore a *synchronization phase*, which waits for the outcome of all the results to value results, that is, the **returned** variable.

Now that we have seen how the SCOOP architecture manages tasks with mapping, let's take a further step by adding the reduction step. From the previous example we have seen how passing an *iterable of n* elements we obtain an *iterable of n* results. Now it is possible to add a reduction phase, adding an *aggregation-reduction function* of the result. For example, we can replace the function **list()** which synchronizes all the results of the different workers and sorts them in a list, with a reduction function such as, for example, the **sum()** function. This function will sum up all the results of the various workers. Regardless of their execution times, it will gradually add up all the results, waiting until the end of the last worker, and then returning the result. Again, we will have a *synchronization mechanism*.

Let's modify the previous code in the following way:

```
if __name__ == "__main__":
    data = np.array([10,3,6,1,4,8,25,9])
    result = sum(futures.map(func, data))
    print("This is the reduction result: %s" %result)
```

Going to execute you will get the result of the reduction, which is the sum of all the results of the workers:

...

This is the reduction result: 21.172245335266624

...

In SCOOP there is another method that incorporates both of the previous operations, that is, both mapping and reduction: **mapReduce()**. We continue to modify the previous code, importing the operator module, which allows us to call operators as methods. In our example, we will use **add()** to add up. Finally, we replace **map()** with **mapReduce()** adding the aggregating method **operator.add**, as a second function to apply:

```
from scoop import futures

import math

import numpy as np

import random

import operator


def func(value):
    result = math.sqrt(value)
    print("The value %s and the elaboration is %s" %(value, result))
    return result


if __name__ == "__main__":
    data = np.array([10,3,6,1,4,8,25,9])
    result = futures.mapReduce(func, operator.add, data)
    print("This is the reduction result: %s" %result)
```

By running the preceding code, you will get the same result as in the previous case. The matter can be further complicated by concatenating the *mapping* and *reduction* functions.

For example, after calculating the square roots of the entered data, we can convert them to *integer values*, and finally calculate the *average*, as done by modifying the code as follows.

```
if __name__ == "__main__":

    data = np.array([10,3,6,1,4,8,25,9])

    result = np.mean(list(futures.map(int, futures.map( func, data))))

    print("This is the reduction result: %s" %result)
```

Executing gives the following result:

```
[2022-09-26 16:09:50,661] launcher  INFO    SCOOP 0.7 2.0 on win32 using
Python 3.10.4 | packaged by conda-forge | (main, Mar 30 2022, 08:38:02)
[MSC v.1916 64 bit (AMD64)], API: 1013

[2022-09-26 16:09:50,661] launcher  INFO    Deploying 4 worker(s) over 1
host(s).

[2022-09-26 16:09:50,661] launcher  INFO    Worker distribution:

[2022-09-26 16:09:50,661] launcher  INFO       127.0.0.1:       3 + origin

Launching 4 worker(s) using an unknown shell.

The value 10 and the elaboration is 3.1622776601683795

The value 3 and the elaboration is 1.7320508075688772

The value 6 and the elaboration is 2.449489742783178

The value 1 and the elaboration is 1.0

The value 4 and the elaboration is 2.0

The value 8 and the elaboration is 2.8284271247461903

The value 25 and the elaboration is 5.0

The value 9 and the elaboration is 3.0

This is the reduction result: 2.375

[2022-09-26 16:09:52,039] launcher  (127.0.0.1:65396) INFO    Root process
is done.

[2022-09-26 16:09:52,054] launcher  (127.0.0.1:65396) INFO       Finished
cleaning spawned subprocesses.
```

As we can see, things can gradually get complicated but making distributed computing more and more powerful.

Conclusion

This chapter introduced the concept of distributed systems and how they can enter the context of parallel programming. In addition, the **Celery** framework was specifically discussed, which currently plays the role of the main reference point for the implementation of distributed systems in Python. In particular, we have seen the most useful features regarding concurrent task computation. Later, we also saw two possible alternatives to this framework that offer similar solutions to our context: **Dramatiq** and **SCOOP**.

In the next chapter, we will see a further possibility of using parallel programming: the use of GPU graphics processors and their libraries. Another possibility is that it allows us to exploit the computing power of this type of processor.

References

- https://www.capitalone.com/tech/software-engineering/distributed-systems-using-python-ray/

- https://scoop.readthedocs.io/en/0.7/

- https://pypi.org/project/scoop/

- https://www.pedaldrivenprogramming.com/2018/07/dramatiq-celery-alternative/

- https://dramatiq.io/

## CHAPTER 6

Maximizing Performance with GPU Programming using CUDA

So far we have considered the CPUs present in our computing systems in the context of parallel programming. But CPUs aren't the only processors capable of doing parallel calculations, there are also **Graphics Processing Units (GPUs)**. These processors are designed to process vector data extremely quickly and efficiently for image rendering, 3D engines and manipulation of polygonal primitives. Their development is mainly due to the great push of the gaming market, which has led to exceptional results over the years. The interesting development is that this technology and GPUs have also turned out to be very powerful tools for scientific computing.

Structure

In this chapter, we will cover the following topics:

- GPU architecture
- GPU programming
- Numba for CUDA
- OpenCL

GPU architecture

In practice, GPUs can be considered to be made up of millions of light cores in parallel, each of which is able to carry out calculations independently. This highly parallel structure is able to perform calculations on very large vectors and matrices in a very short time, something that certainly cannot be done by the CPUs. These characteristics have therefore quite recently captured the attention of the scientific world, leading to the development of development models and tools and highly specialized libraries in this area.

Let's see in detail how a GPU is structured inside. These concepts will then come in handy to better understand GPU programming models. Inside, the GPUs are structured to be divided into *two* levels of parallelism. The first level consists of several processing units that make up the GPU, called **Streaming Multiprocessor (SM)**. Each of these units' works *independently* of the others and all together performs tasks *simultaneously*. The second level of parallelism occurs within the **SM -itself**. Each SM is in turn subdivided into further computing units called **Stream Processor (SP)**. Each SP has a core capable of executing a *thread*, which works independently and simultaneously with the other SPs. The schematic of this structure is shown in *Figure 6.1*:

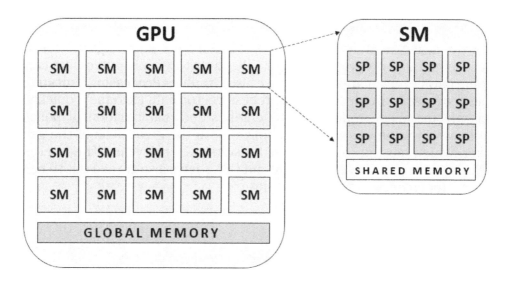

Figure 6.1: *Internal structure of a GPU*

The subdivision into **SM** and **SP** is structural and based on it, a logical organization can be created that we will use for the GPU programming model. The SPs which are the basic unit of calculation of the GPUs can be grouped into blocks. These logic blocks will be used to execute a specific execution mode. That is, all the cores within them will execute the same instruction simultaneously, pointing however to different memory areas, each processing a particular portion of data assigned to them. The memory they will access will be inside the GPU itself, in order to make access to the values inside it as quick and fast as possible. This data will then be transferred and reloaded by the CPU again for further processing.

The highly parallel nature with thousands or millions of *processing units* (or *threads*) capable of doing just as many calculations in parallel, therefore makes GPUs extremely powerful, yet completely different from the CPU. It was therefore necessary to develop specific programming methods different from conventional ones. You will have to take advantage of different drivers and compilers capable of compiling portions of code for the specific language that can be processed by the GPUs, which in turn are produced by different manufacturers, and therefore require a specific approach for each of them.

At present, there are some more efficient solutions that allow us to take advantage of the computing power of GPUs and integrate it with the classic, and often sequential execution of CPUs. Among the various manufacturers of graphics cards, **NVIDIA** is perhaps the one that goes the most, both in terms of computing power and diffusion on our PCs. For this type of card, there is a specific development environment, called **Compute Unified Device Architecture (CUDA)** created specifically to work with NVIDIA cards. This development environment is mainly based on the C language which makes use of particular extensions that allow the use of specific features of GPUs, but other programming languages such as Fortran, Java, and especially Python can also be used.

Another technology that allows us to program the GPUs together with the CPU to exploit its parallel computing potential is the **OpenCL framework**. This too is based on the C and C ++ languages, but over time it has also been possible to integrate it into other programming languages such as Python. This technology is more general than CUDA created specifically for NVIDIA cards. In fact, OpenCL is able to use GPU cards from other manufacturers (Intel, AMD, and so on) as well as NVIDIA cards, thanks to the release of SDK *toolkits* and specific drivers for the integration of OpenCL. As for NVIDIA GPU cards, OpenCL will still rely on CUDA technology that is fully compatible and can be integrated with it.

GPU programming in Python

Limited to Python, GPU programming has been made possible; thanks to a series of libraries, often wrappers in Python of corresponding C libraries, which have developed enormously in recent years. Their development is so rapid that often some of them have been more or less successful over time, alternating with the continuous evolution of these technologies. Currently, *two* libraries are particularly suitable for programming GPUs in parallel:

- Numba
- pyOpenCL

They are certainly not the only ones in this regard. Many other libraries are available and often use the same basic technologies, such as **CUDA** and **OpenCL**, but some of these are quite difficult in their use, often being *incompatible* with other libraries, and requiring compilations of the base in C (with installations of compilers specifications that must comply with particular versions). Often, setting up development environments with these libraries takes days, with little updated documentation, and doesn't always lead to success. **Numba** and **pyOpenCL** are perfectly integrated with Python package management environments such as **Pip** and **Anaconda**, and therefore their *installation* is *quick* and *easy*, allowing you to start working immediately.

Numba

Numba is an open-source library that includes a *JIT compiler* capable of translating portions of Python code and NumPy objects directly into specific machine code, using *LLVM technology*. This technology, provided by the **llvmilite** package, is integrated within **Numba**. Thanks to this integrated compilation system, Numba allows us to be able to create code that uses the characteristics of the CPU and GPU in an easy way without making too many changes to the Python language.

Therefore, Numba allows us to write classic codes in Python to which we will add particular notations (appropriate Python decorators) that will identify portions of code to be compiled specifically for the different GPU cards.

Numba for CUDA

As part of our book, we will be using Numba to work specifically with NVIDIA GPUs and will therefore be relying on CUDA. In order to work with this technology, it will first be necessary to take a look at its programming model and understand its basic concepts. Only thanks to them will we be able to understand well the various steps to be implemented if we want to make the most of the potential of the GPU.

First, in this programming model, you need to identify the CPU on which the program written in Python will run and the GPUs connected to it. The CPU will be identified as the *host* since it will host the mainstream of program execution, often sequentially. GPUs will instead be identified as devices since they can be heterogeneous and require different drivers and compilers in order to function. Python code written specifically to work on CPU and GPUs at the same time will be coded and executed in the traditional way on the host. When portions of code intended to run on GPUs are found, they will be compiled specifically based on the technology to which they will be addressed. Since we are considering NVIDIA GPU cards, Numba will use *CUDA technology* and the compiler inside it to create particular compiled packages, called **kernels**, to send to these cards, on which they will run. As we will see as follows, these kernels are easily *identifiable* within the code, taking the form of functions identified by particular decorators.

In addition to kernels, there are other functions intended for GPUs, called **device functions**. These are always functions compiled specifically to be run on different devices but are called by the kernels while they are running on the GPU (and not by the host).

Also with regard to *memory*, it is necessary to make some clarifications. The portions of the program executed on the CPU have access, like all traditional Python programs, to the system memory, which we will define as **host memory**. As for the kernels, these will be executed on the GPUs and therefore will have to access a specific memory present on these cards, which we will define as **device memory**.

In the GPU programming model, you will have to explicitly allocate this type of memory (host memory and device memory) and manage the transfer between them. Since GPUs work optimally with vectors, they will be used in the CUDA-based model of **NumPy** arrays, specifically optimized for these transfer and allocation operations on the GPUs.

By re-listing the protagonists of the GPU programming model with CUDA, we will obtain the following list:

- **Host** (CPU)
- **Device** (GPU)
- **Kernel** (a GPU function launched by the host and executed on the device)
- **Device function** (a GPU function launched on the device and executed on the device)
- **Host memory** (the main memory of the system)
- **Device memory** (the memory on the GPU card)

Logical hierarchy of the GPU programming model

As we have seen, CUDA responds to a different execution model than the traditional sequential model used for CPU programming. With CUDA, the code will be executed by *multiple threads at a time* (often hundreds or thousands). In addition to a multi-level physical structure that includes the SM and SP units, the CUDA programming model provides for a logical subdivision organized through a hierarchy of *threads*, grouped into *grids* and *blocks*. A representative diagram of the logical hierarchy is shown in *Figure 6.2*:

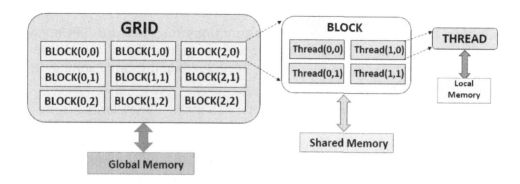

Figure 6.2: *Logical hierarchy of threads in GPU*

Numba provides a whole series of functions, classes and attributes that allow you to manage this hierarchy and the elements that compose it. As shown in *Figure 6.2*, it can be seen that at each hierarchical level corresponds a specific type of memory present in the GPU:

- Global memory
- Shared memory
- Local memory

When implementing a program with Numba (but also with other libraries that make use of CUDA) you must always keep in mind these different types of memory. The creation of efficient algorithms necessarily requires their optimized use, minimizing access and data exchange, and operations that require time resources.

Installation of CUDA

The first thing to do is to install the **CUDA toolkit** from the internet. It can be downloaded for free on the NVIDIA developer site at the dedicated page (**https://developer.nvidia.com/cuda-downloads**). Once the page is loaded, you will be shown a window where you can choose between different options to select your development environment, as shown in the following *Figure 6.3*:

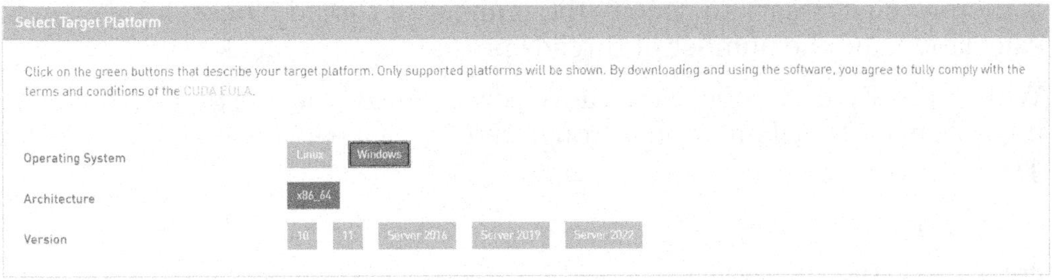

Figure 6.3: *Development system options window*

In our case, after selecting the characteristics of the system (*Windows* 11, *x86_64*), the following version has been automatically downloaded:

cuda_11.7.1_516.94_windows.exe

But certainly, in your case, you will get the most recent release. Once you have downloaded the executable, install it on your computer. Follow the instructions indicated during installation.

Installing Numba for CUDA

Numba installation is very simple with the *Anaconda platform*. To install Numba, simply open the console of the virtual environment that you have specially prepared to work with GPUs and enter the following command:

conda install numba cudatoolkit

As you can see, the **cudatoolkit** package must also be installed. Many libraries that make use of NVIDIA GPUs already have the dependencies for this package inside, but Numba is a library that has many uses and does not always have to be used to work with this type of GPU. So, it is necessary to install **cudatoolkit** separately as well.

Declaration and invocation of Kernel

Before starting the program we saw that the portions of code intended for execution on GPUs are defined as kernel functions. This type of function has *two* fundamental characteristics that differentiate them from normal functions in Python. First, kernels are functions that *cannot* return a value explicitly, that is, they cannot, therefore, use the return to return a value outside the function. These functions work exclusively on the data contained in arrays passed as arguments to the function, and therefore one of these arrays must be destined to contain the results of the calculation. Also in the kernel declaration, you have to take into account the *thread hierarchy* that will be set when invoked. It is therefore necessary to specify the number of thread blocks involved in the calculation and the number of threads present in each block.

Within the Python code, you can easily identify the portion of code that implements a *kernel* function, through the use of a particular decoder: **@cuda. jit**:

```
@cuda.jit

def kernel_func(array):

    """"

    Code here

    """"
```

Once you have a kernel defined, you will then have to invoke it when needed in your code. Before doing this, however, as we said, it will be necessary to express the thread hierarchy that must be set up and used for its execution. We will then set the number of threads for each block and then the *number of blocks per grid*:

```
threadsperblock = 32

blockspergrid = (array.size // threadsperblock) + 1
```

It is clear that by defining these two parameters in this way, we will ensure that the *size* of the array used is taken into account each time and a corresponding number of threads is arranged in a hierarchy suitable for calculating them in the most optimal way are used.

Then we will invoke the **kernel** function, specifying these parameters as indexes of the function. The product of these two values will actually match the threads used in the computation:

```
kernel_func[blockspergrid, threadsperblock](array)
```

Once invoked, the **kernel** function will be compiled and sent as a kernel to the corresponding device to be executed by all the invoked threads. All kernels will run parallel *asynchronously*, each running the kernel *independently*. It is possible to synchronize their calculations by adding **cuda.synchronize()**. In this case, the code will wait for all kernels to finish their execution before continuing with the code.

As we will see in the following examples, choosing the correct thread hierarchy is essential for optimal computing performance on the GPU. The *block size* determines how many threads will share a certain memory area (shared memory) and also must be large enough to be able to take care of the calculation of the input data in a single step.

Furthermore, within the kernel function declaration, we will have to optimally manage the indexes of the threads involved and of the blocks to ensure that each thread knows exactly which element of the input array to deal with. There are special objects supplied by CUDA in this regard. For example, **threadIdx**, **threadIdy**, and **threadIdz** specify the indices of the various threads used within a block along the three dimensions. While **blockIdx**, **blockIdy**, and **blockIdz** specify the indices of the various blocks enclosed within the grid. The size of the blocks can instead be specified through **blockDim.x**, **blockDim.y**, and **blocDim.z**.

In light of this, if you wanted, for example, to implement a kernel that does only the increment of **1** for all the elements present within an array, we will have to use the previous index objects as follows:

```
@cuda.jit

def add_one(array):
    tx = cuda.threadIdx.x

    ty = cuda.blockIdx.x

    dim = cuda.blockDim.x


    pos = tx + ty * dim

    if pos < array.size:

        array[pos] += 1
```

Since the array we are considering is *one-dimensional*, we can consider a 1D geometry inside the kernel where only **x** is present. So the iteration between all the indices involved in the calculation can be related to the position of the array elements with the expression:

pos = tx + ty dim*

Furthermore, during the calculation, it is useful to set a condition to ensure that the index obtained is contained in the dimensions of the array. We then add the condition:

if pos < array.size:

Eventually, all kernels indexed with *pos* with each element of the array will increase their value by one unit simultaneously in a *parallel* and *asynchronous* manner.

Device functions

As for the device functions, they differ slightly from the point of view of the declaration compared to the kernel functions. Just add **device = True** to the decorator:

```
@cuda.jit(device=True)

def device_func(a, b):

    return a + b
```

Unlike **kernel** functions, a **device** function can return a value like all normal functions.

Programming example with Numba

The notions we have accumulated so far about Numba are enough for us to put them into practice and compile a small sample code. We use the kernel seen before which will increase the values of the elements of an array by one unit.

Let's write the following code:

```
import numpy as np

from numba import cuda


@cuda.jit

def add_one(a):

    tx = cuda.threadIdx.x

    ty = cuda.blockIdx.x

    dim = cuda.blockDim.x


    pos = tx + ty * dim

    if pos < a.size:

        a[pos] += 1


n = 10

a_host = np.random.random(n)

print("Vector a: %s" %a_host)

a_dev = cuda.to_device(a_host)
```

```
threadsperblock = 128

blockspergrid = (a_host.size // threadsperblock) + 1

add_one[threadsperblock, blockspergrid](a_dev)


a_host = a_dev.copy_to_host()

print("New Vector a: %s" %a_host)
```

As we can see, we first imported the necessary modules to be able to integrate the kernels into the code. In particular, for those who want to work with NVIDIA GPUs, we will import the part related to CUDA:

```
from numba import cuda
```

The **numpy** library is also essential since the preferred data for this technology, both for memory allocation and for transfer, are precisely the NumPy arrays. So, we also imported this module:

```
import numpy asn p
```

We then copied the kernel we had defined for example earlier:

```
@cuda.jit

def add_one(a):
    tx = cuda.threadIdx.x

    ty = cuda.blockIdx.x

    dim = cuda.blockDim.x


    pos = tx + ty * dim

    if pos < a.size:
        a[pos] += 1
```

Then we defined a simple array **a_host** (because it is on the Host Memory) of **10** elements whose values are randomly generated (floating numbers):

```
n = 10

a_host = np.random.random(n)

print("Vector a: %s" %a_host)
```

At this point we have transferred this array to the Device Memory, through the use of the function **cuda.to_device()** which allocates a memory space identical to the vector **a_host** on the Device Memory and then copies the content, identified with the array **a_dev** (because located on the Device Memory).

The next step is to define the hierarchy of threads involved in running the kernel. Here too, we have copied the definitions seen previously:

```
threadsperblock = 128

blockspergrid = (a_host.size // threadsperblock) + 1
```

We have inserted a large number of threads (**n = 128**) to avoid the output of the warning message in execution:

NumbaPerformanceWarning: Grid size 10 will likely result in GPU under-utilization due to low occupancy.

This error message appears to us because the program recommends using grids of a size comparable to the number of SPs present in the GPU and not too small to avoid that the potential of this hardware is not sufficiently exploited.

After defining an appropriate hierarchy for the threads, the **kernel** function is invoked on the **a_dev** array with the parameters just defined:

```
add_one[threadsperblock, blockspergrid](a_dev)
```

Once the kernel has been invoked, you will then have to manage the result of the calculation that is the vector **a_dev** whose elements have been increased by *one unit*. But this vector is on the GPU, so you will need to transfer it back to the Host Memory. To do this, use the **copy_to_host()** function which copies a memory area from the GPU (device) to the host:

```
a_host = a_dev.copy_to_host()
```

The variable **a_host** will now contain the updated values. We can print it in the output and compare the results with the values prior to the *calculation*:

```
print("New Vector a: %s" %a_host)
```

By running the code in its entirety, we will get a result similar to the following.

Vector a: [0.41384874 0.45213153 0.65042446 0.08814434 0.1537844 0.1184357

 0.61263638 0.86474909 0.91423873 0.34284854]

New Vector a: [1.41384874 1.45213153 1.65042446 1.08814434 1.1537844 1.1184357

 1.61263638 1.86474909 1.91423873 1.34284854]

As we can see, the calculations were done correctly.

Further changes

Let's continue with modifying the previous code while illustrating some other useful concepts. Let's consider the definition of *thread geometry*. We have seen that its management can be complicated and difficult to understand at a simple level. In our favor, there is another alternative method that greatly facilitates things for us: the definition of the absolute position.

In fact, very simple algorithms, such as the one examined in our example, will tend to use all thread indexes in the same way. Numba provides us with functions that greatly facilitate the task of defining the positions of the thread indexes within the kernel.

The **cuda.grid(ndim)** function allows us to know the absolute position of the current thread in the current hierarchy. With **ndim**, we define the number of dimensions the kernel is based on. Thanks to this function, the **kernel** function code is greatly simplified:

```
@cuda.jit

def increment_by_one(an_array):

    pos = cuda.grid(1)

    if pos < a.size:

        a[pos] += 1
```

Replacing it in the previous code does not change the results.

Extension to matrices (2D array)

Another change we can make is to extend the previous example to the case of 2D arrays, so we will talk about *matrices* instead of vectors.

To do this extension you need to make some changes to the code. First, we can define a matrix **A** instead of the vector **a**. We then make the appropriate changes and reduce the number of elements to **4** for better readability of the result:

```
n = 4

A_host = np.random.random(n*n).reshape(n,n)

print("Matrix A: \n %s" %A_host)

A_dev = cuda.to_device(A_host)
```

We have therefore replaced the previous vector with a 4x4 *matrix* both on the host, **A_host**, and on the device, **A_dev**. We then modify the **kernel** function to make it possible to increase all the elements within a matrix by *one unit*:

```
@cuda.jit

def add_one_2D(A):

    x, y = cuda.grid(2)

    if x < A.shape[0] and y < A.shape[1]:

        A[x, y] += 1
```

Thanks to absolute position, it is very easy to define a *two-dimensional kernel function.* As for the thread hierarchy, these will need to have a new geometry capable of responding optimally to working with two-dimensional vectors. So, to make it possible to assign a thread for each element of the matrix, you will have to define the new hierarchy as follows:

```
import math

threadsperblock = (128,128)

blockspergrid_x = math.ceil(A_host.shape[0] / threadsperblock[0])

blockspergrid_y = math.ceil(A_host.shape[1] / threadsperblock[1])

blockspergrid = (blockspergrid_x, blockspergrid_y)

add_one_2D[threadsperblock, blockspergrid](A_dev)
```

Finally, we will retransfer the result obtained from the device to the host and display it in the output:

```
A_host = A_dev.copy_to_host()

print("New Matrix A: \n %s" %A_host)
```

Let's review the modified code in its entirety:

```
import numpy as np

from numba import cuda

import math


@cuda.jit

def add_one_2D(A):

    x, y = cuda.grid(2)

    if x < A.shape[0] and y < A.shape[1]:

        A[x, y] += 1


n = 4
```

```
A_host = np.random.random(n*n).reshape(n,n)
print("Matrix A: \n %s" %A_host)
A_dev = cuda.to_device(A_host)


threadsperblock = (128,128)
blockspergrid_x = math.ceil(A_host.shape[0] / threadsperblock[0])
blockspergrid_y = math.ceil(A_host.shape[1] / threadsperblock[1])
blockspergrid = (blockspergrid_x, blockspergrid_y)
add_one_2D[threadsperblock, blockspergrid](A_dev)


A_host = A_dev.copy_to_host()
print("New Matrix A: \n %s" %A_host)
```

Running the code, we will get a result similar to the following:

```
Matrix A:
 [[0.00993464 0.99662295 0.6271492  0.39916735]
 [0.81896746 0.9282727  0.74802307 0.06418345]
 [0.54618904 0.92098866 0.13560085 0.41312367]
 [0.34544717 0.90828693 0.8784179  0.96724232]]
New Matrix A:
 [[1.00993464 1.99662295 1.6271492  1.39916735]
 [1.81896746 1.9282727  1.74802307 1.06418345]
 [1.54618904 1.92098866 1.13560085 1.41312367]
 [1.34544717 1.90828693 1.8784179  1.96724232]]
```

Transfer of data through the queue

Another change that can be made and that applies to all examples (both for **vectors** and **matrices**) is to use a *queue* for transferring data to and from the GPU. Editing is very simple, just create a CUDA stream:

```
stream = cuda.stream()
```

Then, add it to the two functions that manage data transfer:

```
A_dev = cuda.to_device(A_host, stream=stream)
A_host = A_dev.copy_to_host(stream=stream)
```

In this way, you will have a more efficient data transfer managed by a specific queue to manage the passage of data correctly and efficiently between host and device.

Sum between two matrices

We further extend the case of matrices, introducing an operation between multiple 2D vectors. In this case, we will add the elements of *two matrices* **A** and **B** to obtain the third matrix. This example shows how to introduce multiple input vectors to the kernel and how to manage them in the rest of the code.

Now, we no longer have a single vector (matrix) but three to define, one of which will be empty because it will host the results of the calculation:

```
n = 4

A_host = np.random.random(n*n).reshape(n,n)

B_host = np.random.random(n*n).reshape(n,n)

C_host = np.zeros((n,n))

print("Matrix A: \n %s" %A_host)

print("Matrix B: \n %s" %B_host)
```

Regarding the transfer of data from the *host to the device* and *vice versa*, these must be done individually:

```
Stream = cuda.stream()

A_dev = cuda.to_device(A_host, stream=stream)

B_dev = cuda.to_device(B_host, stream=stream)

C_dev = cuda.to_device(C_host, stream=stream)
```

As for the data transferred from the *device to the host*, in this case, we will need to transfer only **C_dev**, since it is the only one that contains the results of the kernel calculation. While **A_dev** and **B_dev** are used for *read-only* and are identical to those on the host, **A_dev** and **B_dev** do not need to be copied again:

```
C_host = C_dev.copy_to_host(stream=stream)

print("Matrix C: \n %s" %C_host)
```

Now that we have managed the 2D vectors, let's move on to the kernel which will require some changes, even if everything remains very simple:

```
@cuda.jit

def add_one_2D(A,B,C):

    x, y = cuda.grid(2)
```

```
    if x < A.shape[0] and y < A.shape[1]:
        C[x,y] = A[x, y] + B[x, y]
```

The position of the threads remains *unchanged* in the previous example since the correspondence of the calculation between the elements of the *two matrices* **A** and **B** remains. Only the corresponding elements of **A** and **B**, those with the same **x** and **y** to be clear, will be added and the result will be the element of **C** always in the same position. In this case, it was sufficient to add the sum of the elements between the various matrices:

```
C[x,y] = A[x, y] + B[x, y]
```

As far as the thread hierarchy is concerned, things remain the same.

What remains to be changed is the *invocation* of the **kernel** function, which this time requires three arguments, which are precisely the three matrices **A**, **B**, and **C**:

```
add_one_2D[threadsperblock, blockspergrid](A_dev, B_dev, C_dev)
```

Let's rewrite the modified code in its entirety:

```
import numpy as np

from numba import cuda

import math


@cuda.jit
def add_one_2D(A,B,C):
    x, y = cuda.grid(2)
    if x < A.shape[0] and y < A.shape[1]:
        C[x,y] = A[x, y] + B[x, y]


n = 4
A_host = np.random.random(n*n).reshape(n,n)
B_host = np.random.random(n*n).reshape(n,n)
C_host = np.zeros((n,n))
print("Matrix A: \n %s" %A_host)
print("Matrix B: \n %s" %B_host)
```

```
stream = cuda.stream()
A_dev = cuda.to_device(A_host, stream=stream)
B_dev = cuda.to_device(B_host, stream=stream)
C_dev = cuda.to_device(C_host, stream=stream)


threadsperblock = (128,128)
blockspergrid_x = math.ceil(A_host.shape[0] / threadsperblock[0])
blockspergrid_y = math.ceil(A_host.shape[1] / threadsperblock[1])
blockspergrid = (blockspergrid_x, blockspergrid_y)
add_one_2D[threadsperblock, blockspergrid](A_dev, B_dev, C_dev)


C_host = C_dev.copy_to_host(stream=stream)
print("Matrix C: \n %s" %C_host)
```

Running the code will produce a result similar to the following:

```
Matrix A:
 [[0.82645664 0.14077644 0.36426624 0.65039297]
 [0.10257125 0.30826244 0.82165832 0.90301203]
 [0.19817223 0.95656813 0.61620533 0.1200333 ]
 [0.8798604  0.11889796 0.31937825 0.0725755 ]]
Matrix B:
 [[0.83451822 0.37569725 0.91302873 0.061711   ]
 [0.04279979 0.13255439 0.96567441 0.51154525]
 [0.8677725  0.34670277 0.2593976  0.50304275]
 [0.91463535 0.96564344 0.91629866 0.17960097]]
Matrix C:
 [[1.66097486 0.51647368 1.27729497 0.71210397]
 [0.14537104 0.44081682 1.78733273 1.41455728]
 [1.06594473 1.3032709  0.87560292 0.62307604]
 [1.79449575 1.0845414  1.23567691 0.25217646]]
```

Multiplication between matrices

The last modification of the previous code is to consider multiplication between matrices, such as A * B = C. This is quite expensive for a sequential program running on the CPU. Instead, we will discover that this operation lends itself perfectly to being processed on GPUs with truly remarkable performance compared to the CPU:

```python
import numpy as np

from numba import cuda

import math


@cuda.jit
def matmul(A, B, C):


    i, j = cuda.grid(2)
    if i < C.shape[0] and j < C.shape[1]:
        tmp = 0.
        for k in range(A.shape[1]):
            tmp += A[i, k] * B[k, j]
        C[i, j] = tmp


n = 4
A_host = np.random.random(n*n).reshape(n,n)

B_host = np.random.random(n*n).reshape(n,n)

C_host = np.zeros((n,n))

print("Matrix A: \n %s" %A_host)

print("Matrix B: \n %s" %B_host)


stream = cuda.stream()

A_dev = cuda.to_device(A_host, stream=stream)

B_dev = cuda.to_device(B_host, stream=stream)
```

```
C_dev = cuda.to_device(C_host, stream=stream)


threadsperblock = (128,128)
blockspergrid_x = math.ceil(A_host.shape[0] / threadsperblock[0])
blockspergrid_y = math.ceil(A_host.shape[1] / threadsperblock[1])
blockspergrid = (blockspergrid_x, blockspergrid_y)
matmul[threadsperblock, blockspergrid](A_dev, B_dev, C_dev)


C_host = C_dev.copy_to_host(stream=stream)
print("Matrix C: \n %s" %C_host)
```

As we can see, the differences made if we exclude the **kernel** are very minimal. By running the preceding code, we will get a result similar to the following:

Matrix A:
```
[[0.75926968 0.92657886 0.68471105 0.17324253]
 [0.40790221 0.45988319 0.39122078 0.6198121 ]
 [0.10698571 0.43140089 0.58631454 0.38644777]
 [0.17504734 0.76003441 0.68634873 0.94149139]]
```
Matrix B:
```
[[0.79381329 0.96132662 0.16316954 0.5995909 ]
 [0.74119391 0.85658564 0.85753895 0.65944347]
 [0.98787907 0.04619411 0.70690497 0.51689578]
 [0.85581547 0.67852783 0.84931887 0.30510469]]
```
Matrix C:
```
[[2.11416833 1.6727798  1.54963095 1.47305894]
 [1.58158443 1.22468845 1.263899   0.93916938]
 [1.31461425 0.76167987 1.13008593 0.76960271]
 [2.18606024 1.48984562 1.96513125 1.24818073]]
```

The example we have chosen requires *little execution time* since we have chosen to use small-sized matrices. But as the size grows, the situation soon becomes different. We will now add **time** meters via the **time** module. We will see for example how the execution times vary with this kind of operation as the number of threads per block varies. Let's modify the code to record execution times:

```python
import numpy as np
from numba import cuda
import time
import math


@cuda.jit
def matmul(A, B, C):

    i, j = cuda.grid(2)
    if i < C.shape[0] and j < C.shape[1]:
        tmp = 0.
        for k in range(A.shape[1]):
            tmp += A[i, k] * B[k, j]
        C[i, j] = tmp


print("Matrix Size: ")
n = input()
print("\n")
A_host = np.random.random(n*n).reshape(n,n)
B_host = np.random.random(n*n).reshape(n,n)
C_host = np.zeros((n,n))


stream = cuda.stream()
A_dev = cuda.to_device(A_host, stream=stream)
B_dev = cuda.to_device(B_host, stream=stream)
C_dev = cuda.to_device(C_host, stream=stream)


threadsperblock = (128,128)
```

```
blockspergrid_x = math.ceil(A_host.shape[0] / threadsperblock[0])
blockspergrid_y = math.ceil(A_host.shape[1] / threadsperblock[1])
blockspergrid = (blockspergrid_x, blockspergrid_y)
matmul[threadsperblock, blockspergrid](A_dev, B_dev, C_dev)


t1 = time.perf_counter()
C_host = C_dev.copy_to_host(stream=stream)
t2 = time.perf_counter()
elapsed_time = t2 - t1
print("Elapsed time %s" %elapsed_time)
```

As we can see from the code, we have eliminated the printing of the values of the matrices and inserted the size of the matrices from the console during the execution of the program, so as not to have to modify the code every time. Another solution could be to use input parameters during the *program launch*.

If we measure the time taken as the *size of the matrices varies* and the *size of the blocks* (number of threads per block) varies, we obtain a table similar to the following (see *Table 6.1*):

Matrix size	threads in block			
	n=128	n=256	n=512	n=1024
1024	0,06	0,06	0,22	0,71
2048	0,68	0,42	0,42	1,36
3072	2,14	1,78	1,28	2,26
4092	7,24	4,87	2,04	3,28
5120	N/A	12,32	7,22	5,29
6144	N/A	17,08	14,79	10,37
7168	N/A	40,73	25,6	17,51
8192	N/A	67,36	40,24	23,36
9216	N/A	N/A	63,97	46,58
10240	N/A	N/A	121,47	60,23

Table 6.1: *Elapsed times for matrices multiplication*

If we graph the values shown in *Table* 6.1, we obtain an interesting result (see *Figure* 6.4):

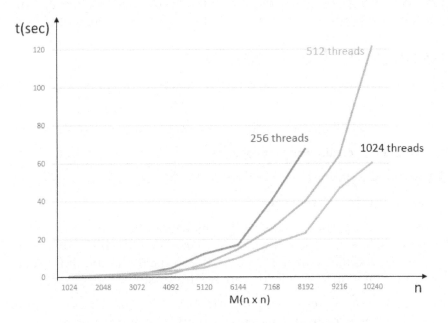

Figure 6.4: *Elapsed time for matrices multiplication with Numba for CUDA, varying threads for block*

You can see the *trend of the times* used in calculating the multiplication of the matrices as their size increases. *Three* trends are reported, each with a different number of threads per block. As you can see the higher this number, the better the GPU performance.

PyOpenCL

Another library that allows us to exploit the potential of GPUs through Python is **pyOpenCL**. This package is a Python wrapper of **Open Computing Language (OpenCL)**. This framework, based on the use of the *C99 language*, allows you to work on different and heterogeneous platforms that include both CPU and GPU. The programs implemented with OpenCL will then be compiled by appropriate drivers, in different languages specific to each technology. So its use is not limited exclusively to NVIDIA cards and the use of CUDA. OpenCL is therefore an excellent solution for extending programming to many other different environments that make use of GPU cards made by different manufacturers such as IBM, AMD, or Intel.

OpenCL was initially created by *Apple*, but later this project was passed to *Khronos Group*, a non-profit consortium, which to this day keeps the project active, releasing new releases that are always updated. Since OpenCL is not based exclusively on CUDA, it is an excellent alternative for anyone who does not have NVIDIA graphics cards but wants to take advantage of other GPUs from different manufacturers for parallel computing in the same way.

Installation of pyOpenCL

Getting your *Windows* machine ready to work with OpenCL is quite simple. The latest drivers must be installed for all *OpenCL-compatible devices*.

You can simply install **pyOpenCL** through a common **conda** installation:

```
conda install -c conda-forge pyopencl
```

to take advantage of Intel's CPU drivers can also be added:

```
conda install intel-opencl-rt
```

For other platforms, there are specific packages that you will need to search for on the web. It is clear that if we want to use NVIDIA GPUs, the CUDA toolkit will have to be installed on the system. If you used Numba in the first part of this chapter, you won't need to do any further installations.

Once you have completed the installation of these packages on your system, you can check if everything went well with the following example. A very useful function in this regard that allows us to investigate the system we are working on is **get_platforms()**. This function gives us the list of platforms on our system that are enabled to work with OpenCL, and from which it is possible to obtain further information on the devices inside them (the GPUs) using the **get_devices()** function. We then use these *two* functions to get a general picture of the system we are working on by writing the following code:

```
import pyopencl as cl


for platform in cl.get_platforms():
    print("Platform %s " %platform.name)
    print(" Vendor: %s " %platform.vendor)
    print(" Version: %s " %platform.version)
    for device in platform.get_devices():
        print("    Device %s " %device.name)
        print("      Max Clock Speed: %s MHz " %device.max_clock_frequency)
        print("      Compute Units: %s " %device.max_compute_units)
        print("      Local Memory: %s Kb" %(device.local_mem_size/1024.0))
```

```
    print("        Global Memory: %s Gb " %(round(device.global_mem_
size/1073741824.0,2)))
```

Running it we will get a result similar to the following:

```
Platform NVIDIA CUDA

  Vendor: NVIDIA Corporation

  Version: OpenCL 3.0 CUDA 11.7.101

    Device NVIDIA GeForce GTX 1650 Ti

      Max Clock Speed: 1485 MHz

      Compute Units: 16

      Local Memory: 48.0 Kb

      Global Memory: 4.0 Gb

Platform Intel(R) OpenCL HD Graphics

  Vendor: Intel(R) Corporation

  Version: OpenCL 2.1

    Device Intel(R) UHD Graphics

      Max Clock Speed: 1150 MHz

      Compute Units: 24

      Local Memory: 64.0 Kb

      Global Memory: 6.31 Gb
```

As we can see, we get the list of platforms in our system that are compatible with OpenCL and which devices can be used within them. In the previous case, we have *two* graphics cards, that of NVIDIA and that of Intel integrated into the motherboard.

PyOpenCL programming model

The programs created with **pyOpenCL** must be structured very precisely in such a way as to take into account the particular architecture of the systems on which you are working, such as GPUs, and the underlying concepts. So within the code, we will always have to refer to the **host** (CPU) and **devices** (GPUs).

First, the program must be developed so that it can be run on the *host*. It will then be coded and compiled, identifying the different portions to be destined for the devices. This will generate several executable packages, each compiled according to the rules of the device they are intended for (models from different manufacturers have different drivers), which will then be dispatched at runtime to be executed. These particular packages are identified by the *kernels*, which are the parts of the code intended to be executed on devices.

The systems managed by the *OpenGL framework* can be seen as distributed systems (we saw them in the previous chapter), in which heterogeneous processors are connected to each other by exchanging *kernels* (instead of messages). So, like distributed systems, there will be a need for a system for managing the exchange and dispatching of these kernels. We, therefore, have in OpenCL the presence of a **Command Queue**, a data structure in which the different kernels that a device receives are collected and accumulated. This structure has the task of managing the order of execution of various kernels. In addition, a **Context** is also defined as part of the OpenCL programming model, which identifies a particular group of devices, facilitating the management of the transfer of kernels and data within the *host-device system* (see Figure 6.5):

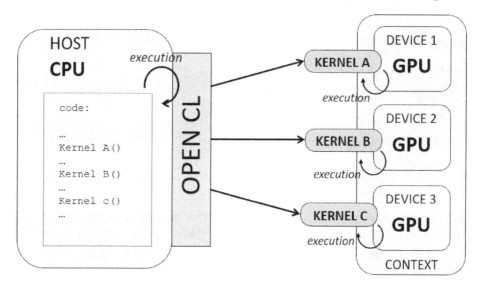

Figure 6.5: *OpenCL programming model*

Developing a program with pyOpenCL

The implementation of a program that makes use of **pyOpenCL** must follow the guidelines of the OpenCL programming model. Since OpenCL is mainly based on operations with NumPy arrays, we can start with a simple example, in which the elements of one of these vectors will be doubled. This operation will be implemented within a *kernel* which will then be compiled to run on a GPU (device).

First, you need to import the basic modules needed to implement a program with pyOpenCL:

```
import numpy as np

import pyopencl as cl
```

At this point, within the GPU programming model, the first step will be to define the memory area in the *host* and the *data* contained in it. With OpenCL this is very simple, using NumPy arrays. In the simple case of our example, we can define a couple of vectors: **a_host** is a vector of **4** elements containing the values to be subjected to the *calculation*, and **res_host** which will be the vector, always of **4** elements which must then contain the results of the calculation:

```
a_host = np.array([0.1 , 1.4, 2.3, 1.7])

a_host = a_host.astype(np.float32)

res_host = np.zeros((4), dtype=np.float32)
```

The next step will be to define the *kernel dispatch management objects*: the context will be created using the **Context()** constructor and its queue with the **CommandQueue()** constructor:

```
ctx = cl.create_some_context()

queue = cl.CommandQueue(ctx)
```

Since we are dealing with GPUs, we have to explicitly manage the memory allocation on the devices and the transfer of data from the host memory to that of the devices. OpenCL does this in a simple way, through the **Buffer** class. We then define a buffer that will take care of transferring the values contained in **a_host** into a memory area of the GPU device identified by the variable **a_dev**. This memory area, since it has only *read* functions, will be defined as **READ_ONLY**. The same will be done with the vector that will contain the results. A **res_dev** vector of the same size as **a_dev** is created, but this being intended to contain the results will be a **WRITE_ONLY** memory:

```
mf = cl.mem_flags

a_dev = cl.Buffer(ctx, mf.READ_ONLY | mf.COPY_HOST_PTR, hostbuf=a_host)

res_dev = cl.Buffer(ctx, mf.WRITE_ONLY, a_host.nbytes)
```

Now, having completed the memory allocation in the device, and the following data transfer, we can move on to implementing the kernel. In pyOpenCL, the **kernel** code is inserted as an argument of the **Program()** class constructor:

```
prg = cl.Program(ctx, """

__kernel void doubled(
```

```
    __global const float *a_dev, __global float *res_dev)
{
  int gid = get_global_id(0);
  res_dev[gid] = a_dev[gid]*2;
}
""").build()
```

As we can see, the kernel has the structure of a *classic function*, where the arguments represent both the input and the returned values. In fact, kernels cannot have return values but operate on vectors passed as arguments. Once the kernel has been defined, it must be invoked to be executed. Once the kernel has been declared and invoked, it is assigned to a *queue*, which will take care not only of its dispatching to the device but also of transferring the memory area containing the result from the device to the host, with the **enqueue_copy()** method:

```
knl = prg.doubled
knl(queue, a_host.shape, None, a_dev, res_dev)
cl.enqueue_copy(queue, res_host, res_dev)
```

Now that the results have been copied to the host, in the **res_host** array, the results obtained can be output:

```
print("Vector a: %s" %a_host)
print("Result: %s" %res_host)
```

Let's review the code just described in its entirety:

```
import numpy as np
import pyopencl as cl


a_host = np.array([0.1 , 1.4, 2.3, 1.7])
a_host = a_host.astype(np.float32)
res_host = np.zeros((4), dtype=np.float32)


ctx = cl.create_some_context()
queue = cl.CommandQueue(ctx)


mf = cl.mem_flags
```

```
a_dev = cl.Buffer(ctx, mf.READ_ONLY | mf.COPY_HOST_PTR, hostbuf=a_host)
res_dev = cl.Buffer(ctx, mf.WRITE_ONLY, a_host.nbytes)


prg = cl.Program(ctx, """
__kernel void doubled(
    __global const float *a_dev, __global float *res_dev)
{
  int gid = get_global_id(0);
  res_dev[gid] = a_dev[gid]*2;
}
""").build()



knl = prg.doubled
knl(queue, a_host.shape, None, a_dev, res_dev)
cl.enqueue_copy(queue, res_host, res_dev)


print("Vector a: %s" %a_host)
print("Result: %s" %res_host)
```

Running the preceding code will give you a result similar to the following:

```
Choose platform:
[0] <pyopencl.Platform 'NVIDIA CUDA' at 0x1612071dd60>
[1] <pyopencl.Platform 'Intel(R) OpenCL HD Graphics' at 0x1611ff6cb80>
Choice [0]:0
Set the environment variable PYOPENCL_CTX='0' to avoid being asked again.
Vector a: [0.1 1.4 2.3 1.7]
Result: [0.2 2.8 4.6 3.4]
```

As you can immediately see, you will be asked first which environment to work in (this happens if your system has multiple platforms that can use OpenCL technology). Enter the value you want. If you press *Enter*, the program will perform the calculation on the default platform (value **0**). To remedy this choice later, you can insert the environment variable in the code, as the program also suggests. We, therefore, insert the following instructions in the initial part of the previous code:

```
import os
os.environ['PYOPENCL_CTX'] = '0'
```

This way we will already tell the compiler that we want to work on the NVIDIA platform. Rerunning the program after the modification, we will have the desired result directly:

Vector a: [0.1 1.4 2.3 1.7]

Result: [0.2 2.8 4.6 3.4]

Multiplication between matrices: an example

As we saw earlier, with the Numba library, a great example of measuring GPU power is *matrix multiplication*. Let's implement it this time using pyOpenCL as a library. For example, we can use the following code to *multiply two matrices* **A * B** of dimension **8** and obtain a third matrix **C** containing the result of this operation:

```
import pyopencl as cl
import numpy as np


import os
os.environ['PYOPENCL_CTX'] = '0'


n = 8


a = np.random.randint(10, size=(n*n))
b = np.random.randint(10, size=(n*n))
c = np.zeros((n*n), dtype=np.float32)


a = a.astype(np.float32)
b = b.astype(np.float32)
```

```
ctx = cl.create_some_context()
queue = cl.CommandQueue(ctx)


mf = cl.mem_flags
a_buf = cl.Buffer(ctx, mf.READ_ONLY | mf.COPY_HOST_PTR, hostbuf=a)
b_buf = cl.Buffer(ctx, mf.READ_ONLY | mf.COPY_HOST_PTR, hostbuf=b)
c_buf = cl.Buffer(ctx, mf.WRITE_ONLY, c.nbytes)


prg = cl.Program(ctx, """
    __kernel void multiply(ushort n,
    ushort m, ushort p, __global float *a,
    __global float *b, __global float *c)
    {
      int gid = get_global_id(0);
      c[gid] = 0.0f;
      int rowC = gid/p;
      int colC = gid%p;
      __global float *pA = &a[rowC*m];
      __global float *pB = &b[colC];
      for(int k=0; k<m; k++)
      {
          pB = &b[colC+k*p];
          c[gid] += (*(pA++))*(*pB);
      }
    }
    """).build()


prg.multiply(queue, c.shape, None,
            np.uint16(n), np.uint16(n), np.uint16(n),
```

```
                    a_buf, b_buf, c_buf)


cl.enqueue_copy(queue, c, c_buf)


print("Matrix A")
print(a.reshape(n,n))
print("Matrix B")
print(b.reshape(n,n))
print("Matrix A*B")
print(c.reshape(n, n))
```

Running this code will give you the following result:

```
Matrix A
[[6. 4. 2. 5. 3. 7. 4. 7.]
 [3. 0. 2. 0. 8. 5. 4. 4.]
 [4. 6. 3. 3. 3. 8. 7. 2.]
 [7. 4. 7. 6. 0. 3. 3. 2.]
 [8. 1. 6. 1. 5. 9. 4. 4.]
 [9. 9. 6. 4. 4. 3. 5. 3.]
 [9. 4. 9. 0. 1. 8. 7. 4.]
 [7. 7. 8. 0. 8. 9. 2. 5.]]
Matrix B
[[6. 3. 1. 0. 0. 6. 8. 7.]
 [3. 0. 1. 0. 9. 3. 3. 4.]
 [2. 4. 7. 1. 5. 1. 8. 1.]
 [3. 3. 4. 8. 1. 4. 6. 3.]
 [7. 3. 3. 8. 4. 0. 8. 9.]
 [6. 3. 0. 6. 0. 8. 8. 4.]
 [3. 0. 8. 9. 2. 6. 3. 4.]
 [2. 0. 2. 7. 8. 6. 5. 3.]]
```

```
Matrix A*B
[[156.  71.  99. 193. 127. 192. 233. 167.]
 [128.  56.  81. 160.  82. 108. 176. 143.]
 [151.  66. 112. 176. 114. 175. 211. 157.]
 [117.  76. 112. 114.  99. 139. 203. 120.]
 [175.  93. 110. 172. 100. 181. 265. 178.]
 [172.  84. 134. 154. 165. 175. 257. 194.]
 [168.  90. 143. 156. 131. 205. 269. 169.]
 [205. 104. 120. 179. 179. 185. 308. 216.]]
```

Now, let's make some changes to the previous program to introduce the measurement of the times used for the calculation of the product between matrices:

```
import pyopencl as cl

import numpy as np

import time


import os

os.environ['PYOPENCL_CTX'] = '0'


n = 8


a = np.random.randint(10, size=(n*n))

b = np.random.randint(10, size=(n*n))

c = np.zeros((n*n), dtype=np.float32)


a = a.astype(np.float32)

b = b.astype(np.float32)


ctx = cl.create_some_context()

queue = cl.CommandQueue(ctx)
```

```python
mf = cl.mem_flags
a_buf = cl.Buffer(ctx, mf.READ_ONLY | mf.COPY_HOST_PTR, hostbuf=a)
b_buf = cl.Buffer(ctx, mf.READ_ONLY | mf.COPY_HOST_PTR, hostbuf=b)
c_buf = cl.Buffer(ctx, mf.WRITE_ONLY, c.nbytes)


prg = cl.Program(ctx, """
    __kernel void multiply(ushort n,
    ushort m, ushort p, __global float *a,
    __global float *b, __global float *c)
    {
      int gid = get_global_id(0);
      c[gid] = 0.0f;
      int rowC = gid/p;
      int colC = gid%p;
      __global float *pA = &a[rowC*m];
      __global float *pB = &b[colC];
      for(int k=0; k<m; k++)
      {
          pB = &b[colC+k*p];
          c[gid] += (*(pA++))*(*pB);
      }
    }
    """).build()


t1 = time.perf_counter()
prg.multiply(queue, c.shape, None,
            np.uint16(n), np.uint16(n), np.uint16(n),
            a_buf, b_buf, c_buf)
t2 = time.perf_counter()
```

```
cl.enqueue_copy(queue, c, c_buf)
elapsed_time = t2 - t1
print("Elapsed time %s" %elapsed_time)
```

We have removed the printing of the output results of the matrices involved in the calculation, and instead, we have inserted the **perf_counter()** functions of the time module in order to calculate the times used during the product between matrices.

By running the previous code we will get a result similar to the following:

Elapsed time 0.007469899996067397

That is, we obtained the *time taken in seconds* as output. This information will be useful for making considerations on the time taken for the multiplication between matrices as their size increases, which in our code is expressed by the variable **n**. We perform a series of measurements on our computer, modifying the value of **n** for each execution, assigning it for example the powers of 2 (4, 8, 16, 32, 64, *and so on*). We will get a table of values similar to *Table 6.2*:

n	t(GPU)
4	0,0063
8	0,0056
16	0,0066
32	0,0058
64	0,0058
128	0,0065
256	0,0076
512	0,0082
1024	0,0086
2048	0,0164
4096	0,0484

Table 6.2: *Elapsed time for matrices multiplication*

As we can see from the result, the times used are almost the same up to 1024 and then they increase for *powers of 2 higher*. This makes us guess that this timing is related to the number of threads available in my GPU. Up to a certain value, we will have n threads in parallel which will take the same time to calculate the product between matrices (*n* x *n*). So, according to this mechanism that we calculate the multiplication between two matrices (4 x 4) will take the same time as the multiplication between two matrices (512 x 512).

To better understand the potential offered by GPU programming and computing through them, let's consider the multiplication between two matrices carried out *sequentially*. An example of how to implement the product between *two matrices* **A** and **B** on a classic Python program that does not use GPU could be the following code:

```python
import numpy as np


n = 8
a = np.random.randint(10, size=(n*n))
b = np.random.randint(10, size=(n*n))
c = np.zeros((n*n), dtype=np.float32)


a = a.astype(np.float32)
b = b.astype(np.float32)


def matmul(n, A, B, C):
    # Iterate over the rows of A.
    for i in range(n):
        # Iterate over the columns of B
        for j in range(n):
            tmp = 0.0
            # Iterate over the rows of B.
            for k in range(n):
                tmp += A[i * n + k] * B[k * n + j]
            C[i * n + j] = tmp


matmul(n, a, b, c)
print("Matrix A")
print(a.reshape(n,n))
```

```
print("Matrix B")
```

```
print(b.reshape(n,n))
```

```
print("Matrix A*B")
```

```
print(c.reshape(n,n))
```

By executing the code we will obtain a result identical to that obtained in the previous example with pyOpenCL. The values are randomly generated so the results will vary for *each run*, but the calculation and the results are practically the same:

```
Matrix A
[[9. 6. 2. 0. 1. 5. 4. 2.]
 [4. 6. 1. 2. 1. 3. 0. 2.]
 [8. 9. 3. 3. 4. 3. 3. 0.]
 [5. 2. 0. 1. 4. 7. 6. 6.]
 [3. 5. 2. 6. 7. 6. 1. 8.]
 [0. 2. 2. 4. 0. 2. 5. 6.]
 [9. 9. 0. 2. 6. 7. 7. 3.]
 [8. 1. 4. 5. 8. 7. 7. 2.]]
Matrix B
[[6. 6. 8. 3. 0. 6. 6. 8.]
 [9. 8. 5. 9. 3. 9. 4. 4.]
 [9. 9. 6. 1. 9. 9. 0. 5.]
 [2. 6. 0. 7. 0. 7. 5. 2.]
 [2. 9. 9. 4. 9. 5. 1. 9.]
 [2. 4. 6. 3. 8. 0. 1. 7.]
 [5. 3. 3. 6. 0. 8. 8. 8.]
 [8. 4. 4. 7. 0. 5. 4. 3.]]
Matrix A*B
[[174. 169. 173. 140.  85. 173. 124. 188.]
 [115. 122. 103. 108.  60. 116.  70. 101.]
 [191. 222. 190. 172. 114. 221. 130. 202.]
 [150. 158. 170. 155.  98. 153. 126. 201.]
```

```
[188. 234. 195. 206. 144. 206. 121. 203.]
[121. 105.  73. 126.  40. 134.  94.  98.]
[224. 253. 246. 230. 137. 250. 181. 280.]
[184. 251. 236. 181. 167. 234. 156. 281.]]
```

At this point, we also modify this code in order to be able to carry out measurements on the time taken by the multiplication between matrices as their *size varies*, also varying the value of **n**:

```
import numpy as np

import time


n = 8

a = np.random.randint(10, size=(n*n))

b = np.random.randint(10, size=(n*n))

c = np.zeros((n*n), dtype=np.float32)


a = a.astype(np.float32)

b = b.astype(np.float32)


def matmul(n, A, B, C):
    # Iterate over the rows of A.
    for i in range(n):
        # Iterate over the columns of B
        for j in range(n):
            tmp = 0.0
            # Iterate over the rows of B.
            for k in range(n):
                tmp += A[i * n + k] * B[k * n + j]
            C[i * n + j] = tmp
```

```
t1 = time.perf_counter()
matmul(n, a, b, c)
t2 = time.perf_counter()
elapsed_time = t2 - t1
print("Elapsed time %s" %elapsed_time)
```

By executing a series of executions for the values of n used with the code in pyOpenCL we will get a series of times as shown in *Table 6.3*:

n	t(CPU)	t(GPU)
4	0,000074	0,0063
8	0,00035	0,0056
16	0,0034	0,0066
32	0,014	0,0058
64	0,12	0,0058
128	0,8	0,0065
256	6,77	0,0076
512	61,5	0,0082
1024		0,0086
2048		0,0164
4096		0,0484

Table 6.3: *Elapsed times compared between CPU e GPU*

As we can see, the trend of the times, in this case, is completely different from the previous case. We have an exponential increase as the size of the matrices used increases, so much so that beyond a certain size the times become prohibitive. An interesting consideration is that for small arrays (<32) sequential computation is much more efficient than that obtained using GPUs via pyOpenCL. The following figure (*Figure 6.6*) clearly shows the time trends in the two types of programming:

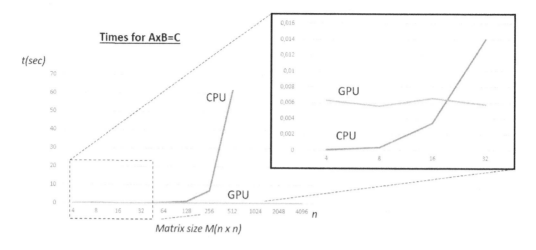

Figure 6.6: *Times used to calculate A * B on CPU (sequential program) and on GPU (with OpenCL)*

As we can see from the graph for small matrices (up to order 16), the sequential calculation performed on the CPU to calculate the *product between matrices* turns out to be more efficient than the one on the GPU that uses threads in parallel. But the trend of times is exponential on the CPU and already for larger size matrices, the calculation is prohibitive, requiring increasingly longer calculation times. Instead, we have a completely different behavior with the GPU that keeps the time taken *constant* despite the growth in the size of the matrices used in multiplication. This is largely due to the large amount of threads on the GPU that are able to handle the parallel computing of thousands of threads at the same time extremely efficiently.

Element-wise calculation with pyOpenCL

PyOpenCL provides the possibility to perform *element-wise calculations* in an implicit way, with the possibility of using complex expressions in a single computational step. The function that is used is **ElementwiseKernel()**.

Let's see an example:

```
import numpy as np

import pyopencl as cl

import pyopencl.array

from pyopencl.elementwise import ElementwiseKernel
```

```
import os
os.environ['PYOPENCL_CTX'] = '0'


a_host = np.array([0.1 , 1.4, 2.3, 1.7])
a_host = a_host.astype(np.float32)
b_host = np.array([0.2 , 0.3, 1.0, 0.5])
b_host = b_host.astype(np.float32)


ctx = cl.create_some_context()
queue = cl.CommandQueue(ctx)


a_dev = cl.array.to_device(queue, a_host)
b_dev = cl.array.to_device(queue, b_host)


sum = ElementwiseKernel(ctx,
    "float *a_dev, float *b_dev, float *res_dev",
    "res_dev[i] = a_dev[i] + b_dev[i]",
    "sum")


res_dev = cl.array.empty_like(a_dev)
sum(a_dev, b_dev, res_dev)


print("Vector A: %s" %a_host)
print("Vector B: %s" %b_host)
print("Vector Result: %s" %res_dev)
```

Running the code will produce a result similar to the following:

Vector A: [0.1 1.4 2.3 1.7]

Vector B: [0.2 0.3 1. 0.5]

Vector Result: [0.3 1.7 3.3 2.2]

MapReduce calculation with pyOpenCL

Like the previous example, there is another construct that allows the implicit use of complex expressions, such as those aimed at **MapReduce**. PyOpenCL provides **ReductionKernel()** for this purpose:

```python
import numpy as np

import pyopencl as cl

import pyopencl.array

import pyopencl.reduction


import os
os.environ['PYOPENCL_CTX'] = '0'


ctx = cl.create_some_context()
queue = cl.CommandQueue(ctx)


ah = np.array([0.1 , 1.4, 2.3, 1.7])
ah = ah.astype(np.float32)
bh = np.array([0.2 , 0.3, 1.0, 0.5])
bh = bh.astype(np.float32)


a = cl.array.to_device(queue, ah)
b = cl.array.to_device(queue, bh)


krnl = pyopencl.reduction.ReductionKernel(ctx, np.float32, neutral="0",
        reduce_expr="a+b", map_expr="x[i]*y[i]",
        arguments="__global float *x, __global float *y")


res = krnl(a, b).get()


print("Vector A: %s" %a)
```

```
print("Vector B: %s" %b)
```

```
print("Vector Result: %s" %res)
```

Running the code produces a result similar to the following:

Vector A: [0.1 1.4 2.3 1.7]

Vector B: [0.2 0.3 1. 0.5]

Vector Result: 3.59

This program will first perform the product between the corresponding elements of the two vectors **a** and **b** (mapping process expressed by the expression **x [i] * y [i]** assigned to the **map_expr** parameter. The vectors **x** and **y** passed as **kernel** arguments must be indexed with the index **i**:

0.1 x 0.2 = 0.02

1.4 x 0.3 = 0.42

2.3 x 1.0 = 2.3

1.7 x 0.5 = 0.85

And all the results will be added together as a reducing operation, expressed by the expression **a + b** assigned to the **reduce_expr** parameter. In this case, the formal values **a** and **b** are used to indicate the operands of a *binary reduction operation*:

0.02 + 0.42 + 2.3 + 0.85 = 3.59

If we want to see another example, we can replace the previous **mapreduce** kernel with this one:

```
krnl = pyopencl.reduction.ReductionKernel(ctx, np.float32, neutral="0",
        reduce_expr='max(a,b)', map_expr="x[i]+y[i]",
        arguments="__global float *x, __global float *y")
```

By running, this time you will get the following result:

Vector A: [0.1 1.4 2.3 1.7]

Vector B: [0.2 0.3 1. 0.5]

Vector Result: 3.3

In this operation, the corresponding elements of the two vectors are added together, with the expression **x [i] + y [i]** assigned to the **map_expr** parameter:

0.1 + 0.2 = 0.3

1.4 + 0.3 = 1.7

2.3 + 1.0 = 3.3

1.7 + 0.5 = 2.2

And from these results, the greater value will be chosen through the binary expression expressed as `max (a, b)` assigned to the `reduce_expr` parameter.

Conclusion

In this chapter, we have seen how to use GPU programming to further enhance parallel computing. *Thanks* to libraries such as **Numba** and **pyOpenCL**, we are now able to exploit the computing potential of GPUs; *thanks* to their particular internal architecture that intrinsically performs even complex calculations in parallel. In particular, these libraries are based on CUDA technology which specializes in NVIDIA graphics cards making the most of their capabilities. We then showed the programming models that are the basis of CUDA and that allow us to insert kernels into the code in Python, portions of code compiled to be executed exclusively on GPUs. With this chapter, we conclude all the parallel programming models and related libraries. In the next chapter, we will analyze all the possible fields of application of these technologies and models covered in the previous chapters.

References

https://www.tutorialspoint.com/cuda/cuda_introduction_to_the_gpu.htm

## CHAPTER 7

Embracing the Parallel Computing Revolution

In this chapter, we introduce the practical aspects of parallel programming that we have seen in the previous chapters. With *parallel computing*, the concept covered expands, which will not only include parallel programming and the aspects related to it, but also the infrastructures that are able to manage it and have been specially designed. Supercomputers are often defined as those high-performance systems formed by many CPUs and GPUs and in which parallel computing and **High-Performance Computing (HPC)** methodologies are applied. This chapter represents an overview of the sectors and disciplines that have found a valid research and innovation tool in parallel computing.

Structure

In this chapter, we will cover the following topics:

- High-Performance Computing (HPC)
- Parallel computing
- Simulation
- Parallel signal processing
- Finite element method
- Molecular docking
- Genomics
- Game engine
- Supercomputer e HPC

High-Performance Computing (HPC)

High-Performance Computing (HPC) is certainly nothing new. Supercomputers have played a vital role in scientific research for decades.

The amount of data has increased rapidly in recent years and there are many application areas that benefit from HPC systems, that is, systems capable of performing computationally intensive operations through shared resources, in order to obtain results in less time.

HPC techniques may work on a single computer or node, but its true power lies in the creation of clusters where many computers are linked together, forming a supercomputer.

Supercomputers are mainly used for *simulation, artificial intelligence*, and *analysis of very large amounts of data*. These are the three operations that underlie the many applications that have found a place and developed in the various scientific and industrial sectors.

While supercomputers aren't new, the new technologies they use have developed tremendously over the past 20 years. The exponential growth of computing speeds and data-carrying networks make parallel architecture not only a good idea but a necessary one. New technologies such as **BigData** and **Internet of Things (IoT)** are producing streams of trillions of data that need to be analyzed in *real-time* and *simultaneously*. It is clear that only parallel computing applied to ever more powerful machines will represent the only solution to be able to process this amount of data.

Parallel computing

Parallel computing is a broader concept that also includes parallel programming. In fact, it is the simultaneous execution of one or more programs on architectures that offer multiple processors simultaneously, whether they are CPUs, cores or GPUs.

So you can have parallel computing both in a simple system in which there is a single CPU in which there are more cores (for example, *Intel Xeon W has 28 cores*) up to supercomputers or clusters of computers in which there are thousands of microprocessors. In the latter case, we speak of massively parallel computing.

So, even if we are not aware, even in our small part of daily life we are using parallel computing. Our smartphones, which we never leave behind even for a few minutes in our daily operations, use this type of technology. For example, if our iPhone could perform one operation at a time, all operations would be much slower. Opening an email could take a few seconds and switching between the different applications would not be so immediate. The latest serial smartphones on the market date back to 2010 (*iPhone4*), prehistory if we think about what current smartphones are capable of doing. Already the next model, *iPhone 5*, has a 1.5GHz *dual-core processor*. While today's *iPhone 11* has *6 cores*. The *Samsung Galaxy Note 10* has *8 cores*. These smartphones are all examples of parallel computing that we squeeze into the palm of our hands.

Benefits of parallel computing

Programs run faster on account of the higher clock speed and might not be completely due to *parallel* execution, while Parallelism allows different parts of the same program to execute at the same time. Parallel computing has the advantage of reducing the execution times of these programs or increasing the amount of data that can be processed simultaneously. The more powerful parallel computing is, the more complex problems it can solve. Saving time often means saving money and this is why parallel computing is becoming a mandatory option for many industrial and engineering sectors. As far as the scientific world is concerned, the main objective is not so much time as the possibility of solving increasingly complex problems. In both cases, the major use mode for parallel computing is *simulation*.

In fact, parallel computing has proven to be ideal for modeling the real world around us. In fact, the real world is not serial, and the things that surround us do not happen one at a time, but simultaneously. Increasingly complex mathematical models are elaborated in parallel in order to reconstruct portions of the real world, both in the macroscopic one, such as *stars* or *black holes*, and in the microscopic one, such as *molecules* and *enzymes*. With the growth of parallel computing, it is possible to use increasingly complex mathematical models, with fewer approximations, and therefore able to generate increasingly accurate simulations. The study of the behavior and properties of the systems reconstructed in the simulations is the basis of innovation and research in many scientific and industrial sectors.

Another application window that has demonstrated the need to use parallel computing is that of monitoring several data signals simultaneously. You often have to work in real-time with several independent data streams that provide massive amounts of data but need to be processed as a whole. Computing must not only process these data streams but at the same time extract real-time information from them that will prove very useful for any actions. This kind of problem can be solved with parallel signal processing algorithms, an extension to the classical methods of signal processing with the contribution of parallel computing. We find this kind of use in medicine with *bio signals*, with finance in the control of stock market trends, in seismology with the study of waves transmitted into the ground and many other applications.

Projects and examples of parallel computing

Having understood the importance of parallel processing for most of analyzes and studies carried out in many scientific and industrial sectors, let's see together some examples in greater detail.

Meteorology

Meteorology is the science that is based on the use of mathematical models of extraordinary complexity, which take into account numerous climatic and environmental factors in continuous change, all in order to be able to make forecasts on the weather trend in the days following the most correct as possible.

It is therefore clear that in order to carry out this type of calculation it will be necessary to use extraordinarily powerful calculators based mainly on parallel computing.

In this particular area, it is necessary to introduce **Numeric Weather Prediction (NWP)**.

It is a weather forecasting method based on a series of dynamic equations describing the flow of fluids. This system of equations is very complex mathematically and in this form, it is not possible to work out solutions. In order to be submitted to computers, these equations must undergo a series of processes in order to convert them into numerical methods. *Parameterizations* are then made and initial and boundary conditions are imposed. Unfortunately, these steps introduce approximations, with omissions, parameter estimates, and other factors that simplify the calculation making it possible, but at the same time introduce inaccuracies.

The purpose of the NWP model is to simulate the atmosphere of a geographical area in its temporal evolution, in order to obtain predictions on climatic trends. The volume occupied by the atmosphere covering the geographical area is divided into a grid of *three-dimensional points* which define its resolution. Advances in parallel computational processing offer the possibility of being able to increase the resolution of the model and increase the speed of computation to obtain results. The higher the *resolution* of the model, the higher the *accuracy* of the predictions. However, manipulating models of this level is increasingly challenging. Despite the increase in resolution and simulation speed, current algorithms are beginning to reach limits due to the communication requirements of the mathematical algorithms used to solve the equations that predict how the weather evolves over time.

At present, these algorithms combine computational parallelism with geographic parallelism. The geographical area under analysis is divided into overlapping parts and each part is assigned to a different processor. During the forecast calculation, each processor will have to exchange data concerning the overlapping area with the other processors involved in the calculation, to take into account the climatic effects of neighboring areas.

The increase in resolution and the speeding up of the NWP model has led to the analysis of ever smaller geographical areas, however increasing the area of overlap between the various processors, thus increasingly increasing the exchange of information and reducing the performance of the model.

Another critical point of the NWP model which requires further progress is the parameterized part. There are many physical processes in meteorology that cannot be predicted directly (see *Figure 7.1*). These are brief, complex or still poorly understood phenomena and are therefore introduced into the model using appropriate parameters based on empirical or statistical considerations. Also, in this case, the development of new algorithms that make the most of parallel computing will be able to respond better to these additional factors, increasing the effectiveness, and accuracy of the forecasts elaborated:

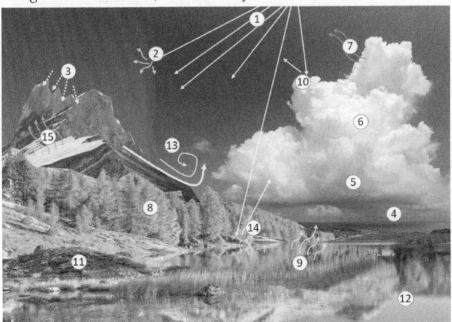

Figure 7.1: *Some factors for weather patterns: 1. Incoming solar radiation, 2. Scattering by aerosols and molecules, 3. Snow, 4. Rain, 5. Condensation, 6. Deep Convection, 7. Emission of longwave radiation from clouds, 8. Vegetation, 9. Evaporation, 10. Reflection/Absorption by clouds, 11. Topography, 12. Water coverage, 13. Turbulence, 14. Reflection/Absorption at Earth's surface, 15. Emission of longwave radiation from Earth's surface.*

As for Python, **Metview** can be reported. This platform provides a useful meteorological workstation designed to provide a comprehensive meteorological data research and analysis environment (see *Figure 7.2*). It includes many tools that facilitate the analysis activity at all stages. Access to the multiple data sources present is facilitated, with converters of different formats. Furthermore, there are many tools for processing and displaying them. All these operations are managed through scripting commands using the Python language:

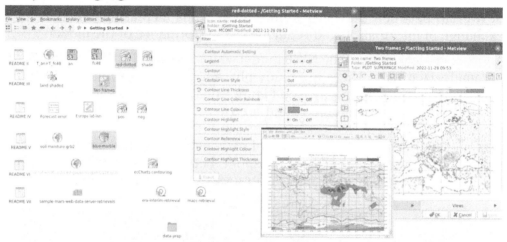

Figure 7.2: *MetView platform*

The **MetView** platform is available on *Anaconda* for *Linux* and *macOS* only. To install it, simply enter the following command:

```
$ conda install -c conda-forge metview
```

After installing it updates its content and related packages via:

```
$ conda update -c conda-forge metview
```

Once installed, the platform is launched using the **metview** command:

```
$ metview
```

After a few seconds, the application will start and a window will appear on the screen as shown in *Figure 7.2*. There are many interesting examples of its use, presented in a series of Jupyter Notebooks on the page:

https://confluence.ecmwf.int/display/METV/Python+Jupyter+Notebooks

Oceanography

A branch of science that applies similar models to meteorology is oceanography. Here, instead of the atmosphere, the immense oceanic volumes and all the factors and processes that describe their evolution over time are taken into account. Here too, to obtain valid simulations, the use of complex models that only high-performance computers can process is envisaged. Here, too, the use of parallel computing is essential.

On the basis of these studies are data that are collected and distributed to researchers and analysts through databases. Most of this data comes from satellite observations, collected by government agencies such as **European Organization for the Exploitation of Meteorological Satellites (EUMETSAT)** or **National Centers for Environmental Information (NOAA)**. These databases provide data regarding parameters observable from space such as surface temperature, water color, wave height, and ice thickness. While other databases provide oceanographic data relating to the seabed and other parameters concerning the intermediate levels.

The type of data most commonly referred to in oceanography is **CTD data**, that is, **conductivity**, **temperature**, and **depth**. These values allow us to determine the physical properties of the various layers of water in the oceans, very useful for obtaining TS *profiles (temperature-salinity)* very commonly used in oceanography.

All these data are then used for simulations (very similar to atmospheric ones for meteorology) which allow us to make predictions on the state of the oceans in the times to come. Also, in this case, the models used are extremely complex and require the support of supercomputers that make the most of parallel computing.

As for Python, there is a site that collects a whole series of Python libraries related to the various operational aspects involved in the oceanographic study:

Sea-Py (https://pyoceans.github.io/sea-py/), as shown in *Figure 7.3*:

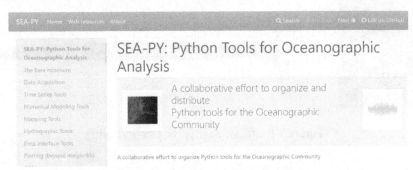

Figure 7.3: *SEA-PY official website*

Seismology

We have seen models for the study of the atmosphere and models for the study of large ocean masses, models for the study of the movements of tectonic plates could not be missing. In particular, the movements of the earth's crust and the prediction of their worst consequence: *earthquakes*.

Seismology is also a complex science whose research is based on the use of complex models that cannot be easily calculated except through the use of numerous acquired data. Making predictions in this field is even more difficult than in meteorology and oceanography. Largely due to the fact that the nature of the underlying terrain is not easily detectable.

In this regard, the method of seismic exploration can be exploited, which is based on the reflection of seismic waves as they cross the earth's crust. When a seismic wave travels through the earth's crust, when it meets an interface that separates two different layers of soil, it reflects part of it. In the end, a whole series of reflected waves of various shapes and intensities are obtained which must be detected, recorded in the form of data, and then extrapolated from them to a model capable of reconstructing the underlying layers of the soil.

The calculations of these models are also based purely on parallel computing:

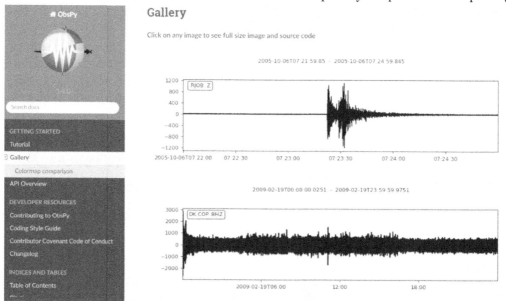

Figure 7.4: *Official page of the Obs-Py library*

As for Python, there is a specific library for this: **Obs-Py** (<u>https://docs.obspy.</u><u>org/</u>). This is an *open-source library* that provides researchers with a useful framework for processing seismological data, providing a whole series of tools dedicated to these specific techniques, such as the signal processing of seismic wave records, as shown in *Figure 7.4*.

Astrophysics

Another branch of science whose recent advances are mainly due to simulations made with parallel processing is astrophysics.

The behavior and evolution of a star is a subject of study in astrophysics and is currently based on simulations that make use of complex physical laws that take into account *hydrodynamics* and *magneto hydrodynamics*. The reference system has spherical geometry and the model makes use of spectral codes, in which physical quantities are subdivided on the basis of spherical harmonics in the orthogonal directions, and *Chebishev polynomials* along the radial direction. It is clear that this type of calculation is quite complex and only the use of high-performance computing systems, such as massively parallel architectures (supercomputers), can process them.

The results obtained from this type of simulation have proved to be very accurate and have allowed enormous progress in this field of *astrophysics*:

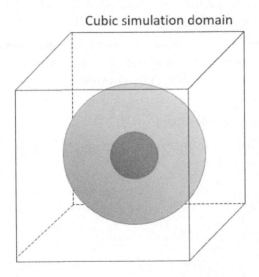

Figure 7.5: *Star-in-a-box model*

In Python, there are simulations of stellar behavior and evolution that follow a more recent approach, called *star-in-a-box*. These simulations are based on a different model, based on Cartesian geometry, in which a star is enclosed inside a cubic box (see *Figure 7.5*). It has been seen that with the scientific libraries provided by Python such as **SciPy**, **NumPy**, **Matplotlib**, and **Pypar** (another library that facilitates parallel implementation with Python), one can get quite accurate results.

In addition to stellar behavior, astrophysics has recently been tackling problems that, until recently, were thought impossible to tackle. The explosion of a **supernova**, the movement of galaxies with their probable collision and merger and the behavior of a black hole, for example when it is engulfing a star, are problems of enormous complexity. The models used for these simulations are so complex they require enormous computing power.

To better understand how these scientific disciplines and their progress are now closely linked to the technological advance of parallel processing, we can give an example. In 2019, a problem that had been tormenting astrophysicists for over forty years, concerning black holes, was solved. Researchers at *Northwestern University*, the *University of Amsterdam*, and the *University of Oxford* have shown in their simulations that the innermost matter that orbits and then collapses into black holes lines up with those black holes. This demonstration was only possible with permission to simulate a powerful supercomputer. It is therefore clear that with the growth of computing power, many other problems that have been insurmountable up to now will be solved.

As regards the study and simulation of the explosion and convective movements of stars such as **supernovae** and **novae**, in Python, there are a series of algorithms implemented in different modules, such as those distributed by *Michael Zingale*:

https://zingale.github.io/index.html

On his site, there are some interesting projects in this regard with the code downloadable from GitHub, see *Figure 7.6*:

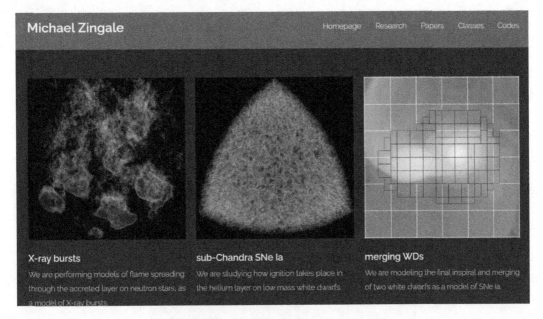

Figure 7.6: *Michael Zingale page*

One toolkit used by the astrophysics community is **yt**, designed for *volumetric data analysis* and *visualization*, in particular its **yt_astro_analysis** extension. This allows us to analyze and visualize the data generated by simulations of astrophysical phenomena on **high-performance computing (HPC)** systems. The data generated on different platforms are often *incompatible*, and such a tool is able to integrate them and create visual representations from them and perform accurate analyzes by exploiting parallel computing. This package is also present on *Anaconda* and can be installed with the following command:

```
conda install -c conda-forge yt_astro_analysis
```

There is an excellent site full of documentation and examples (**https://yt-project.org/doc/cookbook/index.html**), many of which are listed as **Jupyter Notebooks**, as shown in *Figure 7.7*:

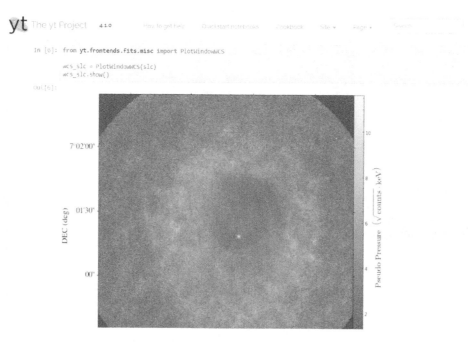

Figure 7.7: *A Jupyter Notebook example of yt_astro_analysis usage in the yt project web page*

Oil and energy industry

Resource exploration is a method of collecting and managing information about energy resources such as *oil, natural gas,* and so on. Computers help in the discovery and management of such resources. Oil and gas companies are exploring every possible new method to increase the probability of finding hydrocarbons in the ground.

The data collected by *Well logging* consists of several gigabytes of information reported by *probes* and *sensors*. These data will have to be analyzed to reconstruct the *presence, extent and depth of layers of rock, oil, gas,* and *water.* For processing this large amount of data, HPC systems and methodologies are necessary. They are the only ones able to process this amount of data and extract the necessary information.

For example, in the *USA*, in *Houston*, there is a supercomputer (among the fastest on the planet) called **Bubba**, made up of thousands of *Intel Xeon Phi* multiprocessors cooled in refrigerated oil baths. This particular technique allows to increase the performance and the calculation speed of this kind of processor. This supercomputer belongs to the geo-processing company *DownUnder GeoSolutions* and is used to perform precisely these kinds of calculations. From this, we understand how every research sector, both *scientific* and *private* companies interested in the business, are now very sensitive to the importance of simulations and the parallel computing on which they are processed.

As far as Python is concerned, in recent years we can find several publications in the literature that report examples of analyzes and simulations with explanations of the pros and cons.

Finance

In addition to academic and governmental research institutes, financial institutions are no less that are increasingly making more and more massive use of processing systems based on parallel computing.

Almost all the main aspects of today's banking are now based on operations carried out on parallel computing systems. **Cryptocurrencies** also require support on advanced computing systems that jointly exploit parallel computing due to the complexity of the underlying Blockchain.

Among the most attractive approaches is **Quantitative Finance**, also called **Quantitative analysis**. This discipline is based on the use of mathematics and statistical methods applied to finance. The underlying processes consist of searching vast quantities of market data for patterns or correlations that can in some way suggest trends and thus apply strategies. Other purposes may be price trends, risk management and investment management.

Today's technologies make it possible to access enormous data flows, through Big Data, and extract from them the data to be used for quantitative finance. There are therefore many algorithms and methods that tend to exploit both BigData technologies and those of data analysis and processing on parallel computing systems.

Also in Python, there are numerous examples reported in the literature and on the web, which describe studies and applications of algorithms and methods that make use of parallel computing. Often many of these applications make use of **Machine Learning**, which in Python finds ample space with numerous libraries provided, but there are also a whole series of specialized libraries for the financial activity that is fundamental for the creation and study of financial models. We describe some of them that could be useful for those interested.

Quandl is a library that allows you to access a vast collection of economic, financial, and market data collected from *central banks*, *governments*, *multinational organizations*, and many other sources. Most of the datasets are free to access upon registration, while others are paid.

Zipline and **Pyfolio** are two other libraries that allow you to perform the initial processing of financial data, for example, collected by Quandl, whose interfacing is well implemented. Both provide tremendous support for specialized algorithms for trading. Furthermore, **Pyfolio** allows you to easily obtain a *tear sheet* containing performance statistics that include important parameters such as *annual/monthly returns, return quantiles, rolling beta/ Sharpe ratios*, and *portfolio turnover* (see Figure 7.8):

Figure 7.8: *The Pyfolio official site*

In addition, there are libraries, such as **QuantLib** and **Technical Analysis Library (TA-Lib)** which have been developed in C++ but made available in Python, which provide even more advanced and specialized tools for the financial world. **QuantLib** allows you to develop models for trading and risk management, offering a set of tools for the design of advanced algorithms including *market conventions, yield curve models, solvers, PDEs,* and *Monte Carlo*. **TA-Lib** provides additional financial tools that can be integrated with the previous library such as *overlap studies, momentum indicators, volume indicators, volatility indicators, price transformations, cycle indicators, pattern recognition,* and *financial statistics functions*.

All these libraries are available on the *Anaconda* platform and can be installed with the following commands:

```
conda install -c anaconda quandl
```

```
conda install -c conda-forge zipline
```

```
conda install -c conda-forge quantlib
```

```
conda install -c conda-forge pyfolio
```

```
conda install -c conda-forge ta-lib
```

Engineering

Finite Element Analysis (FEA) is the simulation of any given physical phenomenon using the numerical technique called the **Finite Element Method (FEM)**.

Engineers use FEA simulations to reproduce the behavior of virtual prototypes under various conditions without physically building them. From the data collected from these simulations, it is possible to optimize the choice of *components*, their *material*, and *shape*, without having to physically create and test them each time, wasting time and money. To do this, however, it is necessary to use mathematical models that simulate reality as much as possible, and that is able to quantify the effects of physical and structural phenomena such as *heat transfer*, *wave propagation*, *resistance to pressure*, and so on. Most of these models are therefore described by **Partial Differential Equations (PDEs)**.

The **Finite Element Analysis** method is the technique that has achieved the most success today for managing this type of calculation and is giving excellent results. It is clear that to carry out an increasingly accurate and efficient FEA, the use of high-performance computers that make use of parallel computing is required. In an FEA, an extremely large number of partial differential equations are solved concurrently and then processed in parallel.

To perform simulations, a mesh, which consists of millions of small elements that together form the shape of the structure, needs to be created.

Calculations are made on each individual element. Combining the individual results, you get the final one that describes the whole structure. This means that an approximation of the interpolation is introduced in the space between the values obtained from the points (nodes) which describe the elements.

That is, you know the value of some points, but not all. **Interpolation** can be improved by using increasingly complex systems, or by increasing the number of finite elements in the analysis. All at the expense of computing power, with the request for more complex calculations and memory. It is therefore clear that to improve the performance, and at the same time the accuracy of these simulations, it is necessary to enhance the calculation tool on which it is performed.

The advances obtained in parallel computing are in fact leading to improvements also in FEA and in the results obtainable from simulations.

As far as FEM methods in Python are concerned, we have many projects and libraries available:

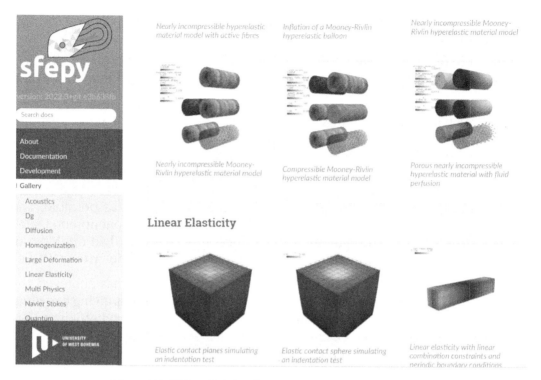

Figure 7.9: SfePy official website with a great set of examples

PolyFem is a library developed in C++ but also released in Python, which provides calculation methods on different PDEs such as:

- Laplace
- Helmholtz
- Linear Elasticity
- St. Venant–Kirchhoff Elasticity
- Neo-Hookean Elasticity
- Stokes
- Navier–Stokes

Where the problems to be submitted to the calculation are easily set via a JSON *interface* or programmatically by defining a class.

This library is also available on the *Anaconda* platform. To install it, you can enter the following command:

```
conda install -c conda-forge polyfempy
```

An alternative is **SfePy**, also a library designed for the resolution of systems of coupled PDEs through the finite element method, both in **1D**, **2D**, and **3D** (see *Figure* 7.9). For its installation, the download of the source code on GitHub and the compilation is recommended, but a pre-built version is available on the *Anaconda* platform:

```
conda install -c conda-forge sfepy
```

Medicine and drug discovery

Parallel computing is also used in medicine, especially in *image processing*. Diagnostic devices that scan the human body and brain use very advanced technologies to produce images. One of the most used techniques in this field is **Magnetic Resonance Imaging (MRI)** reconstruction which is used for the reconstruction of X-ray images and for brain fiber tracking.

Python, as a scientific programming language, offers a series of tools in this area, in particular libraries such as **mripy**, which offer a series of computational tools for MRI reconstruction, such as machine learning functions, Fourier Transform, and specialized neural networks to operate in these purposes. A Python library that fully exploits the potential of parallel computing (both CPU and GPU) is **Sigpy**. This library offers a set of tools for signal processing tasks, but it has been designed to work with MRI reconstruction and it provides a completely dedicated module: **sigpy.mri**. To install the latter you can use the *Anaconda* platform:

```
conda install -c frankong sigpy

# (optional for plot support) conda install matplotlib

# (optional for CUDA support) conda install cupy

# (optional for MPI support) conda install mpi4py
```

But parallel signal processing techniques are also spreading in other diagnostic sectors. Patients with *neuromuscular* or *cardiorespiratory* disease need constant monitoring. This constant monitoring produces a large amount of data in the form of signals which contain useful information of different types that need to be processed as soon as possible. So here too we must make use of signal processing algorithms adapted for this type of application. A peculiar feature is that, however, this data needs to be processed in real-time, therefore with very minimal time. The data produced by monitoring consist of bio signals of different types (generally *electrocardiogram, respiration, electroencephalogram,* and *electromyogram*), all acquired simultaneously. Their processing to extract useful information is not trivial and requires considerable processing time. It is clear that the classical approach generates delays and inefficiencies which could be critical, given that we are talking about human health.

Therefore the transition to parallel processing is an indispensable step to make these current monitoring systems much more efficient and able to give answers in *real-time*, in order to intervene promptly, if necessary. The detection of sudden changes in the patient's vital signs must be rapid and accurate, to avoid serious complications.

In Python, there is a library designed for this kind of signal processing called **BioSPPy**. It is a toolbox that incorporates various signal processing and pattern recognition methods aimed at analyzing the most common bio signals such as **PPG**, **ECG**, **EDA**, **EEG**, **EMG**, and **Respiration**. Unfortunately, this library is not present in the *Anaconda* distribution, but it is possible to install it on **PyPI** using the **pip** command:

```
pip install biosppy
```

Even the research sector, such as *drug discovery* and *genomics*, makes intensive use of complex algorithms in their activity. It is clear that the conversion of these algorithms from serial to parallel and the use of calculation systems (supercomputers) that take advantage of this programming is undergoing strong development and is bringing about significant innovations in this sector as well.

Drug discovery

Drug discovery is one of the most expensive, time-demanding and challenging tasks pharmaceutical companies face. Identification and optimization of molecules or peptides are done on huge scales of available compounds. The molecules to be researched must meet particular requirements, such as high binding affinity and specificity with an associated target, generally an enzyme **(Molecular Docking technique)**. The latter is linked in some way to a disease and its activation-deactivation leads the molecule to have efficacy as a drug. But not only that, the molecule must also have favorable **pharmacodynamics** and **pharmacokinetic** properties, otherwise, it risks being unassimilated or metabolized too quickly so as not to reach the target enzyme. The simulation of such an analysis requires such an amount of computational resources and time that the introduction of parallel computing is very necessary.

Therefore also the thrusts of the pharmaceutical industry are giving a strong impetus to the development and innovation of the current analysis techniques and the calculators on which they are processed.

Drug discovery is a huge market and requires huge economic efforts. Consider that despite this, it has been calculated that only one compound out of 10,000 proposed by *Research and Development* will prove to be a successful drug. So it is clear that all that is necessary to speed up and lighten the simulation and analysis phases of a potential drug will lead to a reduction in expenses.

Molecular docking is a technique that includes sampling and scoring. This activity consists of sampling the possible spatial configurations that the molecule can assume and calculating the scoring functions for each of these configurations when binding to the enzyme.

This activity is computationally very expensive but can be easily parallelized. Also, many algorithms used in the evaluation of a drug can be parallelized, thus increasing the performance of the whole process.

With these techniques, applied to supercomputers, there is an increase in the calculation speed and therefore in the reduction of the time needed for the extraction of potential drugs.

However, research is still very active and therefore opens a scenario for many other innovations:

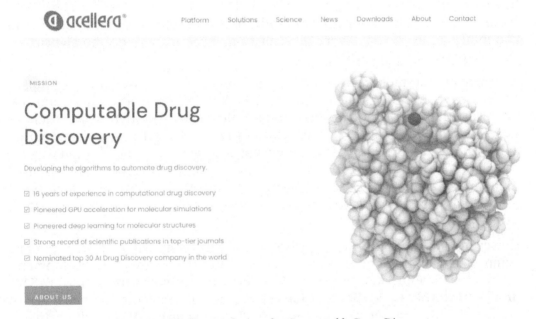

Figure 7.10: *Acellera web page for Computable Drug Discovery*

There are many software for **Molecular Docking**, including **Autodock**, made in C/C++, which has recently been made a new version, called **Autodock-GPU** and which greatly exploits the potential of graphics cards. In fact, it has been found from many scientific works that the speed of operations of this latest version is hundreds of times faster than the original version.

As for Python, there is a version of **Autodock** called **AutodockFR**, which can be downloaded as a suite at **https://ccsb.scripps.edu/adfr/downloads/**.

However, there are other libraries for Molecular Docking. One of these is **pyscreener**, which has an internal tasking system capable of being able to efficiently adapt to the number of available cores, scaling the calculations performed between the cores and the available CPUs in parallel.

Among the paid solutions, it is worth mentioning the libraries provided by **Acellera** (see *Figure 7.10*), which are available for free use (*EULA contract*) and limited to the use of a single GPU. Among these is HTMD, a programmable environment that allows you to *simulate*, *analyze*, and *visualize* molecular systems.

Genomics

As far as *genomics* is concerned, here too the massive use of supercomputers based on parallel computing is necessary. The study of an organism's genome requires being able to manipulate and process a very large amount of data and information, which is very difficult to manage if there are no algorithms capable of working in parallel.

Genomics is the most representative of bioinformatics disciplines. Compare structures such as DNA *sequences*, *genes*, and RNA between different organisms. However, these are data of enormous dimensions (Terabytes) so much so that they can be defined as *Biological Big Data*. Using the usual computers and without the use of parallel computing, a single experiment could require calculation times of several weeks, if not even months. It is therefore essential that parallelization and HPC techniques are applied in order to reduce these *processing times*, in order to make it possible to manage, process and analyze this type of data.

However, the integration of algorithms used in bioinformatics with parallel computing is not a simple matter and is still under study and development. There are *two* approaches to solve this step. Current software such as **FASTA**, **BLAST**, **HMMER**, **ClustalW**, and **RaxML** are being redesigned to make use of parallel computing, for example with MPI (see *Figure 7.11*). An alternative is to use distributed systems, or clouds, in which pipelines are developed for bioinformatics calculations, which can be represented as workflows:

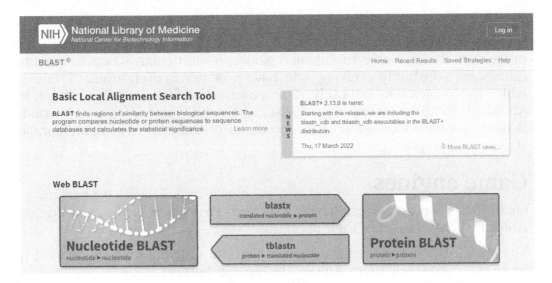

Figure 7.11: BLAST *official page*

There are already workflow systems such as **Tavaxy**, **Pegasus**, **Swift/T**, and **SciCumulus** that can manage bioinformatics processing in distributed infrastructures.

As for Python, there is the **pyrpipe** library, designed to process **RNA-Seq** data by developing computational pipelines entirely in python. This library can be used both on local computers and in HPC environments and can be easily integrated into workflow management systems such as **Snakemake** and **Nextflow**.

This library can be easily installed on the *Anaconda* platform:

```
conda install -c bioconda pyrpipe
```

Along with **pyrpipe**, the *Anaconda* distribution includes a huge amount of bioinformatics-specific libraries, all gathered in a dedicated repository called **bioconda (https://anaconda.org/bioconda/repo)**.

Furthermore, always on *Anaconda*, there is another library called **BioPython** which contains a series of useful tools for molecular biology. It can be downloaded using the command:

```
conda install -c conda-forge biopython
```

Entertainment – games and movies

After so many applications in various scientific and industrial sectors, it will be surprising to discover that parallel computing has its roots in the world of entertainment. This really shouldn't come as a surprise, given that GPUs were initially designed for the heavy graphics loads used in video games. It is in fact the video game market that has strongly pushed the development of particular processors that are able to enhance games, in particular 3D environments. Games are constantly evolving, and have now reached enormous levels, in which the images flow smoothly, rich in interactive features (often guided by AI), which compose increasingly realistic scenarios (sometimes even beyond). It is in fact here that we find the potential of the intrinsic, highly parallel structure of graphics cards.

Game engines

On the basis of most games, there is a complex structure called a **game engine**, which is the very heart of their operation.

There are several game-engine models that are distributed in the market to make video games on them. Among the most important are:

- **The Unreal Engine**
- **Unity**
- **Godot**

These powerful game engines are easy to use and allow intelligent features to be used to create beautiful applications to ensure realistic gaming experiences (see *Figure 7.12*):

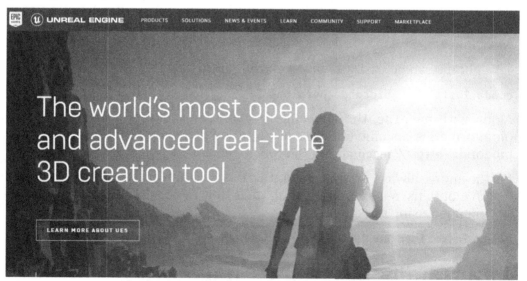

***Figure 7.12**: Unreal Engine official web page*

For developers, user interfaces are provided that allow you to develop games in a simple way, making the most of the most powerful technologies available, both **graphics** (supported by GPUs) and **learning** (AI), giving the possibility of obtaining fluid movements of the subjects in three-dimensional settings and ever greater interactivity. These game engines are constantly evolving, incorporating within them all possible innovations in the field of parallel programming since it makes the most of all available technologies. Often these technologies are then reused in other areas seen previously.

The power of game engines is also based on **3D rendering**. It is this process that allows players to have realistic gaming experience. 3D rendering is nothing more than the creation of an image starting from three-dimensional modeling.

The *three-dimensional models of objects* that make up the virtual environment created by the game engine undergo the texturing phase. Two-dimensional images are applied that cover the surface of these objects, giving them a material appearance, with a sheen calculated based on the orientation of the lighting. Other effects such as shadows are added and in the end, the 2D image is created, which as a photograph, converts virtual reality into a realistic image.

The more powerful the calculators used, the better the results will be, obtaining ever more realistic images. Furthermore, these images will have to be generated for each frame of the video game, which, like the frames of a movie, will have to flow smoothly and therefore it is easy to understand the demands on computing power this kind of technology requires. In addition to this, there are the necessary calculations for the management of sound, artificial intelligence, network and memory.

Parallel computing is a powerful tool for optimizing the underlying processes in a game engine. The most powerful game engines currently make use of CPU cores and GPUs through *multithreading*. In our book, we have seen that Python does not handle multithreading on CPUs well, and in fact, these game engines are based on programming languages such as C# and C++ which instead allow you to apply multithreading on CPUs:

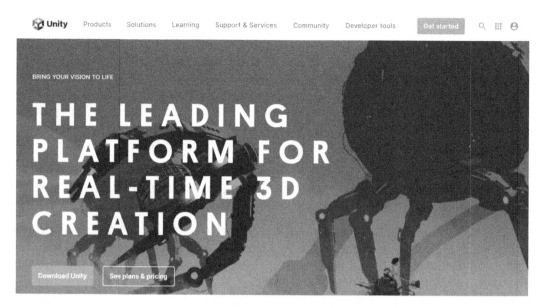

Figure 7.13: *Unity official web page*

In the **Unity** game engine (see *Figure 7.13*), for example, *multithreading* is applied for executing rendering processes in parallel across threads. Parallel execution of multiple threads greatly reduces the *execution time of processes* within a frame. So more frames can be generated per second, and therefore the games will be *smoother*. This is in fact where GPUs come into play, where their architecture is designed in such a way as to resolve the calculation of pixel textures more efficiently than a CPU would. Furthermore, the enormously parallel internal structure allows this computation to be assigned to a large number of threads simultaneously, considerably lightening the workload and reducing execution times.

Furthermore, the CPU is free to carry out further tasks in the meantime. Since the CPUs are powerful in mathematical calculations, they are used in parallel to perform mathematical calculations to make the 3D environment even more realistic. The behavior of objects, the effects of shocks, and the waves transmitted in the water, the responses to user interactions, and even the intelligence of **Non-Player Characters (NPCs)** are processed by algorithms destined for the CPU, whose cores as many threads are allocated for parallel computing.

As said for Python there are no such game engines. Those available are distributed in the form of libraries. **PyGame** and other Python game development libraries cannot multithread on CPUs and have not reached levels of power like those built with other programming languages, such as

Unreal Engine and **Unity**. Nothing prevents new projects from being able to achieve excellent results in the future.

Designing a parallel game engine

There is a wonderful article on the Intel website entitled *Designing the Framework of a Parallel Game Engine*:

https://www.intel.com/content/dam/develop/external/us/en/documents/designing-a-parallel-game-engine-155986.pdf

That illustrates how to design a possible game engine. It could be a good stimulus to develop a new game engine in Python.

A good design for a game engine is to make the most of all available processors. We have seen that other game engines take advantage of multithreading on CPUs. In Python, we don't have this possibility, but we could use *multiprocessing*. As far as GPU is concerned, we have seen that Python is not affected by major limitations compared to other programming languages.

We have seen that a game engine works on a processing loop aimed at creating one frame after another. Each *frame* is the result of a whole series of processes that include the movement of objects in *three-dimensional space*, *texturing*, *rendering*, and *user interactions*. It is clear that the generation of the frame leads to a serial execution of the game, where the *frames* are generated in an ordered sequence one after the other. But between the generation of one frame and another, the full potential of parallel computing can be exploited to the fullest. Between the two frames, *threads* and *processes* will spawn and work in parallel to perform all necessary tasks, greatly reducing processing time. Then the generation of the frame will be the moment of synchronization in which all the threads, or processes, will have to finish their execution and give a result. The exchange of information between them will be done right at this moment greatly reducing the synchronization load, and allowing the system to react more quickly from one frame to another.

The article shows *two* execution modes:

- The **Lock Step Mode** is the one just described and shown in *Figure 7.14*:

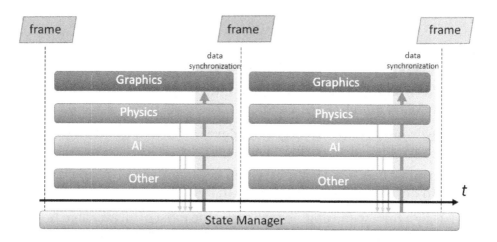

Figure 7.14: *Lock Step Mode*

- The **Free Step Mode**, where not all the components must necessarily synchronize at each frame step, but can extend over several cycles (see *Figure 7.15*):

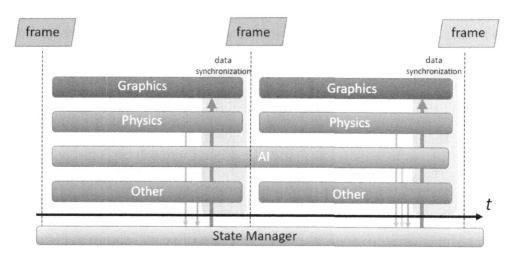

Figure 7.15: *Free Step Mode*

Movies and 3D animations

The power of game engines to create *three-dimensional environments* has come to results that often surpass reality itself. Some of the technologies used in creating images for video games have also been used in making movies. In the post-production phase of many recent films, the use of effects is increasingly frequent (very often taken from video games) which allows to improve the images acquired from reality or to produce new surreal or expensive settings in which actors move.

Some techniques such as color correction and ray tracing harness the power of GPUs to enhance the images shot for a movie. All these visual effects are commonly referred to as VFX (*Visual Effects*) and are the result of processing processes of photorealistic images, digitally generated, or the result of manipulation of other images.

Special effects experts use special software that allows you to do this job. *DaVinci Resolve Studio*, for example, is a special effects processing platform that makes heavy use of GPUs (see *Figure 7.16*). Films such as *Thor: Love and Thunder* (2022) and *Bullet Train* (2022) have used this software to color-correct the images shot by means of high-quality renderings based on *ray-tracing techniques* to accentuate reflections, contrasts and lighting effects. All of this work was done using GPUs in parallel:

Figure 7.16: *DaVinci Resolve Studio web page*

Ray Tracing is a type of rendering algorithm that produces realistic light effects in computer graphics through a series of vector-based calculations and this technique requires a huge amount of resources (*computationally expensive*). So if we imagine the costs of processing parts of images in a film, we can imagine the demand for resources required for animated films such as those from Pixar. These are about 2 *hours* long movies, in which all the images are the result of the rendering of environments completely built on artificial three-dimensional models.

A freelance programmer from *Pixar Animation Studios*, *Peter Collingridge*, has revealed that *Pixar* has one of the 25 *most powerful supercomputers* in the world, consisting of 2,000 *machines* and 24,000 *cores*, for making its animation films. Despite the availability of this computing power, movies like *Monster Inc* (2001) took about two years of computation to render the footage.

It is clear that in recent years *Pixar* has further increased the power of its supercomputer, but it is also clear at the same time that the realization of these films based entirely on 3D *animations* with increasingly realistic rendering effects, requires an enormous computation, even for the best supercomputers on earth.

From *Monster Inc. Pixar*, and not only, have produced increasingly fluid and realistic animated films, where the richness of detail and the complexity of the movements increases.

This is a clear sign that there have been many advances in the underlying technologies, including innovations in parallel computing. Given the properties of these techniques, not much information is available to the public, but it is clear that for those interested in working in this sector, parallel programming is certainly to be taken into close consideration.

Conclusion

With this chapter, we have concluded the overview of the disciplines and application sectors in which parallel computing is proving to be a valid tool for innovation and research. We have excluded data analysis and artificial intelligence which will be the subject of the next chapters of the book and which will be treated in detail.

References

- https://www.intel.in/content/www/in/en/high-performance-computing/what-is-hpc.html

- https://www.hp.com/us-en/shop/tech-takes/parallel-computing-and-its-modern-uses

- https://builtin.com/hardware/parallel-processing-example

- https://www.eoas.ubc.ca/books/Practical_Meteorology/prmet102/Ch20-nwp-v102.pdf

- https://pyoceans.github.io/sea-py/

- https://biostats.w.uib.no/ctd/

- https://library.lanl.gov/cgi-bin/getfile?00285657.pdf

- https://events.ecmwf.int/event/279/contributions/2700/attachments/1869/3361/2022-05-17-nwp-primer-metview-intro.pdf

- https://confluence.ecmwf.int/display/METV/Metview

- https://prappleizer.github.io/textbook.pdf

- https://www.lupm.in2p3.fr/users/jmorin/pres/euroscipy2011-jmorin-pencil.pdf

- https://arxiv.org/pdf/1807.06128.pdf

- https://yt-astro-analysis.readthedocs.io/en/latest/

- https://github.com/yt-project

- https://www.researchgate.net/publication/346249862_DEVELOPING_PARALLEL_COMPUTING_ALGORITHMS_USING_GPU'S_TO_DETERMINE_OIL_AND_GAS_RESERVES_PRESENTED_IN_THE_UPSTREAM_EXPLORATION_SECTOR

- https://iopscience.iop.org/article/10.1088/1742-6596/2032/1/012038/pdf

- https://abhyankar-ameya.medium.com/parallel-computing-for-finance-ec053d8fb20f

- https://www.activestate.com/blog/top-10-python-packages-for-finance-and-financial-modeling/
- https://www.simscale.com/docs/simwiki/fea-finite-element-analysis/what-is-fea-finite-element-analysis/
- https://getfem-examples.readthedocs.io/en/latest/demo_unit_disk.html
- https://sfepy.org/doc-devel/index.html
- https://www.unrealengine.com/en-US
- https://unity.com/
- https://godotengine.org/
- https://www.intel.com/content/dam/develop/external/us/en/documents/designing-a-parallel-game-engine-155986.pdf
- https://www.gamedeveloper.com/blogs/advantages-of-parallel-computing-in-unity
- https://www.dcp.dev/projects/distributed-ray-tracing
- https://sigpy.readthedocs.io/en/latest/mri.html
- https://run.unl.pt/bitstream/10362/8249/1/Chorao_2012.pdf
- https://www.mdpi.com/1424-8247/15/1/63/htm
- https://ccsb.scripps.edu/adfr/
- https://www.ncbi.nlm.nih.gov/pmc/articles/PMC4655901/

## CHAPTER 8

Scaling Your Data Science Applications with Dask

In the previous chapter, we saw an overview of the possible applications of parallel computing in various scientific and industrial disciplines, in particular in the context of Python, suggesting some available tools and libraries related to this language. However, we have deliberately left out *Data Science*, preferring to dedicate an entire chapter to it. In this chapter, in fact, we will mainly deal with a possible application of Data Science in the field of *parallel computing*, in particular, the **Dask** library. Dask is a powerful tool that allows us to extend our commonly used Data Science libraries, such as **Pandas** and **NumPy**, on distributed systems in a very simple and fast way.

Structure

In this chapter, we will cover the following topics:

- Dask library
- Pandas and Dask DataFrames
- Distributed parallel computing
- Dask collections
- Task graphs and computing
- Kaggle
- Saturn.io cluster

Data Science, Pandas library, and parallel computing

Python has proved to be a very suitable language for *Data Science* and *Data Analysis*, gradually competing with languages such as **R** that have been consolidated for years in this area. This is mainly due to the potential of the libraries available today in Python which in recent years have gradually created a place of all merit, among the tools of Data Science. One of these libraries is, for example, **Pandas**, which thanks to the **DataFrame** (see *Figure 8.1*) allows you to manipulate and manage huge amounts of data, in a rather efficient and rapid way. Furthermore, this library, together with other libraries such as **NumPy**, **Scikit-Learn**, **Matplotlib**, and many others, has formed a fundamental tool kit for the Data Scientist activity, creating a study, and analysis environment that exhaustively covers all needs, remaining within the scope of the Python language:

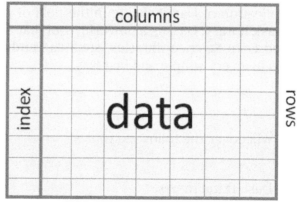

Figure 8.1: A DataFrame

So, the *Data Scientist* soon builds a development and analysis environment, gradually installing all these libraries, such as, for example, a series of specific virtual environments like the ones we created with the *Anaconda* distribution. You import the data (often CSVs available on the web) onto your computer, convert them into DataFrames *thanks* to the **Pandas** library, clean them, manipulate them according to your needs, perform analysis, and extract useful information. Everything would seem perfect. **Pandas** is very efficient as a library and is capable of manipulating hundreds of thousands of lines of data in a few seconds or even less, depending on the computing power of your computer. But however powerful and efficient the computer you are working on may be, sooner or later you will need to import CSV files, or data in other formats, larger in size than your computer's RAM. When trying to import this data, you will get an error message. Furthermore, with the increase in the size of the working DataFrames, and with the use of ever more complicated procedures for processing and manipulating these data, the execution times will lengthen considerably, partly due to the algorithms that underlie the operations but it also depends on computer resources which will gradually become scarcer as the amount of data to be processed increases. This is true the more you approach the world of Big Data.

But *then how to proceed?* Having therefore reached a crisis point, it can certainly be improved by *scaling out* the problem. The best solution, in the case of Data Science, will not be limited only to a concept of parallelization of calculations by exploiting parallel computing, but also to a distribution of data to be processed on different calculation systems with their own memories. Among the systems that we have already seen in the book, distributed systems are the ones that best meet these needs. Systems composed of multiple computing systems, each with its own memory, such as computer clusters, are the best environment for the *Data Scientist* who wants to scale from his *limited, albeit powerful, single computer*, as shown in *Figure 8.2*:

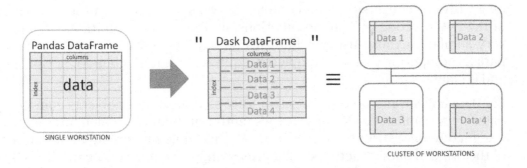

Figure 8.2: *Scaling out of DataFrames*

Pandas is a library that has been designed to work perfectly on single machines, but in moving to a distributed system, such as a cluster of computers, a corresponding library has been devised, with the same characteristics as Pandas, called **Dask**.

Dask library

Dask is a flexible library that allows you to extend many Data Science libraries, such as **Pandas**, but also **NumPy**, **Scikit-learn**, and many others, on distributed systems for parallel computing in Python. These libraries are the bread and butter of anyone working with data analysis in Python. Dask is a library designed to use the *same syntax*, *methods*, and *operating modes* as these libraries. In this way, all users of these libraries will be able to use their already developed codes by extending them with the Dask library in a simple way with very small code changes. In this way, the scaling of the code from a *single-machine system* to *distributed systems* is really immediate.

So, Dask is a real framework that allows us to build distributed applications, a toolbox that allows us to *scale up* in just a few steps, that is, the transition from a purely serial system to one comprising multiple processing systems in parallel, or the *scale out*, that is, the transfer of execution to external distributed systems such as the cloud.

The Dask library is conceptually split into *two* distinct parts:

- Dynamic task scheduling
- Big Data collections

Dynamic task scheduling is the component used to optimize the calculations in the distributed system on which they will have to be performed. It will mainly deal with the conversion, in a completely transparent way to the developer, of the Python code containing functions, methods, and definitions of objects very similar to those used in libraries such as Pandas, into operations for parallel computing that are completely equivalent, but much more performing and efficient.

Big Data collections, on the other hand, are all that series of objects containing data, very similar to NumPy arrays and DataFrames, which are instead designed to be distributed on clusters. All this while preserving the interfaces of the original data structures, thus preserving the names of the methods, the parameters passed and the syntax of the operations generally used on these objects.

In summary, the Dask library is able to provide the *Data Scientist* with the extension to distributed systems with highly parallelized DataFrames and arrays. All while maintaining the same syntax of the original libraries as much as possible, in order to reuse the existing code and extend it to parallel computing in a very simple and rapid way. Furthermore, once the code is integrated with the Dask library, it will be able to work on clusters with over 1000 *cores* as on a single laptop running on a single process. In this case, Dask will take care of optimizing the execution of the code according to the processing environment.

In a simple way, the operation of Dask can be summarized in the representation shown in *Figure 8.3*:

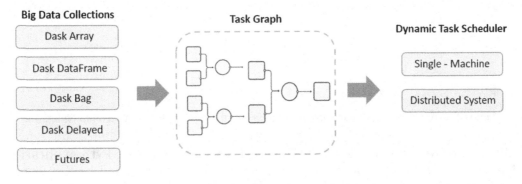

Figure 8.3: Operation diagram of the Dask library

Dask provides *three* different components:

- **Big Data collections**: At a *high level*, this data structure is very similar to the corresponding objects present in other libraries, such as the DataFrame in Pandas. At a *low level*, they are designed to manage parallel computing in distributed.

- **Task graphs**: They are generated by Dask from Big Data collections and from operations to be performed on them. They have the purpose of dividing these operations into smaller parts, the tasks, which will then be distributed to the various processors of the system, the workers, who will have the task to run in a parallel manner.

- **Dynamic task scheduler**: This component has the task of distributing tasks to available workers.

Getting started on a single machine

To begin to familiarize yourself with Dask and its features, there is no better way than to use your own computer. It will then always be possible to pass the code developed on distributed systems such as a cluster (for a fee).

Dask works correctly on all operating systems, so it can be used in both *Linux*, *macOS*, and *Windows*. Again, it is recommended to use **Anaconda Navigator**. We create a new specific virtual environment to work on our projects with Dask, through the **Environments** panel in *Anaconda Navigator* and then we install the *two* packages **dask** and **dask-core** as shown in *Figure 8.4*:

Figure 8.4: *Installing Dask packages in a new virtual environment in Anaconda Navigator*

Since we're working on data analytics, we'll be using two core Python libraries: **NumPy** and **Pandas**. These two libraries need to be installed in the virtual environment, so we will use the following commands from the command shell:

```
conda install numpy
```

```
conda install pandas
```

Or we can always install them via *Anaconda Navigator*, as we did for **Dask** (see *Figure 8.5*):

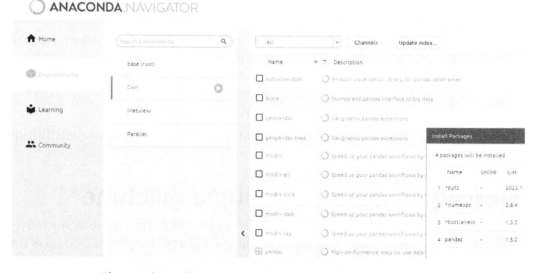

Figure 8.5: *Installing numpy and pandas packages in Anaconda*

Another library that will later come in handy for displaying execution flow and memory distribution patterns through Dask is **graphviz**. We also install this library using the command shell of the virtual environment, via the command:

```
conda install graphviz
```

```
conda install python-graphviz
```

Or graphically, by selecting it from the packages available in Anaconda Navigator.

Once installed, to test the correct installation we will import all the necessary packages into our code, as follows:

```
import numpy as np
```

```
import pandas as pd
```

```
import dask.dataframe as dd
```

```
import dask.array as da
```

```
import dask.bag as db
```

You can use the command shell to launch the programs presented in this chapter as we have done so far, but for data analysis, we will take a different approach: we will use **Jupyter Notebook**, the famous notebook where you can work with Python code in an *interactive* way with the results shown in real time, both in *textual* and *graphical* format. You will find that for data analysis the use of Jupyter Notebook will prove to be a fundamental choice to facilitate the task of the developer and analyst to test the code, but above all to study the data being analyzed at the same time.

To activate Jupyter Notebook, again from *Anaconda*, from the *Home* screen press the **Launch** button directly above the quadrant corresponding to the Jupyter application as shown in *Figure 8.6*:

Figure 8.6: *Jupyter Notebook panel for launching Jupyter Notebook*

By pressing the button, after a few seconds, the application will automatically open on a page on the default browser, which will show the folders in which to *open*, *create*, and *save* the Notebook pages, as shown in *Figure 8.7*:

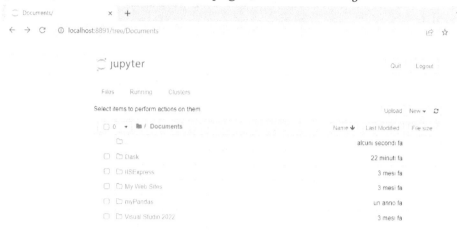

Figure 8.7: *Jupyter Notebook*

So, let's create a new notebook and write in the first cell the modules corresponding to the libraries to be imported. By running the first cell, if we do not get any error message, then the installation will have gone correctly. See *Figure 8.8*:

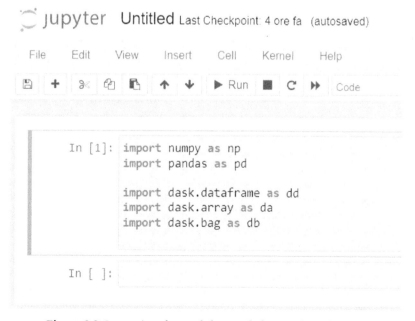

Figure 8.8: *Importing the modules needed to work with Dask*

Dask collections

One of the peculiar characteristics of Dask is to *extend* data structures such as the DataFrame of the **pandas** library and the NumPy arrays to work efficiently in distributed systems. Dask offers the user a set of deployable objects called Collections, including the most relevant ones:

- Dask Array
- Dask DataFrame

Dask DataFrame is represented by many small DataFrame pandas that live in your *cluster*. When you interact with Dask DataFrame, the *functions* and *methods* you call are converted into many smaller functions that run in parallel on multiple smaller Pandas DataFrames.

Dask Array is represented by smaller NumPy arrays that live in your cluster. When you interact with the Dask Array, the functions and methods you call are converted into smaller functions that run in parallel on smaller NumPy arrays.

Now let's look at these concepts in more detail with practice. We create a new *Python 3 Notebook on Jupyter* and in the first cell, we import the libraries and modules we will need:

```
import numpy as np

import pandas as pd


import dask.dataframe as dd

import dask.array as da
```

We execute the cell and then move on to inserting the code in the next one. First, let's see how we can create a simple pandas DataFrame which we will use as a comparison to the Dask DataFrame:

```
df = pd.DataFrame(np.random.rand(60).reshape(10,6))

df
```

Running the cell we will get a result similar to the one shown in *Figure 8.9* (the values change because they are random):

	0	1	2	3	4	5
0	0.149034	0.604988	0.070560	0.298244	0.455134	0.896560
1	0.854942	0.291555	0.686519	0.856187	0.559002	0.737303
2	0.333051	0.779722	0.075977	0.891700	0.577997	0.544064
3	0.032463	0.374616	0.252517	0.291193	0.669397	0.687053
4	0.607324	0.337583	0.270796	0.799909	0.810546	0.530320
5	0.683711	0.048430	0.268431	0.286249	0.526409	0.981537
6	0.903745	0.823235	0.883192	0.379180	0.031492	0.094687
7	0.893327	0.700813	0.876160	0.313225	0.318481	0.726146
8	0.939292	0.308199	0.041690	0.667480	0.076510	0.504596
9	0.153619	0.025283	0.544786	0.339783	0.459579	0.020543

Figure 8.9: *Example of Pandas DataFrame*

As we can see, we have generated a simple DataFrame containing 60 *random values* collected in *six different columns* and *ten records*. We have done this only as an example, but in reality, DataFrames are generally valued using a CSV file containing the data to be imported. On the Internet, there are many data sources that provide CSV files to be imported full of precious data to be analyzed.

So for practice, let's then export the newly generated data to a CSV file that we can use for our examples. This can be done easily via the **to_csv()** method invoked on the DataFrame to be exported:

```
df.to_csv("myDataFrame.csv", index=False)
```

We execute the command in a cell of the Notebook and we go to check the directory we are working on. We will find a new **myDataFrame.csv** file containing the 60 *random data* generated earlier. We used the **index=False** parameter to prevent the row numbering indexes of the DataFrame from being reported in the CSV file.

So if we want to import data into a pandas DataFrame in our notebook, we just need to use the **from_csv()** function to be invoked directly in the library:

```
df = pd.read_csv("myDataFrame.csv")

df
```

If we execute the cell we will obtain as a result a DataFrame identical to the previous one shown in *Figure* 8.9.

Well, we can do the same thing to create a Dask DataFrame. The syntax to use is practically the same.

```
ddf = dd.read_csv("myDataFrame.csv")

ddf
```

But unlike before, we will get the result shown in the following figure (*Figure* 8.10):

Dask DataFrame Structure:

	0	1	2	3	4	5
npartitions=1						
	float64	float64	float64	float64	float64	float64
	...	...	...	...	...	...

Dask Name: read-csv, 1 tasks

Figure 8.10: *Structure of a Dask DataFrame with no data*

As we can see, the data is not present inside the DataFrame and only the internal structure of the DataFrame is displayed with the name of the columns and the relative types of data. But *where did the data go?*

Well, although the syntax between pandas and Dask is very similar, as is the structure of their DataFrames, their behavior is different. Dask is *Lazy*. That is, it does not perform the operations required when invoking a method or in defining an object such as a DataFrame. To do this, I wait for a specific command, called `compute()`.

So, if now in the following cell of the Jupyter Notebook, we run the following command:

```
ddf.compute()
```

We will get as a result the population of DataFrame with the same data as the one created with **pandas**.

Another possible way to import data into a Dask DataFrame is to get it directly from another Pandas DataFrame. This operation is much more frequent than you might imagine, especially when you want to scale an already existing code. In this regard, there is therefore the **from_pandas()** method that allows us to do this operation. In this case, we have the opportunity to choose how many parts the original DataFrame will be divided into, defining it using the

npartitions option, passed as an argument to the function:

```
ddf = dd.from_pandas(df, npartitions=4)

ddf
```

By executing the previous lines of code, we will obtain a result like the one shown in *Figure 8.11*:

Dask DataFrame Structure:

		0	1	2	3	4	5
npartitions=3							
	0	float64	float64	float64	float64	float64	float64
	3	...	...	...	...	...	...
	6	...	...	...	...	...	...
	9	...	...	...	...	...	...

Dask Name: from_pandas, 3 tasks

Figure 8.11: Structure of a Dask DataFrame divided into four partitions

In this case, it can be seen that compared to the previous case, four row indexes corresponding to the first rows of each partition into which the Dask DataFrame will be divided are also reported. If we want to be more explicit, we can also run the following command:

```
ddf.divisions
```

Which will give us as a result a tuple of the indexes corresponding to the first rows of each partition of the DataFrame:

(0, 3, 6, 9)

As we can see the result corresponds to the one shown in *Figure 8.11*.

We just have to enhance the DataFrame as previously done through the **compute()** function:

```
ddf.compute()
```

And we will get the same DataFrame obtained in previous cases.

As for the Dask Arrays, the discussion is very similar, only that in this case instead of talking about the **pandas** DataFrame, NumPy Arrays are used. We then define a NumPy Array of 100 *integer random values between 0 and 9*, collected in a *10x10 matrix*.

```
narr = np.random.randint(0,10,100).reshape(10,10)

narr
```

By executing we will obtain a result similar to the following:

```
array([[5, 2, 5, 7, 2, 3, 9, 8, 2, 6],
       [9, 6, 3, 5, 0, 8, 5, 5, 1, 9],
       [6, 0, 3, 4, 3, 8, 1, 1, 7, 5],
       [3, 5, 5, 5, 3, 8, 3, 9, 3, 9],
       [3, 8, 5, 6, 0, 6, 0, 9, 7, 2],
       [7, 9, 4, 0, 4, 4, 3, 0, 6, 9],
       [9, 1, 7, 2, 4, 8, 9, 2, 6, 6],
       [5, 5, 3, 8, 1, 5, 7, 6, 4, 2],
       [8, 4, 8, 7, 0, 7, 6, 6, 9, 0],
       [1, 2, 8, 6, 8, 8, 0, 3, 0, 8]])
```

You can directly import the values of this NumPy array directly into a Dask Array using this time the **from_array()** function of the Dask library. The **chunks** option requires a tuple containing the size of the **chunks** into which to split the Dask Array:

```
darr = da.from_array(narr, chunks=(5, 5))

darr
```

Executing the previous code, you will get a graphical result as shown in *Figure 8.12*:

	Array	Chunk
Bytes	400 B	100 B
Shape	(10, 10)	(5, 5)
Count	4 Tasks	4 Chunks
Type	int32	numpy.ndarray

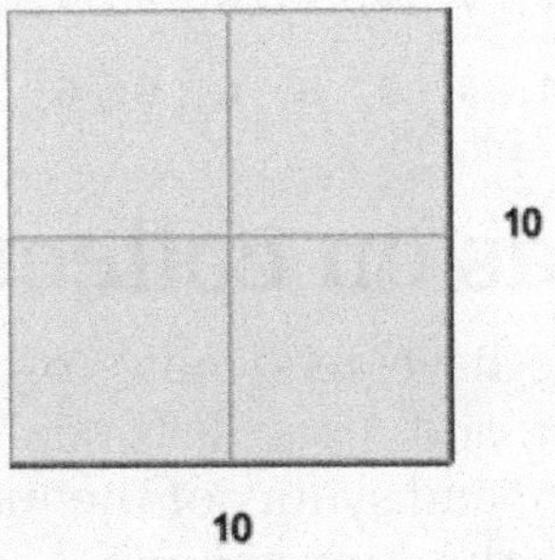

Figure 8.12: *Structure of a Dask Array*

As we can see, also in this case we obtained only the structure of the Dask Array as a result, since this is not yet valued (remember that Dask is *Lazy*). In the indications, we can see the dimensions of each *portion* or *chunk*, into which the Dask Array will be divided. A task will be assigned to each chunk and therefore the populating of the Dask Array will also take place in a parallel manner.

If we want to have textual information about the partition of the Dask Array, this time we will use the **chunks** attribute:

```
darr.chunks
```

```
((5, 5), (5, 5))
```

To evaluate the Dask Array, the **compute()** function is launched once again:

```
darr.compute()
```

As a result, we will have the contents of the array in the output:

```
array([[2, 7, 3, 1, 3, 8, 1, 9, 0, 0],
       [0, 8, 0, 6, 3, 7, 7, 3, 4, 5],
       [0, 1, 2, 8, 6, 4, 3, 8, 5, 6],
       [1, 8, 4, 7, 8, 2, 4, 5, 1, 8],
       [4, 6, 4, 5, 5, 7, 4, 3, 8, 2],
       [8, 5, 3, 3, 9, 4, 5, 4, 2, 5],
       [9, 3, 1, 4, 0, 9, 5, 6, 7, 3],
       [5, 7, 1, 4, 8, 2, 2, 9, 3, 2],
       [1, 7, 9, 4, 7, 8, 9, 7, 2, 0],
       [6, 4, 3, 0, 6, 6, 6, 6, 4, 3]])
```

Methods on collections

Now that we have seen how to define the most common collections such as DataFrame and Array, let's see how to apply methods on them. As for the nomenclature and syntax of the methods, everything should remain the same (or almost) as the corresponding methods of the original libraries.

For example, if we want to calculate the average of the first column of the pandas DataFrame we would write as follows:

```
df['1'].mean()
```

Obtaining as a result the average, which in my specific case is:

`0.42944239885994107`

So, as far as Dask DataFrame is concerned, things shouldn't change much:

`m = ddf['1'].mean()`

In this case, the function is assigned to a variable. In fact, as we have seen for the enhancements of the DataFrame, the same rule also applies to the methods. The methods are not executed until the **compute()** function is called on the *invoked* method. So, to execute the method we have to write:

`m.compute()`

And thus obtain the same result obtained with the pandas DataFrame:

`0.42944239885994107`

The same goes for the Dask Arrays. If you want to calculate the average of the values contained within the array, just write:

`mm = np.mean(darr)`

This calculation will be performed only when the **compute()** method is invoked:

`mm.compute()`

which in my case will give the following result:

`4.52`

So far so simple, but let's analyze the reason for this strange *lazy* behavior of Dask and what actually takes place underneath it.

Computing and task graphs

As seen from the previous examples, the particular difference between the Dask library and that of traditional libraries like Pandas and NumPy is the behavior. Dask is a *Lazy* library and we have seen the enhancement of the data structure, that is, of a collection in the case of Dask, is performed at a later time and not during the definition of the collection itself. At the time of definition, only a *data structure* is built which will have to be populated at a later time. The same thing goes for the invocation of methods which is never followed by the calculation but remains pending through its assignment to a variable.

The population of a collection and the execution of a method on it takes place only when the **compute()** method is invoked in the code on the relative object already defined previously. This operation is called **computing** and it is a particular operation that occurs in a different way from what happens in Pandas or NumPy. In fact, as you have certainly noticed, during the definition of an object there is also its partition, that is the definition of how many parts it will be divided into. Each portion will be assigned a task which in turn will be assigned to a different worker. Valuation and execution of calculations within a collection will then be done in parallel. The different portions, for example, of a DataFrame will be *populated* and processed in *parallel*, thus reducing the time of this operation. With small CSV files, in any case with files smaller than 1 GB, we have never faced this problem, but with larger CSV files, even in data enhancement, there is an enormous consumption of resources, including population time. So, Dask, in addition to arranging its data structures in a distributed manner, such portions of which can be processed in parallel, also reduces the valorization times of these huge objects.

A related concept to computing is that of the **Task Graph**. These graphs are generated before this operation and describe how this will have to be done within the system or a single machine. They represent the kind of execution path that the *Task Scheduler* will have to follow. Task graphs are dynamic and change according to the system being worked on, optimizing parallel computing as much as possible.

You can view these task graphs generated during computing in the Jupyter Notebook. For example, if we want to see the task graph of averaging on the Dask Array in the previous case, we can write:

```
mm.dask
```

Obtaining the list of layers into which the task graph is divided as shown in the following figure (*Figure 8.13*):

HighLevelGraph

HighLevelGraph with 3 layers and 9 keys from all layers.

⬤ **Layer1: array**

⬤ **Layer2: mean_chunk**

⬤ **Layer3: mean_agg-aggregate**

Figure 8.13: *Layers in the task graph*

Meanwhile, if we want to see the task graph we write:

```
mm.visualize()
```

Obtaining a graph as shown in the following figure (*Figure 8.14*):

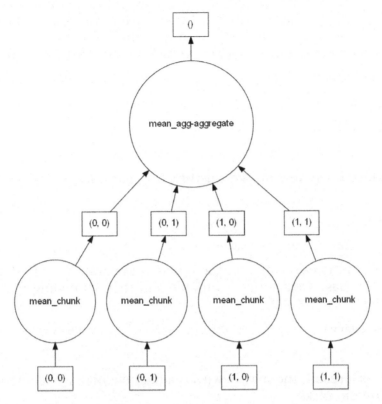

Figure 8.14: *Task graph for calculating the average on the Dask Array*

As we can see, the calculation of the average is performed in parallel between the *four* portions (chunks) into which the matrix was divided. The four results obtained from the individual tasks are then aggregated together to obtain the final result.

Low-level interfacing with the Dask Delayed

In addition to the methods provided by the Pandas and NumPy libraries which were then reproduced in the corresponding collections in Dask, it can often happen in the code that you have to define new methods that apply to this type of object. But *how can we extend, in this case, these new methods to parallel computing with Dask if they have not been implemented within it?*

In this regard, Dask comes to the rescue via the **Dask Delayed**. This tool allows you to wrap individual functions by assigning them a task graph. These functions will be incorporated into the *low-level lazily construction mechanism* and will enter the same behavior as the methods and collections of Dask.

Practically speaking, the functions to be converted will be defined by a **@dask.delayed** decorator. For example, when defining a function that acts on the Dask Array, doubling all its elements, we will anticipate it from the decorator:

```
import dask
```

```
@dask.delayed
```

```
def doubled(x):
```

```
    return 2*x
```

And therefore if we now invoke this function we will obtain a Dask **Delayed** object:

```
doubled(darr)
```

```
Delayed('doubled-5f08d4cc-aaeb-43bb-9577-7c8f055af1fd')
```

So, to perform the calculation of the function in parallel, we first invoke it by assigning the Dask Delayed to a variable and then launching the **compute()** method on it:

```
d = doubled(darr)
```

```
d.compute()
```

Obtaining as a result, the matrix with doubled elements, executed in parallel by four different tasks:

```
array([[ 4, 14,  6,  2,  6, 16,  2, 18,  0,  0],
       [ 0, 16,  0, 12,  6, 14, 14,  6,  8, 10],
       [ 0,  2,  4, 16, 12,  8,  6, 16, 10, 12],
       [ 2, 16,  8, 14, 16,  4,  8, 10,  2, 16],
       [ 8, 12,  8, 10, 10, 14,  8,  6, 16,  4],
       [16, 10,  6,  6, 18,  8, 10,  8,  4, 10],
       [18,  6,  2,  8,  0, 18, 10, 12, 14,  6],
       [10, 14,  2,  8, 16,  4,  4, 18,  6,  4],
       [ 2, 14, 18,  8, 14, 16, 18, 14,  4,  0],
       [12,  8,  6,  0, 12, 12, 12, 12,  8,  6]])
```

Getting started on a cluster of machines

So far we've been working with Dask on a single machine to understand how this works and what the unique characteristics of this library are. Now it's time to work on more realistic cases where you have to deal with huge datasets and run on an environment composed of a cluster of different machines.

Kaggle community

First, let's think about the data. As previously mentioned, there are many sites on the web that make datasets available to consult and analyze. A very interesting site to suggest is Kaggle (**kaggle.com**). **Kaggle** is a *web-based community* of data scientists, primarily specializing in machine learning. In addition to offering many curiosities, competitions and training regarding data analysis and the study of predictive models, it provides its visitors with many datasets covering different topics.

Browsing through the different datasets available, let's choose one that is right for us. Let's choose for example the *Russell 3000 stock history dataset*:

https://www.kaggle.com/datasets/williecosta/russell-3000-stock-history

As shown in the following figure (*Figure 8.15*):

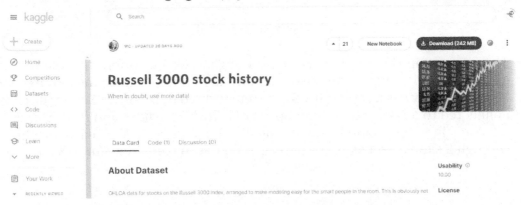

Figure 8.15: *Russell 3000 stock history dataset in Kaggle*

From the dataset page, it is possible to download a 242 MB **archive.zip** file by pressing the *black* button at the top right. Once the ZIP archive file has been downloaded, it must be decompressed and inside you will find a **prices.csv** file which, once extracted, will occupy over 800 MB of memory.

Saturn.io cluster

On the Internet, there are various paid services that make clusters available to be able to perform calculations. Among them is one in particular that supports the Dask library and offers a comfortable environment to work from: Saturn. io. This service offers a series of Data Science applications that allow you to carry out distributed programming with Python and Dask in a simple way, but also with other specific languages in data analysis and statistics such as **R**, as shown in *Figure 8.16*. Furthermore, **Saturn.io** also offers online support via chat and a series of interesting articles on Dask, cluster, and other applications related to Data Science on clusters:

Figure 8.16: *Saturn.io*

The interesting thing is that after user registration, it offers the visitor the opportunity to configure and use a simple cluster of four machines for *free* for *30 hours*. In my case, I configured a system formed by a *Jupyter Server*, directly connected to a Dask cluster composed of a *Task Scheduler* and *three workers*. All done in a few minutes, selecting the characteristics of each machine, through a simple process of options from the web page (see *Figure 8.17*):

Figure 8.17: *Guided configuration of single machines of the cluster on Saturn.io*

Once configured, start all the machines. Press the **Start** button for both the Jupyter Server and the Dask cluster. You will immediately see the startup steps of the individual machines appear in the boxes with the number of machines present in each stage, as shown in Figure 8.18. The entire *boot process* takes a few minutes:

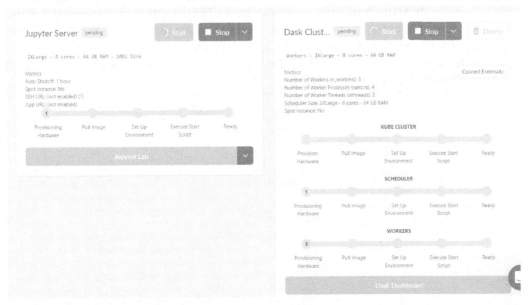

Figure 8.18: *Startup steps of the machines of the Dask cluster*

Finally, when all machines are operational, the boot steps disappear as shown in Figure 8.19:

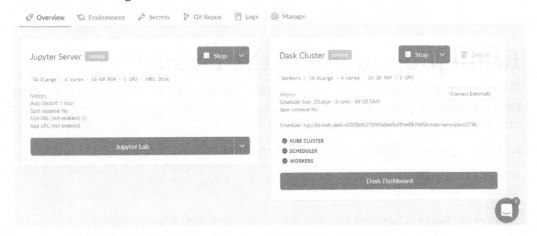

Figure 8.19: *The operational Dask cluster with all machines started*

Uploading data to the cluster

Before you begin programming your cluster, you will need to upload the **prices.csv** data file to your system. To be able to do this, you need to use **Jupyter Lab**. Open the application on the Jupyter Server by pressing the *blue* button at the bottom and once opened, go to the Jupyter file system. Create a folder under *workspace*, calling it for example data, and then start uploading the file. Given the *size* of the file, the operation will take a few minutes. At the end of the operation, you will find the icon of the **prices.csv** file in the newly created directory (see Figure 8.20):

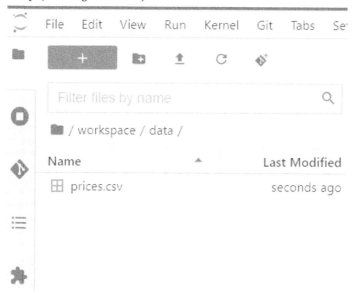

Figure 8.20: *Uploading dataset CSV file to Jupyter Lab*

Begin programming the cluster

Now everything should be ready and configured to start working with programming. Open a new Jupyter Notebook on the Jupyter Server and start importing the following modules:

```
from dask_saturn import SaturnCluster

from distributed import Client


cluster = SaturnCluster()

client = Client(cluster)

client
```

As we can see these were not present in our *single-machine system*. In fact, to work in a cluster it is necessary to import specific modules of the cluster environment on which you are working. However, they are provided by the host system and there is nothing to worry about. Then import the **SaturnCluster** class from the **dask_saturn** module and launch a cluster instance. Furthermore, to make Dask understand that you are working on this type of system and not on a single machine (default situation), you must also instantiate a client provided by the distributed module.

We are finally ready to import the libraries we need for data analysis. They are practically the same that are used in single-machine systems:

```
import dask.dataframe as dd
```

```
import pandas as pd
```

In the previous section, we uploaded the **prices.csv** file to the Jupyter Server. But the work is not yet complete. In fact, our system includes five different machines, each with its own memory. It is therefore necessary to add data synchronization code between the Jupyter Server and the workers so that this data is accessible to all machines:

```
from dask_saturn import RegisterFiles, sync_files
```

```
client.register_worker_plugin(RegisterFiles())
```

```
sync_files(client, 'data')
```

This way, all datasets imported into the Jupyter Server data folder are accessible to all machines in the cluster. Running this cell in the Notebook, you will notice that the operation will take several minutes before being completed. At the end of the execution, you will get as result, in output, the situation of the file system synchronized between all the machines in the cluster:

```
./
```

```
./prices.csv
```

Now, we can finally import the data contained in the **prices.csv** file into a Dask DataFrame. To do this we write the same line of code that we used previously:

```
ddf = dd.read_csv('data/prices.csv')
```

The execution will be very fast because in reality no data will have been loaded. In fact, if we look at the content of the newly created Dask DataFrame we will see that only the structure without data inside will have been loaded:

```
ddf
```

Obtaining the data structure shown in *Figure 8.21*:

Dask DataFrame Structure:

	Unnamed: 0	symbol	date	open	high	low	close	volume	adjusted
npartitions=13									
	int64	object	object	float64	float64	float64	float64	int64	float64
	...	...	...	...	...	...	...	...	...
...	...	...	...	...	...	...	...	...	...
	...	...	...	...	...	...	...	...	...
	...	...	...	...	...	...	...	...	...

Dask Name: read-csv, 13 tasks

Figure 8.21: *Structure of the Dask DataFrame on the cluster*

In order to load it, we have to use:

```
ddf.compute()
```

Only by invoking the **compute()** method do we parse the data contained in the CSV file. In my case, however, I will get an error message informing me of a problem with the data types:

```
ValueError: Mismatched dtypes found in `pd.read_csv`/`pd.read_table`.
```

As we can see, although Pandas and Dask use the same syntax, Dask is more demanding on the **read_csv()** method than its counterpart in **pandas**. In fact, if you try to load the CSV file with the latter, you will not get any error messages. However, in the following output text (*Figure* 8.22), the error suggests how to solve the problem:

```
+--------+---------+----------+
| Column | Found   | Expected |
+--------+---------+----------+
| volume | float64 | int64    |
+--------+---------+----------+

Usually this is due to dask's dtype inference failing, and
*may* be fixed by specifying dtypes manually by adding:

dtype={'volume': 'float64'}

to the call to `read_csv`/`read_table`.

Alternatively, provide `assume_missing=True` to interpret
all unspecified integer columns as floats.
```

Figure 8.22: *Error message while importing the CSV file*

We then rewrite the **read_csv()** method adding the suggested changes:

```
ddf = dd.read_csv('data/prices.csv', dtype={'volume': 'float64'})

ddf.compute()
```

This time everything will be fine and we will get data loading in a Dask DataFrame as shown in *Figure 8.23*:

	Unnamed: 0	symbol	date	open	high	low	close	volume	adjusted
0	1	FLWS	1999-08-03	21.7500	22.2500	17.875	18.1875	9543400.0	18.1875
1	2	FLWS	1999-08-04	18.9375	20.5000	16.875	17.0000	4731800.0	17.0000
2	3	FLWS	1999-08-05	17.0625	17.1250	13.500	16.0000	2851900.0	16.0000
3	4	FLWS	1999-08-06	16.0000	17.7500	16.000	17.0000	1411800.0	17.0000
4	5	FLWS	1999-08-09	17.9375	17.9375	15.875	16.0000	583000.0	16.0000
...	...	...	...	...	...	...	...	...	...
991985	12995441	ZUMZ	2022-11-07	22.4100	22.8800	22.020	22.6700	172900.0	22.6700
991986	12995442	ZUMZ	2022-11-08	22.8700	23.3600	22.220	22.4700	311800.0	22.4700
991987	12995443	ZUMZ	2022-11-09	22.3600	22.4300	20.640	20.7800	239800.0	20.7800
991988	12995444	ZUMZ	2022-11-10	21.8300	23.6900	21.780	23.5100	327600.0	23.5100
991989	12995445	ZUMZ	2022-11-11	23.7700	24.6200	23.670	24.2800	205000.0	24.2800

12995445 rows × 9 columns

Figure 8.23: *DataFrame obtained from prices.csv*

Let's see in more detail the characteristics of DataFrame:

```
ddf.info(memory_usage="deep")

<class 'dask.dataframe.core.DataFrame'>

Columns: 9 entries, Unnamed: 0 to adjusted

dtypes: object(2), float64(6), int64(1)

memory usage: 892.3 MB
```

As we can see the data type of the **Date** column is not **DateTime**, but object. Also, the first column, containing the indexes of the rows in the CSV file is useless and we can delete it. Then we rewrite:

```
ddf = dd.read_csv('data/prices.csv', dtype={'volume': 'float64'}, parse_dates = ['date'])

del ddf['Unnamed: 0']

ddf
```

At this point, the structure and data types are correct as we can see in the following figure (*Figure* 8.24):

Dask DataFrame Structure:

	symbol	date	open	high	low	close	volume	adjusted
npartitions=13								
	object	datetime64[ns]	float64	float64	float64	float64	float64	float64
	...	...	...	...	...	...	...	...
...	...	...	...	...	...	...	...	...
	...	...	...	...	...	...	...	...
	...	...	...	...	...	...	...	...

Dask Name: drop_by_shallow_copy, 26 tasks

Figure 8.24: *Data structure of the correct DataFrame*

It is also interesting to see how our Dask DataFrame has been automatically divided into *thirteen* partitions.

We just have to value it:

```
ddf.compute()
```

Obtaining the desired results as shown in *Figure* 8.25:

	symbol	date	open	high	low	close	volume	adjusted
0	FLWS	1999-08-03	21.7500	22.2500	17.875	18.1875	9543400.0	18.1875
1	FLWS	1999-08-04	18.9375	20.5000	16.875	17.0000	4731800.0	17.0000
2	FLWS	1999-08-05	17.0625	17.1250	13.500	16.0000	2851900.0	16.0000
3	FLWS	1999-08-06	16.0000	17.7500	16.000	17.0000	1411800.0	17.0000
4	FLWS	1999-08-09	17.9375	17.9375	15.875	16.0000	583000.0	16.0000
...	...	...	...	...	...	...	...	...
991985	ZUMZ	2022-11-07	22.4100	22.8800	22.020	22.6700	172900.0	22.6700
991986	ZUMZ	2022-11-08	22.8700	23.3600	22.220	22.4700	311800.0	22.4700
991987	ZUMZ	2022-11-09	22.3600	22.4300	20.640	20.7800	239800.0	20.7800
991988	ZUMZ	2022-11-10	21.8300	23.6900	21.780	23.5100	327600.0	23.5100
991989	ZUMZ	2022-11-11	23.7700	24.6200	23.670	24.2800	205000.0	24.2800

12995445 rows × 8 columns

Figure 8.25: *Computed DataFrame task*

At this point, we can apply an operation on the DataFrame. We choose a medium complex operation that allows us to aggregate the result by grouping values on certain columns:

```
mean = ddf.groupby(['symbol',ddf['date'].dt.year])[['open','high','low',
'close','volume']].mean()
```

At this point, since we are also interested in the performance aspect, we will introduce the Jupyter Notebook magic word, **%%time**, which allows us to measure the time elapsed during the execution of the instructions in the cell. We then perform the grouping operation on the Dask DataFrame:

```
%%time
```

```
mean.compute()
```

Obtaining as calculation times:

CPU times: user 6.23 ms, sys: 12.3 ms, total: 18.5 ms

Wall time: 2.04 s

As a result, the Dask DataFrame is as shown in the following figure (see *Figure 8.26*):

symbol	date	open	high	low	close	volume
A	1999	33.984561	35.447962	33.226037	34.580651	5.739997e+06
	2000	49.966151	51.826004	48.017594	49.877136	4.238259e+06
	2001	23.837856	24.570816	23.174646	23.912350	3.311148e+06
	2002	16.433482	16.814270	16.050480	16.414407	3.700359e+06
	2003	14.447368	14.686315	14.223693	14.478762	3.244672e+06
...	...	...	...	...	...	...
ZUMZ	2018	23.494422	23.925498	22.961633	23.433625	4.686191e+05
	2019	26.504286	26.986825	26.019841	26.532857	4.514512e+05
	2020	27.748182	28.426561	26.997787	27.699881	3.554577e+05
	2021	44.467183	45.372540	43.545119	44.431587	2.604456e+05
	2022	32.647477	33.432982	31.858028	32.622982	3.536784e+05

53124 rows × 5 columns

Figure 8.26: Result of grouping on the Task DataFrame

Now, for comparison, we will perform the same operations but work locally with a **Pandas** DataFrame:

```
df = pd.read_csv('data/prices.csv', dtype={'volume': 'float64'}, parse_
dates = ['date'])
```

```
del df['Unnamed: 0']
```

```
df
```

And in the following cell of the notebook:

```
%%time
```

```
df.groupby(['symbol',df['date'].dt.year])[['open','high','low','close','
volume']].mean()
```

This time we will get the following processing times:

CPU times: user 1.96 s, sys: 396 ms, total: 2.35 s

Wall time: 2.35 s

As we can see, the execution times are much higher than in the previous case. Here we are on the order of seconds, while before with Dask, on the order of *milliseconds*. And things will change more and more as the size of the DataFrame and the complexity of the operations to be performed on it are increasing.

Just as an example, let's quadruple the size of the DataFrame in question, concatenating four copies of it together:

```
mddf = dd.concat([ddf, ddf, ddf, ddf])
```

```
mddf.info(memory_usage="deep")
```

```
mddf
```

In this way, we obtained a considerably larger Dask DataFrame, as we can see from the result of the previous lines of code and in *Figure 8.27*:

```
<class 'dask.dataframe.core.DataFrame'>
```

```
Columns: 8 entries, symbol to adjusted
```

```
dtypes: datetime64[ns](1), object(1), float64(6)
```

```
memory usage: 3.1 GB
```

Dask DataFrame Structure:

	symbol	date	open	high	low	close	volume	adjusted
npartitions=52								
	object	datetime64[ns]	float64	float64	float64	float64	float64	float64
	...	...	...	...	...	...	...	...
...	...		...	...	...	...	...	...
	...		...	...	...	...	...	...
		...	...	...	...	...	...	...

Dask Name: concat, 78 tasks

Figure 8.27: *Structure of the quadrupled DataFrame*

We repeat the same operations performed previously:

```
mddf.compute()
```

```
mean = mddf.groupby(['symbol',mddf['date'].dt.year])[['open','high','low','close','volume']].mean()
```

```
%%time
```

```
mean.compute()
```

This time, we get the following result:

CPU times: user 15.9 ms, sys: 5.77 ms, total: 21.7 ms

Wall time: 2.92 s

As we can see, things haven't changed much since the previous case. Now, let us try to do the same DataFrame quadrupled but working on **pandas**:

```
mdf = pd.concat([df, df, df, df])
```

```
mdf.info(memory_usage="deep")
```

```
mdf
```

```
%%time
```

```
mdf.groupby(['symbol',mdf['date'].dt.year])[['open','high','low','close','volume']].mean()
```

And I get *four* times as long as we expected without parallelization:

CPU times: user 7.98 s, sys: 1.39 s, total: 9.37 s

Wall time: 9.36 s

Conclusion

In this chapter, we have seen how it is possible to extend the computing capabilities of Data Science using systems distributed as clusters using the Dask library. We have seen how it is possible to scale our code built with pandas from a single-machine system to distributed systems. You have also seen how there are clusters on the web that offer specific services and allow you to work through Jupyter Notebook on codes that use the Dask library. Through some practical examples, you have become so familiar with these environments and how they are much more performing than using a single machine, allowing us to also approach Big Data. In the next chapter, we will also extend these concepts to **Artificial Intelligence (AI)** in particular to those branches such as *Machine Learning* and *Deep Learning* with *neural networks* that are enormously gaining ground thanks to parallel computing on distributed systems.

References

- https://saturncloud.io/blog/what-is-dask/
- https://saturncloud.io/blog/should-i-use-dask/

## CHAPTER 9

Exploring the Potential of AI with Parallel Computing

With this chapter, we complete the part of parallel computing applications by closing with the last topic which is **Artificial Intelligence**. This computer science discipline deals with the development of applications that are able to simulate human intelligence. It is a complex objective that requires enormous studies and powerful technologies but which in recent years has been making great strides. Among all the possible applications there is **Machine Learning**, which in particular is the branch of artificial intelligence that focuses on the simulation of human learning. This one, in particular, has found its most representative programming language in Python, having a series of well-stocked libraries of algorithms and pre-set models, such as **sci-kit-learn**. Even more advanced is **Deep Learning**, a subgroup of Machine Learning that is characterized by the use of artificial neural networks that lead to the creation of applications capable of recognizing information and analyzing data such as images, sounds and texts. All these disciplines require a large computational effort for the processing of very complex algorithms and huge data necessary for their learning phase. The use of parallel computing is therefore necessary with the integration of GPUs in parallel computing, significantly reducing processing times. Furthermore, recently, for these systems, their processing on distributed systems such as clusters of computers equipped with GPUs has been proposed, and this is through the **Dask** framework. We will therefore see a series of examples that will cover all these cases, thus providing some basic ideas on how to approach these systems and for those wishing to learn more, it will offer a basis on which to start working.

Structure

In this chapter, we will cover the following topics:

- AI and parallel computing
- Parallel and distributed Machine Learning
- Parallel and distributed Deep Learning
- PyTorch and TensorFlow
- Dask e SaturnCloud clusters

Artificial Intelligence (AI)

A recent field of development that closely involves computers and data analysis is **Artificial Intelligence (AI)**. With this term, we generally refer to *systems*, or *machines*, which somehow manage to imitate human intelligence, especially as regards learning. These systems, often composed of various very complex algorithms, are able to continuously improve themselves in carrying out a given activity, thanks to learning processes that *gain experience* on the basis of the information collected. The more information they collect, the better their ability will be.

Although the term *Artificial Intelligence* is always mentally associated with images of *robots* similar to human beings, in reality, they are completely different realities. Today these AI systems are already quite widespread and operate in different forms in our daily lives. They are at most incorporeal, almost abstract entities that manifest themselves in very different ways from what the common image sees as androids. More commonly they manage search engines or operate behind social networks and other service distributors to study our habits, our tastes and our needs. These systems study our past choices and on the basis of them reconstruct what our future needs could be, proposing, for example, a series of films on *YouTube* or topics in which we might be interested. Their purpose (at least the most obvious one) is therefore to facilitate the user's choice of material of greatest interest, without wasting time among thousands and thousands of possible choices.

Another recent application of artificial intelligence systems is that of **Chatbots**. These chats, often present on the websites of service providers, are available to the customer to collect requests for information or problems encountered and suggest to the customer the shortest way to obtain a solution, such as suggesting the completion and delivery of a form, a phone number of a specific employee or even some steps to solve the problem from home. The skill required by these chatbots is to best replace a human operator by offering customer listening services 24 *hours a day*.

On the other hand, the more profound use of artificial intelligence is less evident, than that of learning by parameterizable model systems, using the flow of large amounts of incoming data to become increasingly accurate and be able to make forecasts of complex phenomena. This approach has given rise to a number of disciplines such as **Machine Learning** and **Deep Learning**.

AI, Machine Learning, and Deep Learning

Artificial intelligence is often used interchangeably with the terms Machine Learning and Deep Learning. However, there are clear differences between these concepts. Machine Learning is a *computational technique* focused on the development of systems capable of learning and improving performance in specific activities, based on the data provided. So it can certainly be asserted that Machine Learning is a phenomenon of artificial intelligence, but the opposite cannot be said, that is, that artificial intelligence is equivalent to Machine Learning. A scheme that can help to understand the differences between these concepts is shown in the following figure (*Figure.9.1*):

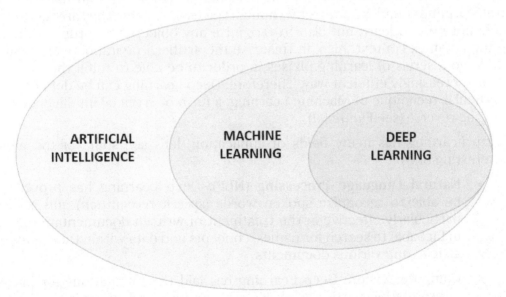

Figure 9.1: *Differences between AI, Machine Learning, and Deep Learning*

Deep Learning is something even more complex. It is still focused on developing systems that can learn but are even more similar in doing so to humans. These systems are based on *artificial neural networks* distributed in multiple layers similar to neurons in the human brain, as shown in *Figure 9.2*:

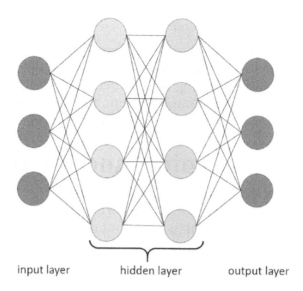

input layer   hidden layer   output layer

Figure 9.2: *An example of an artificial neural network*

They are complex systems that are capable of extracting information and transforming complex data such as human voices or images. They are therefore able not only to learn but also to *recognize* any objects or words within an often complex context. Also, in this case the artificial neural networks must undergo a series of learning phases in order to be able to fulfill their duties in an increasingly efficient way. Therefore, Deep Learning can be defined as a particular technique of Machine Learning, a form of artificial intelligence but not the reverse (see *Figure 9.1*).

Deep Learning has many fields of application, let's see some of the most interesting ones:

- **Natural Language Processing (NLP)**: Deep Learning has proven to be able to recognize spoken words (*speech recognition*) and is also particularly effective in the treatment of written documentation. It is in fact able to search for names, concepts and data within thousands of articles and various documents.

- **Computer vision**: Deep Learning has laid the foundations for image interpretation, particularly in *facial recognition*, and for solving problems such as locating vehicles and pedestrians from webcam images.

- **Pharmacology**: Deep Learning is able to analyze diagnostic images and learn the recognition of any anomalies. It can also learn from physiological characteristics and the discovery of pathologies.

- **Biology**: Deep Learning is proving to be very useful in *protein classification*, genomics, *cell classification*, and *analysis of protein-protein interactions*.

- **Image generation**: Deep Learning is capable of intelligently modifying images, with complex operations such as coloring black and white images, increasing image resolution, removing noise from images, and being able to compose artwork using styles of famous artists starting from basic images.

- **Web search**: Web search engines make use of Deep Learning.

- **Games**: More and more games make use of artificial intelligence, to improve strategy, and simulate human behavior in artificial opponents.

- **Robotics**: Deep Learning is finding applications in the calculation of the trajectories and dynamics of complex robotic systems for object manipulation.

Artificial intelligence, whether it is Machine Learning, Deep Learning, or something else, will soon represent the fundamental pillars of corporate *decision-making processes* of the future.

Supervised and unsupervised learning

Once the areas of learning within artificial intelligence have been defined, it is very important to introduce another fundamental concept before talking about their application in parallel computing.

All learning techniques, both Machine Learning and Deep Learning can follow *two* different approaches regarding the type of data used in the learning phase:

- Supervised learning
- Unsupervised learning

These *two* approaches differ on whether the data used is labeled or not. By *labeled*, we mean that the data is tagged with the correct answer or *not*.

Supervised learning uses data labeled with the correct answers to train models. Knowing the correct answer will be used to refine the model's capabilities in its predictions. This approach is used in *two* particular techniques:

- Classification
- Regression

Classification uses algorithms to classify the data under study. Some of the most used algorithms are:

- Logistic Regression
- K-Nearest Neighbors
- Random Forest
- Naïve Bayes
- Stochastic Gradient Descent
- Decision Trees

Regression instead uses algorithms that measure the relationship between a *dependent variable* and one or more *independent variables*. Some of the more famous ones:

- Ridge Regression
- Lasso
- Neural Network Regression
- Logistic Regression

As far as the unsupervised learning approach is concerned, the data has no additional information about their nature other than the data itself. So, algorithms of this type can work without any human supervision. This approach is the preferred one for Deep Learning.

There are *three* different techniques that follow this approach:

- Clustering
- Association
- Dimensionality reduction

Clustering is based on the similarity or differences of the data under study by grouping them according to certain characteristics. The best-known algorithm that follows this technique is **K-means clustering**.

Association is able to identify the relationship between the variables within a dataset. Relationships are not yet defined before studying the dataset.

Dimensionality reduction is a technique that serves to reduce the number of features to be studied within a dataset that can sometimes be too large. Algorithms that follow this technique must be able to reduce the number of features that distinguish the data in the dataset without compromising their integrity.

Artificial intelligence and parallel computing

As we can certainly guess, the creation of complex computer systems that are capable of carrying out forms of artificial intelligence requires enormous computing resources, and as their capabilities grow, ever more powerful computers will be required. This is why these AI systems have only become widespread in recent years. It is therefore clear that in order to be able to operate in this sector and develop AI systems that are increasingly capable of carrying out their tasks, we will have to exploit systems based on parallel computing, the only ones able to provide the necessary computing resources.

Clouds, for example, provide an abundance of computational power enabling operators and developers to easily obtain high-performance computational power at affordable prices. Prior to this development, the only computing environments available for AI had to work on only a small set of cost-prohibitive supercomputers. While if you work on single computers, you can only create simple models with long processing times and which in any case require the additional support of different GPU cards to operate. It is therefore clear that the latter case can be a choice for a study or development environment.

Parallel and distributed machine learning

As far as Machine Learning is concerned, the Python language offers ample opportunities, indeed it can be said with some certainty, that Python is the reference language for this discipline. There are many libraries available that provide Machine Learning algorithms, here are some:

- scikit-learn
- XGBoost
- LightGBM
- TensorFlow

Furthermore, many of these libraries are designed so that they can also operate on parallel systems (*parallel computing*) or even be extended in environments formed by multiple machines (*distributed computing*). This is precisely due to the fact that Machine Learning requires a lot of computing resources and therefore it is *natural* to use its algorithms on powerful systems capable of providing parallel computing.

In particular, for Machine Learning, we have some operations to carry out in which the parallel computing approach is fundamental. The most important of these is *matrix multiplication*. We have already seen in the first chapters of the book how this can greatly benefit from a correct parallel implementation, especially, if GPUs are used to perform this calculation. Multiplication between matrices is the basis of linear regression algorithms that are widely used in Machine Learning. Considerably, reducing the time of this type of calculation clearly affects the general performance of the learning phases and in the calculation of the predictions of the Machine Learning models.

Another very common operation in Machine Learning is calculating the *distance between two points*. This operation is very common in many algorithms (such as **k-means clustering**) and is performed many times within the same algorithm. Exploiting the fact that the individual distance calculation of subsequent iterations is not dependent on the other calculations in the same iteration, these calculations can be performed in parallel greatly reducing processing times.

Also, in the context of operations that could be onerous in terms of Machine Learning execution, there is **k-fold cross-validation**, which is based on the intense processing of different segments of the dataset. This method is used to validate a model and is based on excluding from the calculation one of the *k segments (fold)* into which the dataset is divided. All other *k-1 segments* are trained and then the *k-th* element is used as a test dataset. Since we are dealing with k segments, this operation is performed *k times*, each of which will exclude a different segment from training. Once *k results* are obtained, an average of them is performed. As can be understood, the *k-fold cross-validation* algorithm, if performed sequentially, will take a large amount of time, having to repeat the same operations k times. If instead brought in parallel form, where each calculation performed on one of the *k folds* is performed simultaneously, there will be a large gain from the point of view of performance.

All these operations, and others, if they are processed in a parallel computing system, make the Machine Learning activity much more efficient and capable of tackling more complex problems and processing larger datasets, with an increase in the forecasting capacity of the models thus generated, and also reducing processing times, which in a single machine system would soon become prohibitive.

Machine learning with scikit-learn

Scikit-learn is currently the most used Python library in Machine Learning and provides users with all the main algorithms to cover the most commonly used types:

- Classification
- Clustering

- Regression
- Dimensionality reduction

Scikit-learn is a well-documented library and there are many examples, documentation and various applications available on the web. So it is normal to start working with Machine Learning starting from this library.

To get familiar with how Machine Learning works with **scikit-learn**, let's look at a simple example of *linear regression*. Among the various examples, this one is very simple to understand and therefore lends itself perfectly as an illustrative case even for people who are not familiar with Machine Learning. This technique is based on the construction of a very simple model of a system that is supposed to behave linearly, to predict the result from a given value of a variable of this system.

For simplicity, we use as study data points generated around a straight line that distances themselves by a random value from the correct linear trend. In this way, we will simulate the data coming from a phenomenon that responds to a linear behavior from which we will have to obtain the linear trend (intercept and coefficient of the slope of the straight line). To do this, we generate a dataset of 30 *values* from the equation of a straight line with slope **0.3** and coefficient **1.0** to which we add a random noise that simulates the deviation of the values from the correct trend:

```
import numpy as np

x = 50 * np.random.random((30, 1))

y = 0.3 * x + 1.0 + np.random.normal(size=x.shape)
```

Once the **dataset(x,y)** has been generated, in which **x** will be the variables and **y** will represent the labels with the results, we can divide it into *two* parts. We will use one of these as a *training set* and the other as a *testing set*. To do this, there is a convenient function provided by **scikit-learn** called **train_test_split()** which allows us to split a dataset based on a percentage defined by the **test_size** parameter. So, if we want *20% of the dataset* to be for testing we will write the following code:

```
from sklearn.model_selection import train_test_split

x_train, x_test, y_train, y_test = train_test_split(x, y, test_size=0.2)
```

Now that we have all the data necessary for learning and validating the model, we need to create one. Since this is a Linear Regression, it is possible to instantiate a specific model simply by defining the **LinearRegression()** constructor. Once the model has been generated, we will move on to the learning phase, using the **fit()** method and passing it to the training set as an argument:

```
from sklearn.linear_model import LinearRegression
model = LinearRegression()
model.fit(x_train, y_train)
```

As we can see, **scikit-learn** makes the implementation of Machine Learning very simple for us, condensing everything into just *two lines of code*. Once executed, we will have a model that will be able to predict the corresponding values of **y** by passing it values of the variable **x**. We have said that this model is very simple and is based on the parameterization of the equation of a straight line in which the two parameters (intercept and slope coefficient) are gradually evaluated based on the learning phase. If we want to see what the values of these two parameters are, we write the following code:

```
print(model.intercept_)
print(model.coef_)
```

Obtaining as a result, the two parameters evaluated:

```
[1.41274643]
[[0.29301879]]
```

These values differ slightly from the real ones: **1** and **3**. Let's now move on to the evaluation of this model by testing its forecasting capabilities. To submit the model to an evaluation test, the **predict()** method is used, to which the testing set is passed as an argument:

```
y_new = model.predict(x_test)
```

The result will be a list of y values corresponding to the **x** passed in the testing set. By checking the difference between the expected values **y_new** and the real ones **y_test** it is possible to evaluate the goodness of the model just created. Since these are numerical values that describe points around a straight line in a *Cartesian graph*, the best way to evaluate the goodness of this model will be to represent them graphically. To do this we can use the **matplotlib** library which is very useful for creating graphs to be displayed in the Jupyter Notebook with a few lines of code:

```
import matplotlib.pyplot as plt
plt.figure()
plt.scatter(x,y)
plt.scatter(x_test,y_new, c='red')
```

By executing the cell of the Notebook containing the previous code, we will obtain as a result a graph very similar to the one shown in the following figure (*Figure 9.3*):

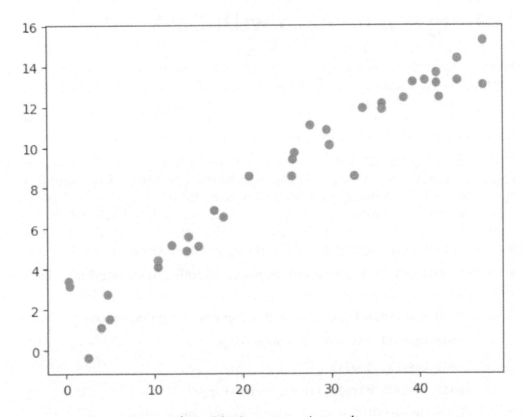

Figure 9.3: *Linear regression results*
(in blue points from the training set, in red the points evaluated by the testing set)

To evaluate the goodness of the model we are using, the **score()** method can be used. This method allows us to calculate the coefficient of determination, known as **R^2**, for both *training* and *test* data. The maximum value is **1** and the minimum value is **0**. The closer this value is to 1, the better the *fit* of the model will be. So, this value is a great parameter to judge the forecasting abilities of a trained model:

```
model.score(x_train, y_train)
```

```
0.920774873832153
```

```
model.score(x_test, y_test)
```

```
0.9011230374736323
```

Scaling scikit-learn with Dask-ML

In a similar way to what we saw in the previous *Chapter 8, Scaling Your Data Science Applications with Dask*, can be an excellent solution for scaling machine learning applications in distributed environments. Like the **Dask DataFrames** for the **Pandas** library and the **Dask Arrays** for **NumPy**, there is a consideration for Machine Learning too: the **Dask-ML module** is able to extend the **scikit-learn** library on distributed environments such as clusters.

This module takes advantage of one of scikit-learn's parallel computing features: **joblib**. Many scikit-learn algorithms have been implemented to run in parallel when using **joblib**, which provides *thread-based* and *process-based* parallelism natively. Dask-ML will use this capability to distribute these computations across a cluster. This same mechanism is also used to implement machine learning models of other libraries such as **XGboost**.

To install **Dask-ML** in a virtual environment specifically created for Machine Learning:

1. Open a command shell, and enter the following command:

   ```
   conda install dask-ml -c conda-forge
   conda install joblib
   conda install matplotlib -c conda-forge
   ```

2. Once the installation is complete, we will open a Notebook on Jupyter:

   ```
   from dask.distributed import Client
   client = Client()
   ```

3. Also, **Dask-ML**, similar to Dask, provides a set of methods and functions corresponding to the original libraries but which are able to work on distributed environments. In this case, the **train_test_split()** function of scikit-learn will be replaced with the same function of the Dask-ML library:

   ```
   from dask_ml.model_selection import train_test_split
   x_train, x_test, y_train, y_test = train_test_split(x, y, test_size=0.2)
   ```

4. Like the scikit-learn functions, the models are also provided in their own version distributed by Dask-ML. Let's replace in the code the **LineaRegression** class of scikit-learn with that of Dask-ML. At this point, also the learning methods **fit()** and evaluation **predict()** will be those provided by Dask-ML, adapted to work in distributed environments:

```
from dask_ml.linear_model import LinearRegression
```

```
model = LinearRegression()
```

But before moving on to the learning phase, we need to add the **joblib** library. This particular library allows Python libraries like scikit-learn to work in parallel on a single machine. With **parallel_backend** provided by this library, it is possible to do it also taking into account the features of Dask. In this way, we activate the execution of the code in parallel computing mode even in a *distributed environment*: a further enhancement to the performance of this library:

```
import joblib
```

```
from joblib import parallel_backend
```

```
with parallel_backend('dask'):
 model.fit(x_train,y_train)
 y_new = model.predict(x_test)
```

5. Now that we have trained and evaluated the model in parallel, we can check the results graphically, as we did before:

```
import matplotlib.pyplot as plt
```

```
plt.figure()
plt.scatter(x_train,y_train)
plt.scatter(x_test,y_new, c='red')
```

6. Running the code, you will get a graph similar to the one shown in the following figure (*Figure 9.4*):

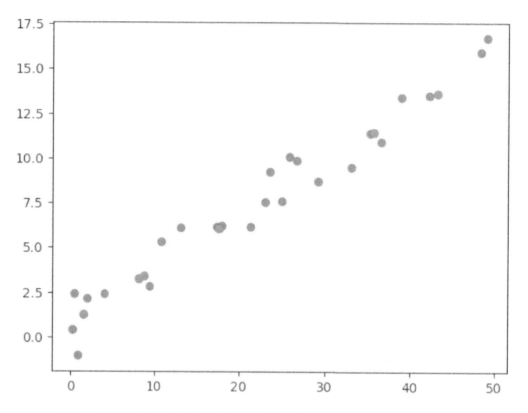

Figure 9.4: *Results obtained by the model with Dask and parallel computing*

Parallel and distributed deep learning

At the base of Deep Learning are neural networks and due to their particular nature, they are excellent for discovering the relationships and structures that are hidden behind unsupervised data. Their ability to *learn* and *analyze*, which in a certain way simulates the way the human brain learns, makes them suitable for working on data that is not strictly numerical in nature, such as images and sounds. This is why Deep Learning is particularly focused on *Natural Language Processing* and *Computer Vision*.

Artificial neural networks are complex structures that require huge computing resources to operate efficiently. The typical neural networks used in Deep Learning make use of millions of parameters that make up a model. These systems will also have to take advantage of a large amount of data for their learning. So, this process is computationally intensive that will take an enormous amount of time in *single-machine systems*, often several days. Furthermore, it must be considered that many datasets are too large to be contained within the memory of a single machine. Fortunately, the particular layered structure of neurons in a neural network is perfectly suited to distributed systems and therefore allows you to make the most of parallel computing. The models used for Deep Learning can in turn be distributed over the different layers of the neural network, and its parameters (weights) are in turn distributed among the different neurons present in each layer. So it is clear that we can take advantage of these features to distribute the load and information of the models used and their relative calculation on different machines in a distributed system.

There are several methods to distribute and thereby parallelize computation when training on clusters of machines. These methods can be used singly or in combination:

- **Parallel processing**
    - Multi-core processing
    - GPU processing
- **Distributed training**
    - Data parallelism
    - Model parallelism

By applying these methods, it will be possible to convert Deep Learning algorithms into parallel algorithms, in which the single tasks will be assigned to the different cores (multi-core processing), or even more efficiently, to the different GPUs present on the machines (GPUs processing). As for the datasets, since these tend to be enormous in size, they can be divided and then distributed on different machines (*data parallelism*), thus reducing memory overloads. Even Deep Learning models, in turn, can be divided into smaller parts, assigning a set of parameters for each machine (*model parallelism*). Both of these methods will help reduce learning time significantly. However, **data parallelism** is often preferred over **model parallelism**. In fact, in the latter case, there are some synchronization operations that require more processing time, and therefore data parallelism is the fastest approach between the *two*. On the other hand, model parallelism produces better predictive results.

PyTorch and TensorFlow

Among the various possibilities offered by the Python language to work with Deep Learning, there are *two open-source frameworks* that are very popular lately:

- PyTorch
- TensorFlow

PyTorch is a relatively new Deep Learning framework. This library was developed by the *Facebook AI Lab research group* and open-sourced on *GitHub* in 2017. Its main purpose was to implement applications for **Natural Language Processing (NLP)**. PyTorch soon gained some success for some of its characteristics such as simplicity, efficient use of memory and being largely native, it produces code with higher processing speed.

TensorFlow is also an *open-source framework* built specifically for Deep Learning. This library was developed by *Google* and first released in 2015. Compared to PyTorch, **TensorFlow** is much more *used* and *popular*. This is not only because it has been present for longer, but above all because of the large amount of documentation available and the abundant support from other technologies that facilitate scalability on distributed systems and on different platforms, including *Android*. Furthermore, since 2017, TensorFlow has integrated **Keras**, another framework for Deep Learning that has existed for several years and boasts a large literature in this discipline. TensorFlow is currently the *preferred tool* for many professionals and researchers, and already has many models already trained.

Deep learning example with PyTorch

Moving on to the practical part, we will see one of these two libraries together. Let's choose PyTorch to implement a Deep Learning example. We will use a neural network to analyze a dataset of images and somehow recognize their content.

PyTorch installation

To install PyTorch on *Anaconda*, go to **Anaconda Navigator** and in the **Environments** panel select the virtual environment dedicated to Deep Learning. If you haven't done so yet, you can create a new one by pressing the **Create** button as shown in *Figure 9.5*:

Figure 9.5: *Pressing the Create button, a new virtual environment is generated*

At this point, a dialog box will appear in which you will enter the name of the virtual environment to be created and the Python version. Choose version **3.10.9** as shown in *Figure 9.6*:

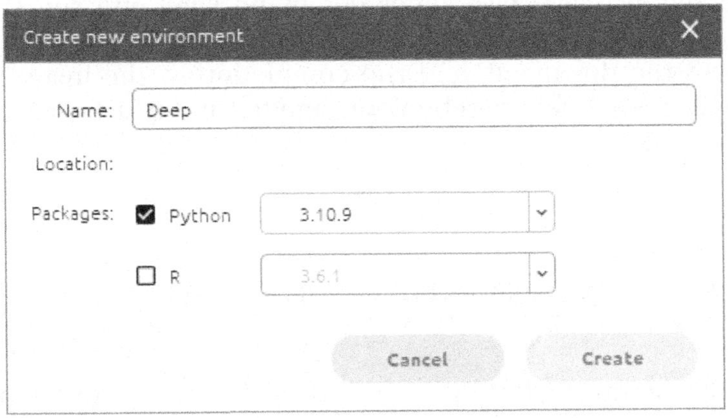

Figure 9.6: Dialog box for creating a new virtual environment

Once the virtual environment dedicated to Deep Learning has been generated and activated, we can start installing the packages needed to work with PyTorch. To do this, visit the PyTorch website (**https://pytorch.org/get-started/locally/**) and make the appropriate selections based on your work platform on the table of system features displayed in the center of the page, such as shown in *Figure 9.7*:

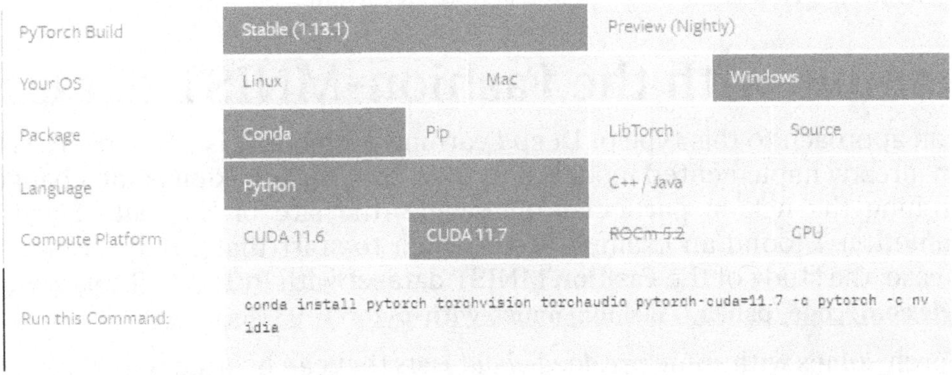

Figure 9.7: *Panel for selecting packages to install from the PyTorch site*

Once you have selected the current configuration of the platform you use, the **conda** command will be shown as follows with a list of all the necessary packages:

```
conda install pytorch torchvision torchaudio pytorch-cuda=11.7 -c pytorch
-c nvidia
```

Then open the virtual environment command shell and run the preceding **conda** command. At the package installation request, enter Y to confirm, and wait for both the download, and the completion of the installation. At this point, we will open a new notebook on Jupyter and test the installation with the following lines:

```
import torch
```

```
torch.__version__
```

Hopefully, you will get the PyTorch version as a result:

'1.13.1'

And then we test interfacing with CUDA through the following code:

```
torch.cuda.is_available()
```

```
True
```


```
torch.version.cuda
```

'11.7'

If you get these results without any error messages, then the installation of these packages went well and they integrate seamlessly with CUDA and NVIDIA drives to use GPUs to process data in parallel.

Example with the Fashion-MNIST dataset

For an approach to this type of Deep Learning problem, it is advisable to start from already implemented models and then continue, making some changes. Searching the net, in particular on **Kaggle** (the site of the *Data Scientist community*), I found an example from which to start that can be useful for our case: the study of the **Fashion MNIST dataset** with PyTorch. (**https://www. kaggle.com/code/pankajj/fashion-mnist-with-pytorch-93-accuracy**).

PyTorch comes with some *pre-loaded datasets* that can be used to test models. Inside the library you can find the following:

- Image datasets
- Text datasets
- Audio datasets

For our example, that is, recognition of objects within images, we can use the **Fashion-MNIST dataset**. This dataset consists of around 60,000 small-sized (*28x28 pixels*) black and white (grayscale) garment images taken from **Zalando**. A dataset that is right up our alley.

As for the model used, on Kaggle we find the convolutional Neural Network **FashionCNN()** implemented which we can use with our example. So, once we open a new Notebook on Jupyter, we import all the necessary modules into the first cell:

```
import torch
import torch.nn as nn
from torch.autograd import Variable


import torchvision
from torchvision import datasets
from torchvision.transforms import ToTensor
from torch.utils.data import DataLoader


import datetime
```

At this point, we start by extracting the data from the dataset and distributing them in a *training* set and a *testing* set, necessary for the *learning* and *testing* phase:

```
training_data = datasets.FashionMNIST(
    root="data",
    train=True,
    download=True,
    transform=ToTensor()
)


test_data = datasets.FashionMNIST(
    root="data",
    train=False,
    download=True,
    transform=ToTensor()
)
```

To understand the type of images used for both the training set and the testing set, let's visualize the first nine images of the *training* set:

```python
import matplotlib.pyplot as plt

labels_map = {
        0: "T-Shirt",
        1: "Trouser",
        2: "Pullover",
        3: "Dress",
        4: "Coat",
        5: "Sandal",
        6: "Shirt",
        7: "Sneaker",
        8: "Bag",
        9: "Ankle Boot",
}
figure = plt.figure(figsize=(8, 8))
cols, rows = 3, 3
for i in range(1, cols * rows + 1):
    sample_idx = torch.randint(len(training_data), size=(1,)).item()
    img, label = training_data[sample_idx]
    figure.add_subplot(rows, cols, i)
    plt.title(labels_map[label])
    plt.axis("off")
    plt.imshow(img.squeeze(), cmap="gray")
plt.show()
```

If we execute the previous code, we will get a table of *nine black and white images* of different garments each of which is labeled with one of the *ten garments* described in the **labels_map**, as shown in the following figure (*Figure 9.8*):

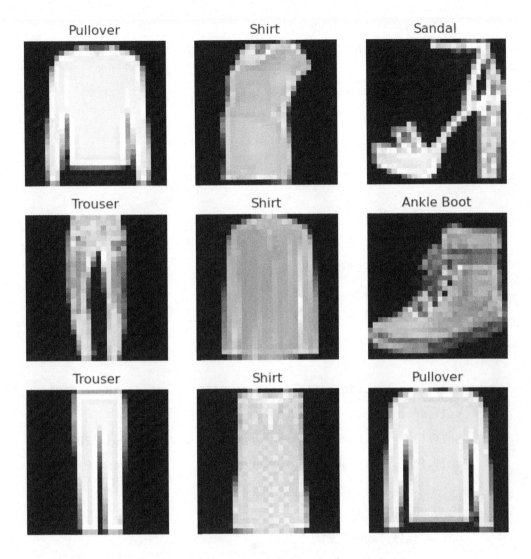

Figure 9.8: *Some images of clothing in the training set*

Now in the next cell of the Jupyter Notebook, we write the code related to the **Convolutionary Neural Network FashionCNN**:

```
class FashionCNN(nn.Module):


    def __init__(self):
        super(FashionCNN, self).__init__()
```

```python
        self.layer1 = nn.Sequential(
                nn.Conv2d(in_channels=1, out_channels=32, kernel_size=3,
padding=1),
            nn.BatchNorm2d(32),
            nn.ReLU(),
            nn.MaxPool2d(kernel_size=2, stride=2)
        )


        self.layer2 = nn.Sequential(
            nn.Conv2d(in_channels=32, out_channels=64, kernel_size=3),
            nn.BatchNorm2d(64),
            nn.ReLU(),
            nn.MaxPool2d(2)
        )


        self.fc1 = nn.Linear(in_features=64*6*6, out_features=600)
        self.drop = nn.Dropout2d(0.25)
        self.fc2 = nn.Linear(in_features=600, out_features=120)
        self.fc3 = nn.Linear(in_features=120, out_features=10)

    def forward(self, x):
        out = self.layer1(x)
        out = self.layer2(out)
        out = out.view(out.size(0), -1)
        out = self.fc1(out)
        out = self.drop(out)
        out = self.fc2(out)
        out = self.fc3(out)
        return out
```

Once both the datasets and the neural network model are ready, we move on to implementing the model learning phases and simultaneously calculating the model's *accuracy* and *loss* during the *learning* phase. These values will be useful later to evaluate the goodness of the model obtained:

```python
def train(bs, lr):

    batch_size = bs
    learning_rate = lr
    train_loader = torch.utils.data.DataLoader(training_data,batch_size)
    test_loader = torch.utils.data.DataLoader(test_data,batch_size)

    #device = torch.device('cuda:0')
    device = torch.device('cpu')
    num_epochs = 5
    count = 0
    model = FashionCNN()
    model.to(device)
    error = nn.CrossEntropyLoss()
    learning_rate = 0.001
    optimizer = torch.optim.Adam(model.parameters(), lr=learning_rate)

    training_start_time = datetime.datetime.now()
    results = []

    for epoch in range(num_epochs):
        for images, labels in train_loader:
            images, labels = images.to(device), labels.to(device)
            train = Variable(images.view(100, 1, 28, 28))
            labels = Variable(labels)
            outputs = model(train)
            loss = error(outputs, labels)
```

```
            optimizer.zero_grad()
            loss.backward()
            optimizer.step()
            count += 1


    # Testing the model
        if not (count % 50):      # It's same as "if count % 50 == 0"
            total = 0
            correct = 0
            for images, labels in test_loader:
                images, labels = images.to(device), labels.to(device)
                test = Variable(images.view(100, 1, 28, 28))
                outputs = model(test)
                predictions = torch.max(outputs, 1)[1].to(device)
                correct += (predictions == labels).sum()
                total += len(labels)

            accuracy = correct * 100 / total
            new_results = {
                "batch_size": batch_size,
                "loss": loss.data.item(),
                "iteration": count,
                "accuracy": accuracy.item(),
                "elapsed_time_sec": (datetime.datetime.now() - training_
start_time).total_seconds(),
                }
            results.append(new_results)
    return results
```

Now we carry out the *training* process of the neural network by invoking the function just defined and passing the **batch_size** and the **learning_rate** as arguments:

```
# batch_size = 100, learning_rate = 0.001
```

```
results = train(100, 0.001)
```

The preceding code will take a while to run. After nearly a minute, the model will complete the *learning* phase. During this phase, we calculated and collected some parameters that take into account the quality of the learning phase such as *loss* and *accuracy*. These values that we have collected in the results variable, we pass them in a Pandas DataFrame so that they can be consulted more easily:

```
import pandas as pd
```

```
results_df = pd.DataFrame.from_dict(results)
```

```
results_df.head(10)
```

By executing the previous code, we will display the *first ten rows* of the DataFrame using the **head()** method, as shown in the following figure (*Figure 9.9*):

	batch_size	loss	iteration	accuracy	elapsed_time_sec
0	100	0.503404	50	79.540001	10.698972
1	100	0.563143	100	81.220001	20.112245
2	100	0.452134	150	84.059998	29.749219
3	100	0.395133	200	85.709999	39.393635
4	100	0.441687	250	85.050003	48.891572
5	100	0.422865	300	84.529999	58.477025
6	100	0.347971	350	86.680000	68.099902
7	100	0.439388	400	86.589996	77.511428
8	100	0.620000	450	84.849998	87.049638
9	100	0.501260	500	87.669998	96.446948

Figure 9.9: The first 10 rows of the DataFrame containing the results

As we can see from the DataFrame, we have collected the value of the *loss*, the *accuracy*, and the *time taken* in the execution of *every 50 iterations*, which in the present case is about 10 *seconds*. To see the time taken for the whole learning (3000 *iterations*), we can see the last rows of the DataFrame through the **tail()** method:

```
results_df.tail()
```

By executing the method, we obtain a table containing the last five results collected, which correspond to the last five steps of the *learning* phase, as shown in the following figure (*Figure* 9.10):

	batch_size	loss	iteration	accuracy	elapsed_time_sec
55	100	0.250286	2800	90.449997	533.636908
56	100	0.484450	2850	89.900002	543.004209
57	100	0.292580	2900	90.570000	552.542618
58	100	0.195649	2950	90.129997	562.113212
59	100	0.211632	3000	89.910004	571.689600

Figure 9.10: *The last five rows of the DataFrame containing the results*

Having put all the data collected from the results into a Pandas DataFrame, we also take advantage of the simplicity with which the data in these objects can be plotted with **matplotlib**. Let's see the trend of the loss throughout the learning phase by writing the following code in the following cell of the Notebook:

```
import matplotlib.pyplot as plt


plt.plot(results_df['iteration'], results_df['loss'])
plt.show()
```

By executing the code, a *linear graph* is obtained in which the trend of the loss is represented throughout the learning phase (3000 *iterations*), as shown in the following figure (*Figure* 9.11):

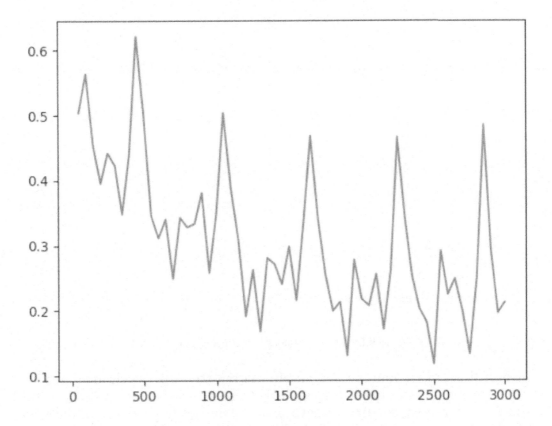

Figure 9.11: Loss trend during the learning phase

As can be seen from the figure, the *loss trend* is *highly variable*, and for each epoch, there is a similar trend with *high and low values*. But for each epoch, there is a gradual improvement in the loss which takes it from the initial **0.5** to a stable value of **0.2** after five *learning* epochs.

The same can be done with accuracy. In order to graph the accuracy trend we can write the following code:

```
plt.plot(results_df['iteration'], results_df['accuracy'])
```

```
plt.show()
```

By executing the previous code, we will obtain a graph similar to the one in the following figure (*Figure 9.12*):

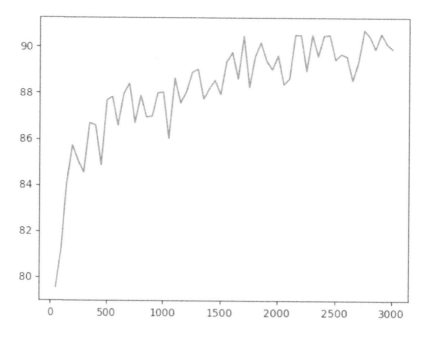

Figure 9.12: *Neural network learning accuracy trend*

Also in this graph, you can see an alternating trend between *high* and *low* peaks, making the accuracy very variable from a few iterations to others. But the general trend of accuracy is always *improving,* leading from an initial value of *80% of accuracy,* to a value of about *90% at the end of the learning phase.*

Another interesting graph could be of the time taken to execute the iterations during the entire learning process:

```
plt.plot(results_df['iteration'], results_df['elapsed_time_sec'])
plt.show()
```

Running the code, we will get a graph very similar to the one shown in the following figure (*Figure 9.13*):

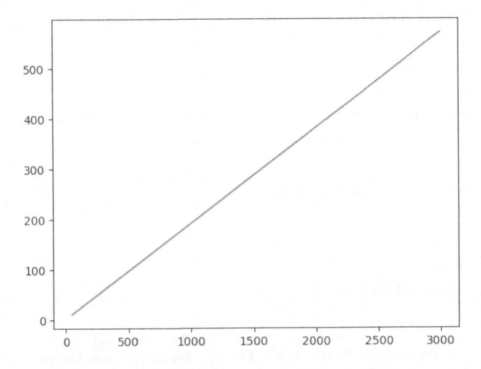

Figure 9.13: *Trend of the time spent learning the neural network*

From the graph, we can see that the execution times are homogeneous, remaining unchanged throughout the learning process.

Deep learning example with PyTorch and GPU

Now that we have a complete example of learning a neural network model on a set of images, performed on a single machine, it is interesting to see how it is possible to exploit the parallel computing technologies we have available. For example, we can integrate the calculation using the PyTorch library with the GPU graphics card on our computer. Starting from the code we have used, we can make some changes and see what differences are obtained in its execution.

In the training function of the neural network that we have defined as **train()** we are going to modify the calculation device, replacing **cpu** with **cuda:0**. Now by rerunning all the code, we will be able to have parallelism support through the NVIDIA graphics card *thanks* to the integration of CUDA:

```
def train(bs, lr):

    batch_size = bs
    learning_rate = lr
    train_loader = torch.utils.data.DataLoader(training_data,batch_size)
    test_loader = torch.utils.data.DataLoader(test_data,batch_size)


    device = torch.device('cuda:0')


    num_epochs = 5
    count = 0
    model = MyCNN()

    . . .
```

We reset the Jupyter notebook by restarting the *kernel* and cleaning all the outputs obtained. To do this, select **Kernel** > **Restart & Clear Output** on the menu as shown in *Figure 9.14* and wait for the Jupyter system to reset:

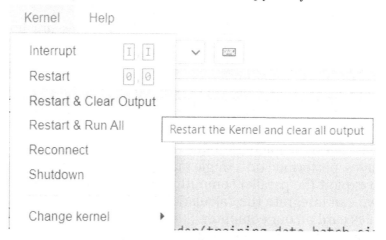

Figure 9.14: *Jupyter Notebook resetting*

Once the Notebook has been reset and the device modified in the code, we re-execute all the cells from *start* to *finish* and observe the difference in the results obtained. Let's check the execution times from the DataFrame containing the calculation parameters of each iteration as shown in *Figure 9.15*:

	batch_size	loss	iteration	accuracy	elapsed_time_sec
0	100	0.549456	50	78.680000	4.770011
1	100	0.449008	100	81.519997	7.666718
2	100	0.513790	150	84.449997	10.254896
3	100	0.434090	200	85.599998	12.682994
4	100	0.424354	250	86.070000	15.455611
5	100	0.348596	300	86.839996	17.886880
6	100	0.338119	350	87.209999	20.646353
7	100	0.411364	400	84.680000	23.106270
8	100	0.621500	450	86.419998	25.801914
9	100	0.430898	500	87.680000	28.419534

Figure 9.15: DataFrame of the results obtained by adding the GPU

As we can see in the previous figure (*Figure* 9.15) and the following one (*Figure* 9.16), times have been reduced by *more than half*. The 10 *seconds* to carry out about 50 *iterations* have become less than four in the case of the use of the GPU:

	batch_size	loss	iteration	accuracy	elapsed_time_sec
55	100	0.259191	2800	89.930000	147.375217
56	100	0.433528	2850	89.629997	150.086596
57	100	0.217143	2900	90.930000	152.501081
58	100	0.207694	2950	89.529999	155.274581
59	100	0.198218	3000	90.290001	157.656414

Figure 9.16: Last rows of the DataFrame of the results obtained by adding the GPU

Let's also see the *loss* and the *accuracy* in the *two* graphs shown in the following figure (*Figure* 9.17):

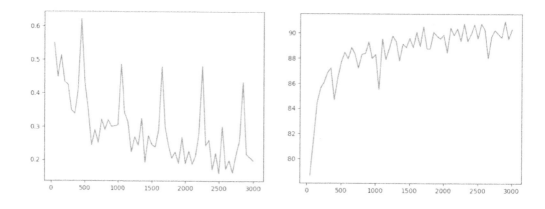

Figure 9.17: *Loss and accuracy trends during GPU learning*

In this case, the addition of parallel computing by the GPU graphics card does not make any difference (neither *improvement* nor *deterioration*) in the learning capabilities of the neural network. Learning is just faster.

Scaling PyTorch with Dask

So far we have seen an example of Deep Learning and the behavior of a neural network in a single machine system, with or without a GPU. Now, let's scale the same example into a distributed system through the use of a cluster of computers. As done in the previous chapter, we will use the service provided by **SaturnCloud.io** to be able to access a cluster of machines for a *30-hour trial period* for *free*. More than enough time to be able to carry out our tests.

In order to scale our PyTorch-based code in a distributed system, we will once again make use of Dask and the technologies it makes available. As we have seen in the previous chapters, it will be very simple to carry out this step, making very small changes to the code we have just used. Dask will then take care of making the appropriate conversions at the time of execution.

We go to **SaturnCloud.io** and once logged in with an account, we *activate* a cluster of machines using this time a template already prepared, created specifically for the use of PyTorch. Go to **Resources** and click on the **New Resource from a Template** button, as shown in *Figure 9.18*:

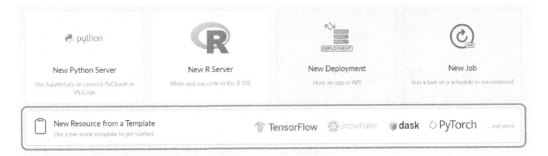

Figure 9.18: *Choice among the possible types of resources available on SaturnCloud.io*

Pressing the button, a series of possible options will appear, where many templates are proposed, each specialized for a particular application, including PyTorch. Click on the *corresponding button* to activate a cluster already prepared for PyTorch with all the necessary libraries already installed (see *Figure 9.19*):

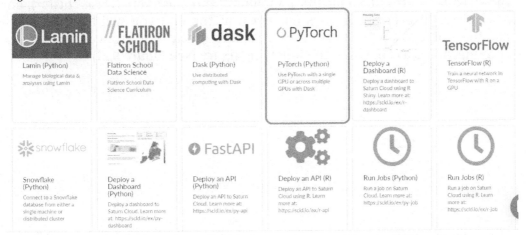

Figure 9.19: *Choose from the different pre-installed cluster templates available on SaturnCloud.io*

Immediately afterwards, a dialog box will appear in which you will have to enter the name of the resource to be created. Feel free to leave the default name **example-pytorch**, or enter a new one as you like, as shown in *Figure 9.20*:

Create Resource

Create a jupyter workspace with settings from **example-pytorch**.

Owner   Name

meccanismocomplesso ⇅   /   example-pytorch

[**Create**] [Cancel]

Figure 9.20: Selection of the name of the resource to be created on SaturnCloud.io

Once the creation of the resource is finished, all the machines that are part of it will begin to activate, including a Jupyter Server on which you will insert the *code and four other machines*, including *three workers (Dask cluster)*, and a *scheduler*. If everything goes correctly, at the end you will find the newly created one among the resources with the *green* indicators indicating the **running** status as shown in the following figure (see *Figure 9.21*):

Figure 9.21: *Name of the newly created Dask Cluster resource on SaturnCloud.io*

Select it to access the resource. You will find on the page *two* different panels, one dedicated to the **Jupyter Server** and one to the **Dask Cluster**. At the bottom of the **Jupyter Server** panel, select the **Jupyter Notebook** button as shown in *Figure 9.22* and click to access the application:

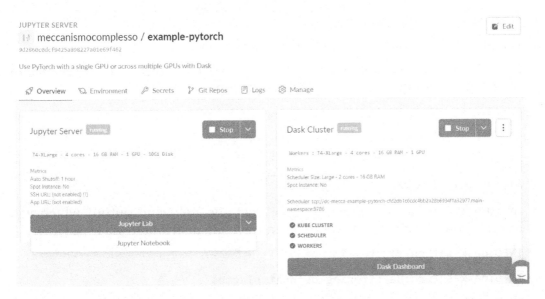

Figure 9.22: *Dashboard of the newly created resource on SaturnCloud.io*

Once Jupyter is open, create a new notebook and start entering the code we used earlier, but with some differences. As for the imports of the various *modules* and *libraries* needed, everything remains unchanged:

```
import torch

import torch.nn as nn

from torch.autograd import Variable


import torchvision

from torchvision import datasets

from torchvision.transforms import ToTensor

from torch.utils.data import DataLoader


import datetime
```

But new libraries need to be added to import Dask and use this code in a distributed system like that of **SaturnCloud**. We will then import some proprietary libraries that will allow you to integrate Dask into a SaturnCloud cluster:

```
import dask

from dask_saturn import SaturnCluster
```

```
from dask.distributed import Client
```

```
from distributed.worker import logger
```

Now in the following cell of the notebook, we signal to Dask the presence of the cluster, and the number of workers present:

```
n_workers = 3
```

```
cluster = SaturnCluster(n_workers=n_workers)
```

```
client = Client(cluster)
```

```
client.wait_for_workers(n_workers)
```

By running the previous cell, you will get the following output which will indicate that the cluster is *ready* to run the code distributed via Dask:

INFO:dask-saturn:Cluster is ready

INFO:dask-saturn:Registering default plugins

INFO:dask-saturn:Success!

Once this is done, the code relating to the import of data for *training* and *testing* of the neural network is inserted. This piece of code has practically remained unchanged:

```
training_data = datasets.FashionMNIST(
    root="data",
    train=True,
    download=True,
    transform=ToTensor()
)


test_data = datasets.FashionMNIST(
    root="data",
    train=False,
    download=True,
    transform=ToTensor()
)
```

By executing this part of the code, you will see the data download start in the output as shown in the following figure (see *Figure 9.23*):

```
Downloading http://fashion-mnist.s3-website.eu-central-1.amazonaws.com/train-images-idx3-ubyte.gz
Downloading http://fashion-mnist.s3-website.eu-central-1.amazonaws.com/train-images-idx3-ubyte.gz to data/FashionMNIST/raw/trai
n-images-idx3-ubyte.gz

            26422272/? [00:01<00:00, 26241060.82it/s]

Extracting data/FashionMNIST/raw/train-images-idx3-ubyte.gz to data/FashionMNIST/raw

Downloading http://fashion-mnist.s3-website.eu-central-1.amazonaws.com/train-labels-idx1-ubyte.gz
Downloading http://fashion-mnist.s3-website.eu-central-1.amazonaws.com/train-labels-idx1-ubyte.gz to data/FashionMNIST/raw/trai
n-labels-idx1-ubyte.gz

            29696/? [00:00<00:00, 132190.39it/s]

Extracting data/FashionMNIST/raw/train-labels-idx1-ubyte.gz to data/FashionMNIST/raw
```

Figure 9.23: Downloading data to Jupyter Server in SaturnCloud.io

The class describing the CNN neural network also remains unchanged:

```
class FashionCNN(nn.Module):


    def __init__(self):
        super(FashionCNN, self).__init__()


        self.layer1 = nn.Sequential(
            nn.Conv2d(in_channels=1, out_channels=32, kernel_size=3,
padding=1),
            nn.BatchNorm2d(32),
            nn.ReLU(),
            nn.MaxPool2d(kernel_size=2, stride=2)
        )


        self.layer2 = nn.Sequential(
            nn.Conv2d(in_channels=32, out_channels=64, kernel_size=3),
            nn.BatchNorm2d(64),
            nn.ReLU(),
            nn.MaxPool2d(2)
        )
```

```
        self.fc1 = nn.Linear(in_features=64*6*6, out_features=600)

        self.drop = nn.Dropout2d(0.25)

        self.fc2 = nn.Linear(in_features=600, out_features=120)

        self.fc3 = nn.Linear(in_features=120, out_features=10)


    def forward(self, x):

        out = self.layer1(x)

        out = self.layer2(out)

        out = out.view(out.size(0), -1)

        out = self.fc1(out)

        out = self.drop(out)

        out = self.fc2(out)

        out = self.fc3(out)

        return out
```

Now we need to insert the neural network training code that we enclosed in a **train()** function. Having already done this greatly facilitates the integration of this code with Dask. In fact, the Dask library provides a **@dask.delayed** decorator that allows you to distribute the code enclosed within the function to which it is related in different tasks to be assigned to as many workers who will execute them in parallel. All in a transparent way to the developer whose only concern will be to add the decorator:

```
@dask.delayed

def train(bs, lr):


    batch_size = bs

    learning_rate = lr

    train_loader = torch.utils.data.DataLoader(training_data,batch_size)

    test_loader = torch.utils.data.DataLoader(test_data,batch_size)


    device = torch.device('cuda:0')

    num_epochs = 5

    count = 0
```

```python
model = FashionCNN()
model.to(device)
error = nn.CrossEntropyLoss()
learning_rate = 0.001
optimizer = torch.optim.Adam(model.parameters(), lr=learning_rate)


training_start_time = datetime.datetime.now()
results = []


for epoch in range(num_epochs):
    for images, labels in train_loader:
        images, labels = images.to(device), labels.to(device)
        train = Variable(images.view(100, 1, 28, 28))
        labels = Variable(labels)
        outputs = model(train)
        loss = error(outputs, labels)
        optimizer.zero_grad()
        loss.backward()
        optimizer.step()
        count += 1

    # Testing the model
        if not (count % 50):
            total = 0
            correct = 0
            for images, labels in test_loader:
                images, labels = images.to(device), labels.to(device)
                test = Variable(images.view(100, 1, 28, 28))
                outputs = model(test)
```

```
        predictions = torch.max(outputs, 1)[1].to(device)

        correct += (predictions == labels).sum()

        total += len(labels)


    accuracy = correct * 100 / total
    new_results = {
        "batch_size": batch_size,
        "loss": loss.data.item(),
        "iteration": count,
        "accuracy": accuracy.item(),
        "elapsed_time_sec": (datetime.datetime.now() - training_
start_time).total_seconds(),
    }
    results.append(new_results)


    return results
```

Until now the code used was almost the same as that used in the case of the single machine, except for some additions. Now begins the different part which is inherent to the particular behavior of Dask. In the following cell, we launch the training execution using the **client.map()** mapping function:

```
experiment = [(100, 0.001)]

train_future = client.map(train, experiment)
```

In executing the previous cell we will see that there will be no execution and the output will be immediate. This happens because Dask is *Lazy* and the invocation of the function does not cause any execution. Parallel code execution will only happen by calling **client.compute()**:

```
futures_gathered = client.gather(train_future)

futures_computed = client.compute(futures_gathered)

results = [x.result() for x in futures_computed]
```

This time by executing the previous cell we will have a long execution time, and the results obtained for each iteration will be collected within results, in a different way, but in the same form as in the previous examples. Once the execution is finished we can go and see the results:

```
import pandas as pd
```

```
results_concatenated = [item for sublist in results for item in sublist]
results_df = pd.DataFrame.from_dict(results_concatenated)
results_df.head(10)
```

You will get a result similar to the one shown in the following figure (see *Figure 9.24*):

	batch_size	loss	iteration	accuracy	elapsed_time_sec
0	100	1.008428	50	61.660000	2.228519
1	100	1.139894	100	61.430000	3.704949
2	100	0.940989	150	65.250000	5.168618
3	100	0.805514	200	66.369995	6.641557
4	100	0.796870	250	65.830002	8.113434
5	100	0.962739	300	66.309998	9.618787
6	100	0.915788	350	64.669998	11.094542
7	100	1.013723	400	66.220001	12.570212
8	100	1.099278	450	65.309998	14.060075
9	100	0.881033	500	65.409996	15.532078

Figure 9.24: *DataFrame with learning outcomes*

Same thing for the last five DataFrame values:

```
results_df.tail()
```

You will get the final part of the DataFrame (see *Figure 9.25*):

	batch_size	loss	iteration	accuracy	elapsed_time_sec
55	100	0.721782	2800	69.250000	83.680797
56	100	0.987083	2850	69.549995	85.286323
57	100	0.778295	2900	70.400002	86.749804
58	100	0.662645	2950	68.739998	88.234482
59	100	0.748363	3000	70.479996	89.732871

Figure 9.25: *Last five rows of the DataFrame with the learning outcomes*

As we can see from the previous figures (see *Figure 9.24* and *Figure 9.25*), the execution of the *3000 iterations* was even faster than the case of parallel execution via GPU on single machines. The times are further halved, with an average of *1.5 seconds* of time spent every *50 iterations*. This is about half the time taken in the preceding single GPU machine case (*about 3 sec*):

```
import matplotlib.pyplot as plt


plt.plot(results_df['iteration'], results_df['loss'])

plt.show()
```

Let's see the loss and accuracy values during the iterations using the graphs shown in *Figure 9.26*:

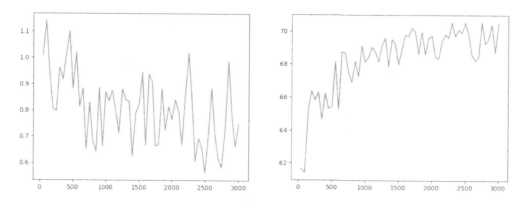

Figure 9.26: Loss and accuracy trends obtained with Dask on SaturnCloud.io

As we can see, this time the system has suffered and both loss and accuracy are no longer as good as the single machine case. This means that despite the increased performance of Deep Learning code execution in a distributed system, the quality of learning of the neural network used has not been preserved. This is due to the fact that we most likely integrated the existing code in Dask on a distributed system making too few changes and therefore neglecting some scaling mechanisms that led to the loss of learning quality of the neural network.

To better understand what may be the origin of the problems just mentioned. Consider analyzing the code you just used on a single machine. Dask, among its many features, allows you to execute its distributed code even in *single-machine architectures*.

To do this, simply change the **Dask Client** settings. On your PC, open a Jupyter Notebook in the *Anaconda* virtual environment dedicated to PyTorch, and copy all the preceding code into it. Then modify the cell relating to the Dask Client as follows:

```
import dask

#from dask_saturn import SaturnCluster

from dask.distributed import Client

#from distributed.worker import logger

#n_workers = 3

#cluster = SaturnCluster(n_workers=n_workers)

#client = Client(cluster)

#client.wait_for_workers(n_workers)


client = Client()
```

Running all the cells, let's see the results obtained in the following *Figure 9.27*:

	batch_size	loss	iteration	accuracy	elapsed_time_sec
0	100	0.446040	50	80.779999	4.762428
1	100	0.545907	100	82.389999	8.147475
2	100	0.513924	150	85.379997	11.207155
3	100	0.406646	200	86.110001	14.164868
4	100	0.388509	250	84.759995	16.760471
5	100	0.372058	300	86.860001	19.718247
6	100	0.360087	350	86.970001	22.391748
7	100	0.461946	400	83.979996	25.316237
8	100	0.668416	450	84.930000	28.051320
9	100	0.486805	500	87.669998	30.677633

	batch_size	loss	iteration	accuracy	elapsed_time_sec
55	100	0.294967	2800	90.099998	158.686704
56	100	0.458460	2850	89.939995	161.465027
57	100	0.235022	2900	90.409996	164.436711
58	100	0.153714	2950	90.029999	167.063556
59	100	0.156465	3000	90.570000	169.751957

Figure 9.27: *DataFrame with the results of the integration with Dask but on a single machine*

Similarly, the *loss* and *accuracy* trends will be represented in the graphs generated by **matplotlib** as shown in *Figure 9.28*:

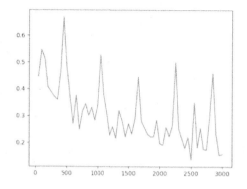 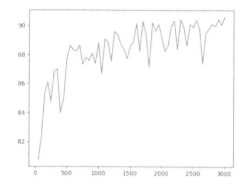

Figure 9.28: *Graphs of loss trends and learning accuracy with Dask but on a single machine*

As we can see in this case the *loss* and the *accuracy* have regained the right trend returning to values similar to the previous examples on a single machine. So most likely the problem is not due to the integration of Dask into the code, but it will be the distribution of tasks to the various tasks or even the distribution of data that will affect the learning mechanisms of the neural network used.

More accurate analysis of the code used and modifications where necessary are therefore required. It is clear that the scaling of complex code such as that of Deep Learning on distributed systems is not yet a simple operation, as that of Pandas or Scikit-learn could be with its Machine Learning models. However, there are other approaches to differently integrate PyTorch models with Dask in a distributed system, for example by wrapping with models that are more integrated with the Dask framework, probably guaranteeing better scaling efficiency. However, these types of analyzes go beyond the simple context of this book, and those interested are invited to seek innovative solutions to this problem.

On the other hand, despite the underlying mechanisms of the code used which have produced less efficient learning, it is evident how the use of a distributed system can lead to a considerable increase in calculation speed, making the learning phases of the networks neural much faster.

Conclusion

Artificial intelligence (AI) has found great development in the world of information technology in the last decade, especially in the development and study of systems capable of learning. It is from this objective that the discipline of Machine Learning has developed, so deeply rooted in artificial intelligence that it has almost become a synonym for it. Machine Learning has found its best representation in the Python language, providing researchers, and operators with powerful libraries capable of providing all the necessary tools for this discipline. The models used, the data sizes and the learning algorithms are becoming more complex and the transition to parallel computing has become necessary.

As far as Deep Learning is concerned, it is the last current frontier of the application of distributed systems. Artificial neural networks and their learning systems represent a complex phenomenon that requires more and more computing resources. The matter is so complex that the results are often unpredictable and require further study. However, Deep Learning is a fascinating discipline, to which much can still be added.

In the next chapter, we will wrap up the topic of parallel computing by discussing the future trends and technological innovations that will greatly develop the concepts presented in the book. Machine Learning and Deep Learning seen in this chapter are only the vanguard of what awaits us shortly. New technologies will bring new disciplines and the contribution of parallel programming developers will be increasingly required, who will bear the burden of having to keep up with the times.

References

- https://www.oracle.com/it/artificial-intelligence/what-is-ai/
- https://www.meccanismocomplesso.org/deep-learning/
- https://medium.com/@gaurav2proud/what-is-the-need-of-parallel-processing-for-machine-learning-in-real-time-7bfc9b66e40c
- https://web.stanford.edu/~rezab/classes/cme323/S16/projects_reports/hedge_usmani.pdf
- https://www.alteryx.com/glossary/supervised-vs-unsupervised-learning
- https://analyticsindiamag.com/a-guide-to-parallel-and-distributed-deep-learning-for-beginners/
- https://www.e2enetworks.com/blog/demystifying-parallel-and-distributed-deep-learning

- https://www.simplilearn.com/keras-vs-tensorflow-vs-pytorch-article
- https://www.simplilearn.com/tutorials/deep-learning-tutorial/deep-learning-frameworks
- https://www.simplilearn.com/tutorials/deep-learning-tutorial/deep-learning-algorithm
- https://pytorch.org/docs/stable/notes/multiprocessing.html#asynchronous-multiprocess-training-e-g-hogwild
- https://pytorch.org/tutorials/intermediate/ddp_tutorial.html
- https://www.tensorflow.org/guide/distributed_training

## CHAPTER 10

Hands-on Applications of Parallel Computing

In the previous chapter (*Chapter 9, Exploring the Potential of AI with Parallel Computing* we saw in detail how Artificial Intelligence is gaining ground among the disciplines that make more use of parallel computing. The success of this approach and the fascination that has always led people to create an intelligent entity to work with pushes this sector ever more towards great progress. The progress that goes hand in hand with the technological potential on which these systems work.

In this chapter, we will see what will be the next technological steps that will involve parallel computing and artificial intelligence in their development. These technological innovations will lead to an evolution not only in the procedures and concepts discussed in this book but will be a boost to the creation of new concepts and paradigms that can keep pace with technological progress. As will be seen, such progress will not be linked only to a strictly scientific and professional environment but will gradually become more and more integrated into everyday social life, involving our customs and habits. In all of this, parallel computing will become more and more integrated so as to become the processing standard. Those who work professionally in this area will be the professionals of the future, and many interesting and stimulating job opportunities will open up.

Structure

In this chapter, we will cover the following topics:

- Massively parallel artificial intelligence
- Edge computing
- Cyber-physical systems

- Cybersecurity
- Exascale computing
- Quantum computing
- New professional opportunities
- Advances in Python libraries

Massively parallel artificial intelligence

Among the innovations to which artificial intelligence will be subject, the most imminent is the development of **Massively Parallel Artificial Intelligence**, which as the name suggests, will be based on the ever-increasing availability of massively parallel systems (see *Figure 10.1*):

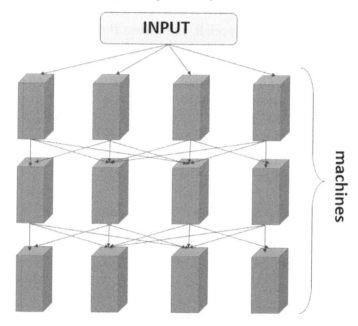

Figure 10.1: *Massively Parallel System Model*

The term massively parallel system refers to a set of many processing units structured in such a way as to be able to carry out a certain operation by working in parallel.

These systems existed before the 1970s, only they have evolved through technological innovations by changing their shape. Generally, we can identify these systems to a particular type of supercomputer, where the processing units, which can be CPUs, GPUs, or entire separate machines (massively parallel machines) are arranged in parallel, and where each of them simultaneously performs a specific portion of a task.

Today, massively parallel systems are more and more numerous and more and more powerful. Facebook and Google make use of these systems, being the only ones capable of managing an immense amount of data arriving from search engines and social networks.

The particular parallel structure, made up of homogeneous and independent units, also allows these systems to be scaled according to the calculation needs.

For example, if one of these systems requires increased resources to keep up with applications, more processing units can easily be added to that system, adding new machines where necessary. If, on the other hand, the computing resources should prove excessive, they could be deactivated when necessary, or allocated to other tasks, saving in this case a waste of resources.

Massively parallel systems are therefore offered for considerable studies and applications and their management (for example performance tuning) can represent a good job opportunity.

The nature of these particular systems, their increasing power and flexibility, makes them suitable for the use of artificial intelligence. The same artificial intelligence is used for its own performance tuning, allowing these systems to adapt dynamically and in an ever more autonomous and efficient way to the calculation needs.

This new area of artificial intelligence research will have unimaginable computing power, the immediate consequence of which will be ever-greater computing performance. But this is not the goal. In fact, as we have seen in the past, with the transition from Machine Learning to Deep Learning, this availability and computing power will certainly lead to a new approach towards the creation of intelligent systems. For example, new methods are being developed to introduce forms of **memory-based reasoning** into applications and no longer simple parametric learning. Another technique that has been talked about lately is **parallel marker passing**, with which new highly parallel algorithms are being developed that are able to reformulate the use of neural networks. These innovations and many others, encouraged by the use of massively parallel machines, offer an opportunity for artificial intelligence to new challenges towards the vastness and irregularities of the world of real-world data. Also, in the field of data, new technologies are being introduced such as the **Very Large Knowledge Bases** (VLKB).

Edge computing

In the last chapters of the book (*Chapter 8, Scaling Your Data Science*

Applications with Dask and *Chapter 9, Exploring the Potential of AI with Parallel Computing*, we have seen how the clusters of machines and Cloud services available on the net are very powerful tools which allow us to have distributed systems and therefore to scale our parallel computing applications from a single machine to clusters of cars. In fact, this is currently the usual approach for those who want to develop and study applications for Machine Learning and Deep Learning. But that's not all, the other disciplines that currently make use of Parallel Computing will also soon switch to this form of calculation, thanks to the ever-increasing availability of these systems.

In the near future, we also expect significant progress for these distributed systems. Recently, **edge computing** has been proposed as a new computing paradigm that will add to those we have covered in the book. In this type of system, the computing and memory resources are located near the data and in general near all information sources. With the introduction of edge computing, new paradigms and implementations will be added to the current distributed computing (or cloud computing) that will take into account the latency and bandwidth of the information involved between the various components of the system. These characteristics will increasingly intertwine with the integration of security and policy systems, which will gradually have to be integrated into data processing with the consequent diffusion of distributed systems in the context of daily activities.

So, the data processing will be divided into two levels: on the one hand the edge and on the other hand, the cloud, as shown in *Figure 10.2*:

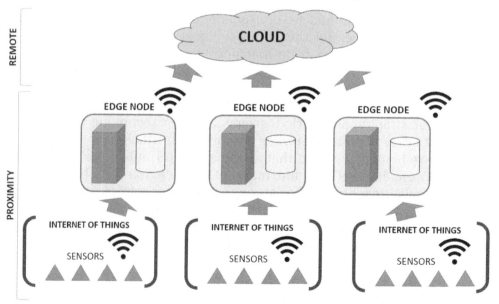

Figure 10.2: *Edge computing in an IOT System*

It is almost useless to add that the types of input data to be processed will be of the most varied types, acquired more and more from everyday objects. Even the form of data during their processing from the source to the edge, to the cloud, ending up with the information extrapolated from appropriate models, will evolve with the ever-increasing integration of intelligent systems. In fact, these systems will convert numerical data, images, sounds, and all current and familiar forms to us at this moment, into abstract and summary information, from forms more suited to artificial intelligence, from forms unusual to us, used by these systems for the generation of knowledge and reasoning (and not just any more as learning).

Such a picture is only a still imprecise image of what is expected of the future, and there are still many steps to take, as well as technological problems to solve. It is, however, a description of the future trend to which all parallel computing applications are pointing.

From a practical point of view, we already have some examples to get some ideas. For example, Google has created the Edge-TPU service (**https://cloud. google.com/edge-tpu**) available online by purchase. This service makes use of ML inference with a number of layered technologies to choose from for your environment, including TensorFlow as a framework (see *Table 10.1*):

	Edge	Cloud
Task	ML inference	ML training and inference
Service	Linux, Windows	AI platform, Kubernetes Engine, Computer Engine, Cloud IoT Core
ML Frameworks	TensorFlow Lite, NN API	TensorFlow, scikit-learn, XGBoost, Keras
HARDWARE ACCELERATORS	Edge CPU, GPU, CPU	Cloud TPU, GPU, CPU

Table 10.1: Services available on Google Edge-TPU

Distributed computing infrastructure with cyber-physical systems

The previous section immediately brings to mind other disciplines and related technologies that are involved with the innovation of artificial intelligence and the integration of increasingly intelligent systems in our society.

We talked about data sources, future edge computing, and the growing use of sensors and other forms of real-world data capture. In recent years, thanks to technological advances in communication technologies and the possibility of coverage by Wi-Fi systems, these have led to the birth and development of the **Internet of Things (IoT)**. **Cyber-Physical Systems (CPS)** play a decisive role in this new *distributed* data acquisition system in the real world.

These are computer systems whose purpose is to interact continuously with the real environment in which it operates. CPS systems must meet three fundamental requirements (3 C properties) to be considered as such:

- Computing
- Communication
- Control

These systems equipped with these three properties must therefore be able to interact with the world in which they operate, collecting data through a network of sensors or other human interfaces, processing them in an increasingly intelligent way, and communicating the processed information with other computer systems connected to them (edge computing). *Figure* 10.3 shows the evolution of the scheme represented in *Figure* 10.2 with the introduction of intelligent systems, Cyber-Physical Systems, in edge computing, capable of processing input data and extrapolating abstract information already at this level and interacting with the external environment, via actuators or **Human-Machine interfaces (HMI)**:

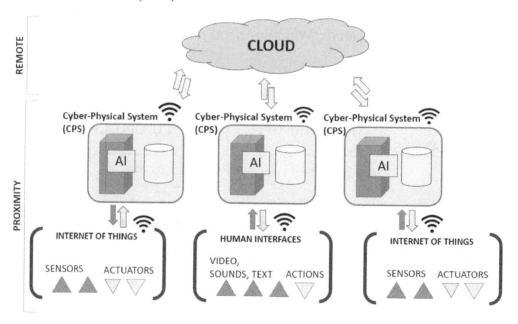

Figure 10.3: *The evolution of edge computing through intelligent systems
(Cyber-Physical Systems)*

Furthermore, this new intelligent system, the Cyber-Physical System, will also be able to *control* the physical environment in which it operates through actuators, or other physical interaction systems, based on the information processed or received. The future goal is to make these systems increasingly intelligent, integrating them with applications capable of learning, reasoning, and actuating in a similar way to humans. So, we will have a development of new technologies, approaches, and methods for the implementation of these new intelligent systems, which will certainly make use of parallel computing.

Artificial intelligence in cybersecurity

The direct consequence of everything we have said in the previous sections is therefore the ever-increasing integration of intelligent systems in all human activities, both professional and social. Entrusting all these operations and visibility more to intelligent systems capable of understanding, but at the same time being able to be controlled, requires an equal development of new security systems that are able to guarantee any problems in their use.

This reality is not that far away. Recent studies show that artificial intelligence has already taken over many fields of application, some of which are sensitive to the security of society. Sectors such as finance, military, transportation, and hospitals already make use of intelligent systems operating in these fields, and their use will spread more in the years to come. Their malfunction or the intrusion of ill-intentioned people who take control of them could cause devastating damage to society. It is therefore clear that at the same time, specific safety systems will have to be developed, capable of keeping these systems under control and acting immediately and appropriately to avoid side effects.

Currently, **Cybersecurity** deals with today's computers, equipped with functional and dumb operating systems and is already busy enough to fight issues such as intrusion detection, privacy protection and social engineering. The extension of these problems to systems equipped with artificial intelligence and increasingly integrated into daily life is a new challenge for those approaching the future.

Even in this case, artificial intelligence can be used to address these security issues. Considering the interconnection between AI and Cybersecurity is a key factor for the future of society and the use of information systems.

In this regard, the **European Union Agency for Cybersecurity (ENISA)** has released an interesting PDF document that can be downloaded for free online (**https://www.enisa.europa.eu/publications/artificial-intelligence-cybersecurity-challenges**), which reports the challenges that Cybersecurity will have to face in the imminent future from which a summary scheme has been represented in *Figure 10.4*:

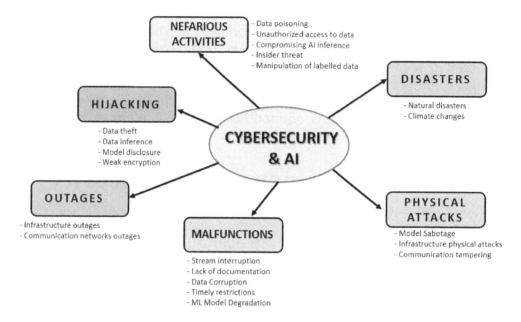

Figure 10.4: *Some of the threats Cybersecurity will have to deal with in the coming years*

Advent of Web 5.0

Even with regard to the Web, we are about to witness a great change. The introduction of Web 5.0, also nicknamed Brain-Net, will revolutionize the way users interact. This new system will in fact add emotions and sensoriality to the flow of data exchange and will also increase the degree of interfacing between man and machine.

Such an innovative system will require a whole new set of new technologies that will produce data in new forms, currently not taken into account by current information systems. This data will take on ever more complex and abstract forms, far from the simple numbers and texts we are used to today.

Given that Data Science, and above all Big Data, are based exclusively on data produced by the web, they will have to adapt to these changes. Furthermore, if we think that the current daily requests for services (for example Google processes around 3.5 billion requests per day) require extremely powerful computing systems which already make use of artificial intelligence, it is clear that innovation in this area will have to work hard if it wants to keep up with the times.

These new forms of data will require not only specific algorithms that have not yet been developed but also artificial intelligence systems capable of understanding them. Therefore, even in this area, considerable efforts will have to be made to bring about the right innovations. All this will be integrated with the concepts expressed previously in the chapter, such as intelligent Edge Computing which will allow the input data to be processed already "close" to the source, thus reducing the costs of the central processing unit and the flow of data.

So, Web 5.0 will make use of **Decentralized Web Nodes (DWNs)** which will perform data storage functions, and which will allow entities of any type (people, organizations, and so on) to send and store encrypted or public data messages, allowing the creation of a wide variety of decentralized apps and protocols (as shown in *Figure 10.5*):

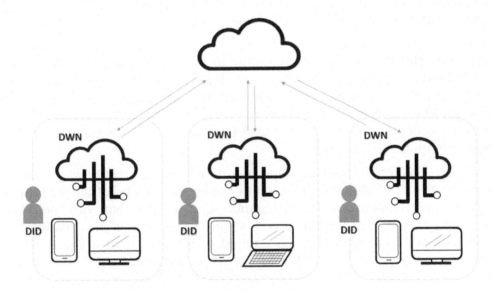

Figure 10.5: *Decentralized Web Nodes in Web 5.0*

Leveraging the introduction of decentralized Web Nodes, another set goal of Web 5.0 will be to decentralize the identity of users and the storage of their data. Account management will also be decentralized through the use of **Decentralized Identifiers (DID)**, self-owned identifiers that will allow authentication and routing to be decentralized. The applications developed in this area, instead of sending the identity data to the central unit, will keep them locally, only sending their elaborations. Even if this seems trivial, it responds to many current cyber security and data privacy needs. It will also greatly revolutionize the forms of data processing, which will require new processing systems. Will the management of countless accounts and passwords be just a bad memory? We will see.

Exascale computing

Returning to a more technological discourse, one of the trendiest future technological innovations is **Exascale computing**. This term indicates a new level of supercomputing capable of performing at least 1,000,000,000,000,000,000 floating point operations per second (Exaflops). Such computing power can only increase the performance of applications that take advantage of parallel computing.

The creation of supercomputers based on these systems will bring enormous benefits to the use of simulations, the development of artificial intelligence and data analysis, thanks to the possibility of solving problems of incredible complexity that not even the best computers of today can deal with.

This reality is upon us. In the United States, the Californian company HPE has built the first exascale supercomputer called Frontier, which will be assembled at the Oak Ridge National Lab (2023), an interdisciplinary science and technology laboratory managed by the United States Department of Energy. This supercomputer recorded a performance of 1.1 exaflops breaking a hitherto unattainable limit and thus positioning itself as the most powerful supercomputer in the world.

Frontier, like other exascale supercomputers under study, was built using combinations of CPUs and GPUs, multi-socket nodes, and other purpose-built devices based solely on parallel computing. It is clear that with the diffusion of such systems, there will be a very strong incentive for the creation of new approaches and methods in the context of parallel programming. It will be interesting what the future developments in programming technologies will be.

Quantum computing

Even the current concept we have of parallel computing is soon destined to evolve with the birth of new computing technologies that are completely different from those we are used to. One of these is **Quantum Computing**. This computing system bases its operation on the quantum properties of matter, such as the superposition of states and entanglement. Thanks to these properties, these systems are able to perform operations on data not through transistors that operate in binary state (0 or 1), but on quantum bits, called qubits, capable of being able to possess multiple values simultaneously, completely distorting the basics of the binary code.

Computers based on quantum computing are already intrinsically parallel at a very low level, in a different way than we are used to, and these characteristics promise upheavals in computing performance. It is clear that these technologies require, due to their very nature, an upheaval of the foundations of parallel computing, leading to new concepts and approaches.

The potential offered by computers of such power has led to a real race among the various nations of the world to create such computing systems. At present, these types of computers already exist, even though it is a very new technology. The first quantum computer was marketed by IBM in 2019 and is called **IBM Q System One**. Subsequently, the USA created a series of quantum computers called **Eagle** (127 qubits) in the form of chips to be adapted to the new system: **IBM System Two**, and the related software for use.

In Canada, the startup Xanadu has joined the *quantum* superpowers with the creation of a quantum computer based on photon entanglement, called **Borealis** with 216 qubits of computing power. This system was used to calculate the gaussian boson sampling of 216 photons, in just 36 microseconds. Such a problem would have required over 9,000 years of computation on today's fastest supercomputers.

As far as Europe is concerned, two quantum computers are already active (Paris in France, and Jülich in Germany) out of the 6 under construction (one of which is in Italy) which will form the first quantum computer network in the world. These machines will be used for research but will also be made accessible to European start-ups and companies in order to stimulate subsequent technological progress. Even more recent (2022) is the news from China on the creation of their first quantum computer, **Wuyan**, equipped with 24 qubits, and built by Origin Quantum Computing.

Quantum technology, integrated with existing HPC systems, will allow for significant advances in all sectors of the industry.

New professional opportunities

A good note on which to hope for those who undertake this profession is what was said at one of the most recent **World Economic Forums (WEF)**. Among the new emerging professions that will define the work of the future are AI and data specialists, whose digital skills will increasingly intersect with human ones. From the Data Scientist to the Cloud Engineer, from the Artificial Intelligence expert to the Cybersecurity expert, all these professions are present among the 96 professions of the future listed in the study "Jobs of Tomorrow: Mapping Opportunity in the New Economy", published by the World Economic Forum.

Among the clusters of new professions, there is Data Science & AI, which confirms the expectations placed in this book and which concentrates most of the topics covered here. Still, in the WEF study, it is expected that in the near future, requests will increase more for Artificial Intelligence specialists, even if the number of open positions is not high, still remaining a niche profession for industry experts. On the other hand, the number of positions for Data Scientists will grow considerably (it is the third emerging job by the number of open positions).

Regarding the skills required in this sector, the study proposes the wording *Tech disruptive skill*, a term which will indicate more advanced digital skills, which allow those who possess them to be able to use and develop business models, thus impacting the market of work in a meaningful and lasting way. In fact, under this term we find the following competencies:

- Data Science
- Natural language processing
- Robotics and Automation
- Cybersecurity

All skills we have seen in the book are linked to artificial intelligence and implicitly to parallel computing.

Required advances in parallel computing for Python

Today all computing hardware is multi-core, so "*it is imperative for Python to increasingly provide high-performance parallelism.*"

This is what was said at EuroPython 2019. This goal is set in the immediate future for all Python library developers who will increasingly suffer the push to innovate their libraries to adapt to this goal.

There is still a long way to go. Despite everything we've seen in the book, a lot of changes will be needed to adapt their APIs more and more to these parallel systems, which will soon become the norm.

Given the nature of Python, this task will also involve the users of these libraries, who will have the task of signaling the major needs of their professional activity and pushing the modifications of the libraries towards these needs.

So also, in this area, a new generation of developers will come into play, in which Parallel programming will be the main form of reasoning and they will be able to devise new constructs and patterns that are more efficient and more intuitive in their use. For example, these new developers will be able to create new libraries by integrating the most modern technologies for parallel computing into them. In fact, Python also lends itself to wrapping native implementations, often developed in C (for example BLAS), a feature that allows this language to be able to take advantage of the innovations made in other languages. An example of this is the recent MPIRE library which is proposed as an evolution of the multiprocessing module. In S. Jansen's article that talks about this library, he carries out some interesting benchmarking tests on the most common libraries in which the performances of the most commonly used libraries for parallel computing are shown, and which we have dealt with in the book. *Figure 10.6* shows his final result, highlighting the performance of the various libraries, and reporting the execution time trends as the number of threads increases:

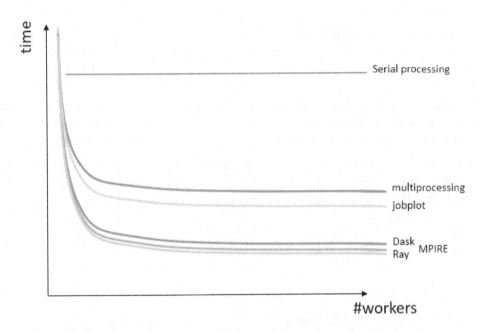

Figure 10.6: *Performance for some libraries for the parallel computing Libraries*

As reported in the article, this library manages to achieve the same performance as distributed systems with libraries such as Dask and Ray, while remaining within the scope of the single machine. In this case, there would be an improvement in performance without having to scale the calculation execution on clusters of machines and therefore keeping costs and making the implementation of the code easier.

MPIRE is certainly only the beginning. Other libraries will take advantage of other mechanisms for parallel computing, most likely wrapping other native libraries (such as CUDA with GPUs).

As far as the Machine Learning and Deep Learning libraries are concerned, here the improvements and innovations will certainly occur not only with the introduction of new libraries but with the improvement of existing ones such as PyTorch and TensorFlow.

Future of PyTorch and TensorFlow

As far as these two libraries are concerned, the interesting factor regarding their future will not only be their ability to incorporate modern technologies to improve their performance but their ability to provide services and models to the community of users.

In fact, an interesting article by AssemblyAI, PyTorch vs TensorFlow in 2023, shows some interesting dynamics between the possible future of these libraries, undoubtedly in competition with each other. For example, it is stated that an important factor is that, at the present time, building new models from scratch may be too expensive for small companies and therefore they will have to make use of pre-trained models. So, it will be the quantity and quality of pre-trained models offered by the two libraries to decide their future fate.

Demonstrate this hypothesis, the article illustrates the success trend of these two frameworks by measuring the number of papers that report them over time. An indicative reconstruction of this graph is shown in *Figure 10.7*:

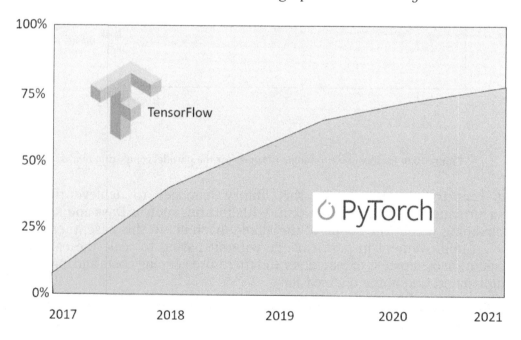

Figure 10.7: *Fractions of Papers using Pytorch or TensorFlow*

As we can easily see, PyTorch has been gaining ground in academic and research environments in recent years, taking over from TensorFlow. This happens despite the goodness and excellent performance of TensorFlow. From this, it can be inferred that a library (such as a programming language) are tools, and the ease and availability in their application of facilities, such as better pre-trained models, makes them preferable to others that may be more efficient, but which are more difficult to use or require more resources.

If we want to remove all doubts, the article proposes another parameter to corroborate his theory: consider the number of repositories that make use of the various Deep Learning frameworks, including PyTorch and TensorFlow. An indicative representation is shown in the following figure (*Figure 10.8*):

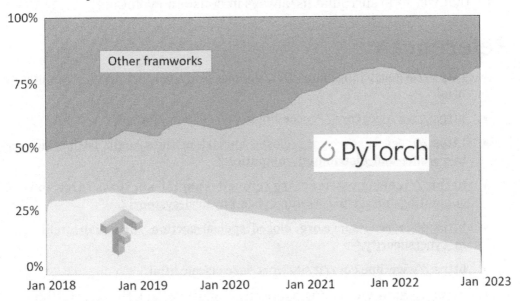

Figure 10.8: *Percentage of Repositories by Deep Learning frameworks*

Also, in this other context, we can see a greater diffusion of PyTorch compared to TensorFlow in the last three years. It is clear that these trends only photograph the trend in the last 5 years, and certainly cannot guarantee that PyTorch will become the reference library for Deep Learning in the near future. An innovation by TensorFlow, a mutation in user needs and the introduction of a new library, will be able to move the balance in a completely different direction.

Conclusion

With this chapter we finish the book, concluding with an overview of the modern technologies and innovations that will impact the world of parallel computing. Having read all the chapters of the book, you will certainly have acquired a clear concept about the world of parallel programming and parallel computing both now and its evolutionary trends in the imminent future. You will have cleared the significant role that these topics will have in the future, not only in the scientific field but above all in the professional and social field. Those who master these systems will certainly hold the keys to access the work of the future, but not only that, they will be able to better understand the world that will soon surround us, always in constant evolution.

References

- https://ai.googleblog.com/2021/03/massively-parallel-graph-computation.html

- https://www.ijcai.org/Proceedings/91-1/Papers/087.pdf

- https://ieeeaccess.ieee.org/closed-special-sections/artificial-intelligence-in-parallel-and-distributed-computing/

- https://ieeeaccess.ieee.org/closed-special-sections/distributed-computing-infrastructure-for-cyber-physical-systems/

- https://ieeeaccess.ieee.org/closed-special-sections/artificial-intelligence-in-cybersecurity/

- https://www.hpe.com/it/it/what-is/exascale.html

- https://www.enisa.europa.eu/publications/artificial-intelligence-cybersecurity-challenges

- https://insidehpc.com/2019/10/parallel-computing-in-python-current-state-and-recent-advances/

- https://towardsdatascience.com/mpire-for-python-multiprocessing-is-really-easy-d2ae7999a3e9

- https://ethz.ch/en/news-and-events/eth-news/news/2020/06/the-first-intuitive-programming-language-for-quantum-computers.html

Index